Monteverdi's Unruly Women

Monteverdi's Unruly Women examines the composer's madrigals and music dramas for what they can tell us about the musical and cultural world of singing and the voice in early modern Italy. Monteverdi's music demanded trained, female voices to make dramatic and expressive statements. At a time when singing was not entirely acceptable for respectable women, his music allowed women to use their voices to gain power.

Bonnie Gordon examines Monteverdi's music as well as the social and musical environment in which the singers lived and worked. Using key primary source material such as singing treatises and Renaissance writings on medicine and acoustics, Gordon contributes to two distinct disciplines: she brings an increased engagement with medical and literary representations of the female body to the growing field of scholarship treating gender and music, and she adds to a well-established industry of scholarship devoted to the perception of gender and the body in early modern Europe.

BONNIE GORDON is Assistant Professor of Music at the State University of New York at Stony Brook. She has published on Renaissance music and culture as well as contemporary female song writers.

New perspectives in music history and criticism

GENERAL EDITORS

JEFFREY KALLBERG, ANTHONY NEWCOMB, AND RUTH SOLIE

This series explores the conceptual frameworks that shape or have shaped the ways in which we understand music and its history, and aims to elaborate structures of explanation, interpretation, commentary, and criticism which make music intelligible and which provide a basis for argument about judgments of value. The intellectual scope of the series is broad. Some investigations will treat, for example, historiographical topics, others will apply cross-disciplinary methods to the criticism of music, and there will also be studies which consider music in its relation to society, culture, and politics. Overall, the series hopes to create a greater presence for music in the ongoing discourse among the human sciences.

PUBLISHED TITLES

Leslie C. Dunn and Nancy A. Jones (eds.), *Embodied Voices: Representing Female Vocality in Western Culture*

Downing A. Thomas, *Music and the Origins of Language: Theories from the French Enlightenment*

Thomas S. Grey, *Wagner's Musical Prose*

Daniel K. L. Chua, *Absolute Music and the Construction of Meaning*

Adam Krims, *Rap Music and the Poetics of Identity*

Annette Richards, *The Free Fantasia and the Musical Picturesque*

Richard Will, *The Characteristic Symphony in the Age of Haydn and Beethoven*

Christopher Morris, *Reading Opera Between the Lines: Orchestral Interludes and Cultural Meaning from Wagner to Berg*

Emma Dillon, *Medieval Music-Making and the "Roman de Fauvel"*

David Yearsley, *Bach and the Meanings of Counterpoint*

David Metzer, *Quotation and Cultural Meaning in the Twentieth Century*

Alexander Rehding, *Hugo Riemann and the Birth of Modern Musical Thought*

Dana Gooley, *The Virtuoso Liszt*

Bonnie Gordon, *Monteverdi's Unruly Women: The Power of Song in Early Modern Italy*

Monteverdi's Unruly Women

The Power of Song in Early Modern Italy

BONNIE GORDON

CAMBRIDGE
UNIVERSITY PRESS

PUBLISHED BY THE PRESS SYNDICATE OF THE UNIVERSITY OF CAMBRIDGE
The Pitt Building, Trumpington Street, Cambridge, United Kingdom

CAMBRIDGE UNIVERSITY PRESS
The Edinburgh Building, Cambridge, CB2 2RU, UK
40 West 20th Street, New York, NY 10011–4211, USA
477 Williamstown Road, Port Melbourne, VIC 3207, Australia
Ruiz de Alarcón 13, 28014 Madrid, Spain
Dock House, The Waterfront, Cape Town 8001, South Africa

http://www.cambridge.org

First published 2004

Printed in the United Kingdom at the University Press, Cambridge

Typeface Palatino 10/12 pt.   *System* LATEX 2$_\varepsilon$ [TB]

A catalogue record for this book is available from the British Library

Library of Congress Cataloguing in Publication data
Gordon, Bonnie, 1968–
Monteverdi's unruly women : the power of song in early modern Italy / Bonnie Gordon.
  p. cm. – (New perspectives in music history and criticism)
Includes bibliographical references and index.
ISBN 0 521 84529 7 (hardback)
1. Feminism and music. 2. Women singers – Italy. 3. Monteverdi, Claudio, 1567–1643.
Vocal music. 4. Vocal music – Italy – 17th century – History and criticism.
5. Madrigals, Italian – Italy – 17th century – History and criticism. I. Title. II. Series.
ML82.G67 2004
782′.0082′0945 – dc22   2004052684

ISBN 0 521 84529 7 hardback

CONTENTS

ILLUSTRATIONS

ACKNOWLEDGMENTS

Perhaps the best part of writing this book is thanking the many people who made it possible. I am deeply grateful to Cambridge University Press and especially to Vicki Cooper and Jeff Kallberg who ushered this project through their system with unparalleled speed and commitment. I would like to thank the Lloyd Hibberd Endowment Fund of the American Musicological Society for a generous book subvention. A Mellon Post Doctoral fellowship in Music and Women's Studies at Brandeis provided me with the time to begin writing a book. A Professional Development Grant from SUNY at Stony Brook provided support for summer research, and a Bunting Fellowship at the Radcliffe Institute for Advanced Study gave me time and space to complete this book. It seemed perfectly appropriate to write a book about unruly women while I was surrounded by a collective of fascinating and hilarious women who offered a constant exchange of ideas, wit, support, fun, and encouragement.

Graduate students at Brandeis University and the State University of Stony Brook helped shape this project through several seminars where they willingly endured hefty readings that must, at times, have seemed bizarre. Matt Vandergiff set the musical examples in record time. Deborah Heckert deserves special mention, and perhaps even a medal, for her comments on countless drafts and for reading the whole thing more times than either of us cares to remember. The project simply would not have been completed without her.

The real pleasure of this project has been the people it gave me the opportunity to work with. The following very patient colleagues and friends read the countless drafts and helped in other crucial ways. They include, Joe Auner, Linda Austern, Johanna Beaver, Jane Bernstein, Alix Cooper, Sarah Babb, Olivia Bloechl, Julie Crawford, Gabriella Cruz, Natasha Corda, Margreta de Grazia, Monique Deveaux, Mario Digangi, Martha Deary, Will Fisher, Dana Gooley, Monica Green, Rebeca Bloom, Mai Kawabata, Rebecca Lee, Ellen Linquest, Sara Lipton, Lily Panoussi, Roger Parker, Judith Plascow, Megan Prado, Gabriella Safran, Alison Sneider, Kate Van Orden, Eugene Wolf, Deborah Wong, and Sue Woodward. Several others filled special roles that deserve specific mention. I was lucky enough to go through graduate school with a fabulous cohort, Mathew Butterfield, Maribeth Clark, and Youyoung Kang. They are still my most faithful readers, and their influences are everywhere in these pages.

Kirsten Wood has earned a prize for responding within seconds to panicked emails and for reading most of the book. Eric Chafe, Susan McClary, and Suzanne Cusick all read the entire manuscript. Susan McClary caught countless errors and helped keep the arguments focused. Eric Chafe's unparalleled commitment to musical detail kept me honest and never failed to give me new insight. With her characteristic wit and generosity of spirit, Suzanne Cusick shared private and public comments that helped in the early stages of the project and offered the most detailed and generous reading of the whole book that anyone could hope for. Since my first days of graduate school Nathan Macbrien has been a constant source of support and a brilliant reader; his encouragement and ideas helped at every step of the process. Toward the end of this project, and in all of my academic endeavors, Martha Feldman, Cristle Judd, and Jessie Ann Owens were more helpful than they can know; they are models in many ways. Gary Tomlinson first served as a superb dissertation advisor and has become that rare combination of friend and colleague who makes thinking fun.

Finally I owe an immeasurable debt to my family. My parents, Joyce and Richard Gordon, taught me the pleasures of ideas and passed on to me the drive to pursue them. My sister, Pam Gordon, spent long runs assuaging my writing anxiety, kept me grounded in the real world, and made me laugh. My husband, Manuel Lerdau, endured a year of commuting, fixed my computer hundreds of times, found a way to care about early music, and read every word with a loving and critical mind. Finally, to our miracles, Jonathan and Rebecca, whose imminent arrival hastened – and of course delayed – the book's completion and whose smiles and unruly voices make it all worthwhile, I dedicate this book.

Introduction

This is not a book about Monteverdi in the traditional sense. Instead, it is a book about the embodied female voices, real and imagined, through which his music circulated. It re-hears singing as an embodied activity and argues that when women sang they made themselves into unruly women: that is, women who break the rules and occupy the spaces between the lines. Unruly women do things with their bodies, consciously or not. Unruly women say no when they are meant to say yes, and yes when they are meant to say no. In the Renaissance women acquired their unruliness simply from their form. Their bodies – understood as inherently excessive, leaky, and oversexed – threatened those around them. Their mouths opened up the dark and scary abyss of their bodies, while long hair symbolized a freedom that society tried again and again to contain. Their minds moved toward ideas forbidden to their kind. And their voices expressed joy, sorrow, lust, and adventure, which not even restrictive clothes could hide. This is a book about the ways in which singing women – of the corporeal and fictitious varieties – embodied that unruliness. These women are not the kind of rebels seen today in the form of skimpily clad pop singers, of the quirky, unwieldy protagonists of Margaret Atwood's novels, or even of television heroines like Xena or Buffy the Vampire Slayer. Their unruliness worked at a much subtler level. It operated in a world where what one did on the outside of the body directly implicated the inside, and where women were not supposed to reveal their bare arms, dance, sing, or be overly merry. In this world the voice could be a woman's most potent possession. As such, Monteverdi did not need to make his women misbehave. That they did themselves.

The book attempts to re-hear the female voice through the music of Monteverdi. Though Monteverdi's music makes the same demands on singers who perform his music today as it did for singers four hundred years ago, the experience of that voice depended on a set of truths about the gendered body and its inner workings that diverges from modern sensibilities. An exceedingly malleable instrument, the human voice varies according to anatomy, taste, time, and place, and thus, like the body from which it emerges, it is anything but essential. Furthermore, at the end of the Italian Renaissance the voice must have been experienced in ways unimaginable to us since it came from a very different elemental body, one imagined as a small but fiery corpus in which hearts and veins pumped the same vital spirits as the universe and in which there existed no natural separation between inner and outer states. Taking the body as the medium through which music was experienced suggests that musical practice was one of the key ways in which early modern singers and listeners inhabited their bodies.

Monteverdi's madrigals and music dramas written between 1600 and 1640 serve as textual and performative accounts of the musical and cultural production of the voice in early modern Italy. My story about gender and the body revolves around the music of Monteverdi and thus shifts the balance of power away from the composer as an omnipotent entity. I chose Monteverdi both because he is *the* riveting musical personality of his generation and because he serves as a representative of musical culture and the forces with which it interacted. In other words, Monteverdi is certainly special, but not so special that he fails to exemplify the world in which he lived. Straddling the Renaissance and what we tentatively call the Modern so precariously that scholars have touted him as the last gasp of the Renaissance and the father of modern music, his compositions bring into relief points of tension in a rapidly changing culture. Though many scholars have made good use of the composer's prolific and self-conscious prose to expound upon musical culture, few have considered his music in the context of ideas about sense and body. Given that my approach to the music moves in a different direction than that of most musicologists, I hope that focusing on a composer about whom scholars care deeply will help to ground my arguments within a musicological tradition.

This book contributes to and interrogates two distinct literatures: it adds sound to a well-established industry of scholarship devoted to gender and the body in early modern Europe, and it brings an increased engagement with medical and literary representations of the female body to the growing field of scholarship treating gender and music. By accounting for the sonic dynamism of individual female voices in specific sung performances, rather than just reading metaphors of voice, I diverge from scholars of social and literary history who often depict early modern culture as a world of silenced women and creative men. To be sure, social mores in the decades around 1600 demanded tacit women whose quieted voices supposedly reflected their chastity and distanced them from inappropriate eroticism. But music from that time regularly depended upon and displayed trained women's voices. This paradox inflected musical productions with tantalizing contradictions that situated both women's bodies and sonorous expression precariously between harmless pleasure and threatening excess. It also created a space in which women could, through singing, seize power. Just as

2

neglecting the intoxicating sounds of early modern women limits the methods of literary scholars and historians, so too has musicology's frequent tendency to sever canonic works from their ideological contexts constrained the discipline's interpretive scope.

By bringing sound to literary models and context to musicological models, I bring new perspective to several well-studied pieces. For instance, Monteverdi's final piece for the gargantuan 1608 wedding festivities in Mantua, *Il ballo delle ingrate*, which ends with a solo *ingrata* bemoaning her sentence to the dark and fiery underworld where she never again will have an individual voice, is easily read as a mechanism for disciplining the female voice. However, because vocalist Virginia Ramponi animated that song through her powerful performance, the means of delivering the message exceeded the message itself. Even though the *ingrata* ends up in hell, Ramponi's song defied social injunctions to silence. As for *L'Arianna*, musicologists have sought to prove the musical genius of its final lament by citing court chroniclers who proclaimed that at its conclusion, "there was not one lady who failed to shed a tear."[1] But since the ladies supposedly cried in response to most early modern dramatic productions, this statement reflects neither an actual flood of tears nor the genius of the lament. Instead, it reinscribes a gendered discourse that imagined women as "leaky vessels" whose excess fluids rendered them inherently incontinent, unruly, and lascivious. Such an interpretation depends on the reading of different discursive systems against one another and the juxtaposition of dramatic and lyric representations with other facets of social life.

Let me stress from the beginning that I have not chosen to isolate real living women composers, characters, or historical subjects. My interest in the female voice and the bodies from which it emanated, as well as the ways that gender difference was figured, necessitates moving freely between traces of real embodied women, imaginary and idealized women, male fantasies of women, and female characters – categories that are radically contingent on one another. For instance male fantasies enabled and circumscribed the lives and sounds of women who sang, while female performers stimulated those fantasies.

Real women exist for us as represented by male writers and serve as entrées into larger issues. Two young women of whom we know very little – Caterina Martinelli and Margherita of Savoy – serve as examples and were each unruly in their own way: Caterina because she sang, and Margherita because she was sung to. The Roman prodigy Caterina Martinelli, known as La Romana, would have sung the title role of Monteverdi's *L'Arianna* at the Mantuan Court but for her death

---

[1] As translated in Paolo Fabbri, *Monteverdi*, trans. Tim Carter. (Cambridge: Cambridge University Press, 1994), 9.

from smallpox shortly before the first performance. Before the Duke of Mantua would let her even rehearse at his court, he forced her to endure a virginity test. She was thirteen. Caterina's mandated virginity test brings to the fore the early modern connections between acting vocally and acting sexually for women – an entanglement that implies something zestier than the Neoplatonic non-fulfillment and spiritual arousal generally associated with performances of Monteverdi's Petrarchan madrigals. Teasing out these connections inspires a very detailed exploration of contemporaneous accounts of female anatomy and brings together fragments of evidence often overlooked by modern scholars. For example, statements by Renaissance medical practitioners espoused the ancient belief that a woman's voice changes when she has intercourse because "her upper neck responds in sympathy to her lower neck."[2]

The slightly older Margherita of Savoy, aged eighteen, attended the production of *L'Arianna* during the spectacles written to honor her wedding to Francesco Gonzaga in 1608. These spectacles staged a stream of violated, punished women, including a ballet in which her groom dressed as one of a group of women eternally condemned to the smoky infernos of the underworld. In that role, he danced in and out of the gaping mouth of hell while Mantuans and visiting dignitaries from all over Europe gazed upon his young bride. The productions centered around her nuptials emphasized clashes between representations of women in music dramas and conduct books and the female singers who envoiced them.

This focus on women could seem to perpetuate the very structures of difference it aims to illuminate by recreating fictions of femaleness, rehearsing traditional notions of sexual difference, and disempowering women through the act of figuring them only as subjects of patriarchal control. Keeping these methodological problems in mind, I move toward an examination of the ways that gendered bodies were produced and deployed in early modern Italy, and the ways that music-making worked to reinforce and challenge ideologies of difference. Rather than suggesting that anatomy means everything, in the pages that follow biological difference stands as something that translates into social distinctions, behavioral codes, and institutional forces.

A focus on women also raises the question of men's voices. Were they sexual? Were they threatening? At the simplest level I might say that this book does not address men's voices directly, and that such a fascinating project is sorely needed. At the next level, the book does argue for an inextricable connection between music, love, and women. As Linda

---

[2] As quoted from Hippocratic gynecology in Ann Hanson and David Armstrong's "The Virgin's Voice and Neck: Aeschylus, Agamemnon 245 and Other Texts," *British Institute of Classical Studies* 33 (1986): 99.

Austern has argued, associations between music and femininity could threaten the masculinity of those who performed it.[3] In his famous *Il cortegiano*, Castiglione's interlocutor Gaspare insisted that "music, like so many other vanities, is most certainly very suited to women, and perhaps also to some of those who have the appearance of men, but not to real men who should not indulge in pleasures which render their minds effeminate and so cause them to fear death."[4]

At the deepest and most important level, the question of men forces the issue of difference, which lies at the very center of this endeavor. In the early modern period women served as sites around which sexual difference circulated. Masculine identity existed in relation to the fantasy of difference – an abstraction used to denote women's marginality and to create a marked space that existed apart from the male universal. That women were imagined as always threatening to exceed boundaries made it especially crucial for men to constantly reinforce limits placed upon them.

The sexualization of the female voice emerged from the sexualization of their bodies, which meant that male voices were less contentious and less eroticized than their female counterparts. Particular understandings of women's bodies, grounded in reigning scientific and medical philosophies, implicated their singing in ways that did not affect men. The body parts that made singing possible – mouths, lips, tongues, and throats – were imagined differently when attached to women. For instance, early modern associations of mouths and wombs related women's singing to a sexually productive part that men lacked. Similarly women's bodies, imagined as colder and leakier then men's, were necessarily affected in their own special way by the temperature-altering and fluid-exuding act of singing. In men, on the contrary, voice was associated with virility.[5] The Paduan doctor Giulio Casseri directly associates voice and power, suggesting that a man needs the appropriate tone and pitch to command domestic power.[6]

These physical differences play out in accounts of listening. Responses to male singers reflect the belief that music could, in the proper hands

[3] Linda Phyllis Austern, "Alluring the Auditorie to Effeminacie: Music and The Idea of The Feminine in Early Modern England," *Music and Letters* 74 (1993): 343–354.

[4] Baldassare Castiglione, *Il libro del cortegiano*, ed. Giulio Carnazzi (Milan: Biblioteca Universale Rizzoli, 1987).

[5] Valeria Finucci discusses the associations of virility, semen, and voice in *The Manly Masquerade: Masculinity, Paternity and Castration in the Italian Renaissance* (Durham, NC: Duke University Press, 2003). Her book appeared too late for me to fully digest in time for the publication of my study, but she cites the Venetian traveler Nicolò di Conti's account of ritual in which men enact their newly achieved manhood by making their penises literally sing through the attachment of gold, silver, and copper bells.

[6] Giulio Casseri, "The Larynx, Organ of the Voice," trans. Malcolm Hast and Erling Holtsmark (Uppsala: Almqvist and Wiksells, 1969), 15.

(and mouths), educate with delight, whereas responses to female singers tend to show the dangers of music exuding from the wrong mouths. In effect, this contrast inverts the eye of the beholder. Women's singing reflected their natural tendency toward the lascivious, while their essential inability to control themselves made it impossible to trust them with such a powerful instrument as song. Because women's voices, like their bodies, existed on the contested margins, men's voices came under less scrutiny and received less adulation: correspondingly, descriptions of them tend to traffic in much tamer adjectives. The best poets serenaded in verse the best female singers, lavishing upon them conventional but effusive adjectives, while men seldom received such double-edged honor. The power ascribed to male voices related to an imagined orphic rhetorical fluency, which was distinct from ravishing pleasure. Their praise reflected the humanist celebration of rhetorical persuasion and elegance and the sense of these skills as the distinguishing features of poets, courtiers and politicians.

Marco da Gagliano explains the experience of listening to Jacopo Peri, a renowned tenor and composer of *L'Euridice*, writing that he "gave them such grace and style that he so impressed in others the emotion of the words that one was forced to weep or rejoice as the singer wished."[7] Similarly, descriptions of the Florentine tenor Francesco Rasi, who played the title role in Monteverdi's *L'Orfeo*, tend to stay within the realm of Neoplatonic adoration, as in the claim that he "who to the harp made the woods echo with celestial harmony."[8] Even castrati had not yet reached the pyrotechnical heights that would eventually lead to overzealous descriptions of their virtuosity. Expressing his satisfaction with the castrato Giovanni Gualberto, who sang in the first performance of *L'Orfeo*, Francesco Gonzaga wrote that, "he has done very well and given immense pleasure to all who have heard him sing . . ."[9] Such a bland description contrasts markedly with the exuberance that pervades descriptions of women, which will be the focus of the fourth chapter of this book.

Each of the book's five chapters uses a piece or group of pieces to illuminate issues surrounding the female voice at the turn of the seventeenth century. Embodied readings take musical compositions as performances constituted by a constellation of discourses, not tacit texts. Though each chapter explores different contexts for the voice, they all circle around

---

[7] As cited in Carol MacClintock, *Readings in the History of Music in Performance* (Bloomington: Indiana University Press, 1979), 189.

[8] Warren Kirkendale, *The Court Musicians in Florence During the Principate of the Medici* (Florence: Leo S. Olschki Editore, 1993), 571.

[9] As cited in John Whenham's *Claudio Monteverdi, Orfeo* (Cambridge: Cambridge University Press, 1986), 170.

issues of agency, erotics, and body. They also face the challenge of simultaneously doing cultural work and accounting for the music. I have resisted claiming a direct one-to-one correspondence between specific musical gestures and larger ideological issues, but like many scholars exploring these issues, I have not, I am sure, found an ideal solution to the problem. The book, then, asks how to approach this challenge but does not propose a codified method for it. I use analysis sparingly as a mechanism for exploring sonorous moments that open up questions about cultural issues. In an attempt to think through the experience of the music, I have tended to avoid discussing architectural elements of the music, even though they are clearly germane to the production and composition of the pieces.

A book that uses Monteverdi's music to illuminate widespread phenomena must confront the relationship between changes in his musical style and structures of knowledge. As other scholars have already discussed, Monteverdi composed during a pivotal shift in European sensibilities and epistemologies. His involvement in new solo-voiced genres, public opera, and abstract tonal systems have led scholars to characterize his music as moving from what Foucault called an epistemology of resemblance to one of representation, a move that reflects the emergence of new world views that were ultimately capstoned by Descartes. By relating issues of female vocality and the physicality of song to shifts that have been understood in largely metaphysical terms, this book explores what those important changes meant for women, real and represented, and particularly for the subversive potential of their voices.

The first chapter, devoted to vocal anatomies, opens up a space for a unique engagement with early modern music by recovering the materiality of the human voice and its imagined organic relation to bodily processes. The chapter begins with a reading of "O come sei gentile," a soprano duet from Monteverdi's seventh book of madrigals, as a textual and performative account of the voice. It then examines the philosophical, medical, and literary contexts for the corporeal rhetorics embedded in early modern singing treatises by Camillo Maffei, Giulio Caccini, and others. Understood in early modern Italy as a kinesthetic entity with a physical substance, the voice consisted of vibrating air that flowed through the throat of the singer into the vulnerable ear of the listener, where it was thought to work with essential animating spirits composed of air and heat that coursed through the body. This theory reflected the continued dominance of humoral understandings of the voice first put forth by Aristotle and Galen. These treatises presented virtuosic embellishments such as ornaments, which manipulated throat, tongue, and breath, as processes that physically disciplined singers in a manner similar to vocal compositions and descriptions of singers.

The second chapter moves from the material voice to musico-dramatic and literary representations of the female voice and the complicated matrix of agency and constraint in which it was embedded. I examine Monteverdi and Rinuccini's *Il ballo delle ingrate* and *L'Arianna* in light of the recent scholarly tendency to portray early modern culture as an opposition between female silence and male creative expression. Rendering this dichotomy more dynamic, these pieces reveal resistant voices whose performances enacted early modern struggles over the female voice – struggles in which constraints were defied and then redoubled. On and off the stage, women continually asserted the unsettling force of their voices, despite the attempts of discursive and social systems to mold them into passive and closed-mouthed projections of patriarchal ideals. In contrast to literary, artistic, and philosophical representations, these women were not quiet, chaste, and absent. Moreover, then as now, real women rarely acted quite like the ideal figures described and prescribed by patriarchal discourses.

Bringing to the fore the erotic potential of song around which the first two chapters circled, the third explores the libidinal economy of sung performances through an examination of selections from Monteverdi's fourth book of madrigals (1603). The pieces in this collection sing of desire, but mostly of its unfulfillment. The sexual buildup of "Sì ch'io vorei morire" and the spiritual climax of "Cor mio, mentre vi miro" enact an experience that encompasses the spiritual Neoplatonic love immortalized by Petrarch and the *trattati d'amore*, as well as the corporeal voices that stand in complex relation to it. Within this collection, the textual and musical excesses of "Sì ch'io vorei morire" present physical pleasure so graphically that it resembles the works of the sixteenth-century erotic satirist Pietro Aretino. I argue, however, that the piece is anomalous only in degree, not in kind. While poetry and philosophical writings could separate virtuous from vulgar love, sung performance propelled bodily motions homologous to the sensations underlying sex and spiritual love.

The fourth chapter moves from the erotics of song to the desire and fantasy that it inspires. It takes as a starting point the continuo madrigal "Mentre vaga Angioletta" (1638), in which two tenors enact Guarini's 1582 lyric description of an erotic encounter between a seductive female singer and her admirer. Imbuing the words with the sensuality of song, the music propels the performers through a dizzying course of passaggi, gorgia, diminutions, and other flourishes popular at the turn of the seventeenth century. Reflecting connected discourses – literary, social, musical, and medical – this piece imagines the ravishing female voice as dangerously alluring. In effect, "Mentre vaga Angioletta" uses male singing voices to animate a poem that rationally analyzes the female voice, presenting virtuosic song as a series of effects and sensations working on the male lover/listener. At the same time, it partakes of a dismembering and controlling manipulation of the female voice that resonates with medical dissections, early modern singing treatises, descriptions of singing virtuose, and Petrarchan blazons.

The fifth chapter broadens the focus from specific pieces to an inquiry into shifting ways of knowing, one that brings together the diverse issues touched upon in the previous case studies. It relates gender to the experience of song in general, and thus insists that a book about gender is necessarily a book about larger cultural issues – in other words, gender does not exist in a vacuum. I read musical and scientific discourses against each other in order to illuminate the ways in which the experiences of singing and listening changed during the seventeenth century. For example, the discovery by astronomers that the universe was not held together by the music of the spheres rendered untenable the notion of music as a microcosm of the universe's divine harmony. And the shift from a conception of the body as a vessel that depended on the maintenance of an appropriate balance of humors and temperament to theories of the circulatory system undermined notions of song as a material force that helped keep the body in motion.

The book closes with an epilogue devoted to conceptions of the female voice and body at the end of Monteverdi's career. I juxtapose two pivotal characters: Clorinda, Tasso's virginal heroine to whom Monteverdi gave voice in the *Combattimento di Tancredi e Clorinda*, and the luscious Poppea of *L'incoronazione di Poppea*. An unlikely pair, these female figures can be read as an axis around which orders of knowledge rotated during the seventeenth century, and they exemplify the representations and enactments of voice that fill the pages of this book.

In writing this book I have used my students as muses not just because many of them helped me work through the ideas contained here, but because the challenge of making the early modern world accessible to them has kept me historically honest and challenged. Having come of age with a generation that finds Madonna's lace bra feminism passé, my students always doubt me when I try to convince them that the women who sang Monteverdi's madrigals and music dramas also transgressed social boundaries. They find it unimaginable that ladies who had to cover even their naked arms and whose music trafficked in a noise level several decibels below most sounds familiar to them used their voices and bodies in ways that caused trouble. They inhabit a world where female musicians assault the senses. The assault on the senses by Monteverdi's unruly women did something even more visceral and more body-altering than what most of us experience today.

1

Vocal anatomies: mouths, breath, and throats in early modern Italy

Breath, throats, tongues, lungs, and chests comprise the stuff of the voice. From our twenty-first-century vantage point, we can see that the rush of air from the lungs as a singer exhales causes the vocal cords to vibrate. The long and thick male cords produce low pitches, while the short thin female cords produce high pitches. Thanks to the singer Manuel García, who, seeking the causes of a cracked voice, plunged a dentist's mirror down his own throat in 1854, doctors or anyone with enough nerve and either a mirror or a good web browser can look at their vocal cords.[1] In early modern Italy, the understanding and hence the experience of the voice was different, conditioned by a set of truths about the gendered body and its inner workings that diverge from modern sensibilities. A kinesthetic entity with physical substance, the early modern voice was imagined to be vibrating air that flowed through the throat of the singer into the vulnerable ear of the listener. In keeping with Galenic and Aristotelian notions of the body, the voice – a physical substance – was understood to work with essential spirits composed of the air and heat that kept living things alive.

Today, however, it is impossible to escape completely our post-Renaissance, post-MRI sense of anatomy and enter the heads of early modern listeners. We are left with only traces of an experience that must have been stunningly powerful. Theirs was a world where laments that to us sound almost recitative-like made ladies cry, and the sound of a low bass voice could send shivers through even the bravest soldiers. The effects of close parallel thirds derived from the erotic friction that led to sexual reproduction could manifest themselves in body parts, words, or sounds. When women did fantastic things with their mouths and throats, they did so in a world that imagined the uterus as a closed mouth and tested a woman's fertility by sitting her over potent garlic and checking the smell of her breath.

---

[1] Manuel García, *Traité complet de l'art du chant*, trans. L. J. Rondeleux (Geneva: Minkoff, 1985).

This impossibility of inhabiting that world explains, at least in part, the difficulty of making pre-common practice music exciting to today's undergraduates, and why the shocking effects about which Monteverdi's commentators wrote seem merely quaint to post-Wagnerian ears. The marvels of the voice depended on glottal articulations accompanied by continuo textures that hardly achieved the volume of today's loud Punk concerts or even operatic productions with bel canto sopranos and full orchestras. How terrifying can the infernal shades of *Il ballo delle ingrate*, with their suspensions and four-part texture, really be after hearing a car alarm in the middle of the night? And after seeing *Silence of the Lambs* or *Star Wars*, how impressive and frightening is a flaming *bocca d'inferno*?

Exploring the impossibility of inhabiting an early modern experience of song assumes that, since our ears are conditioned by everything we have heard, they cannot take in Monteverdi's music in the way that early modern listeners did. Rather than suggesting that we can understand the embodiment of that experience, the discussions that follow approach the process of experiencing music discursively. They examine the musical and cultural production of the female voice through the bodies that made and received music – the gendering of those bodies and the peculiar inflections of song with ideologies of gender and sex. Considering music as sung, not just as heard or in relation to text, illuminates the inextricable intertwining of song and body. A familiarity with vocal anatomies opens up an engagement with early modern music that recuperates the physical stuff of the human voice and its imagined organic relation to the body's inner processes. Such an engagement also reinserts the corporeality of the performer's body into musicological inquiry. Unfortunately no one left a record of exactly what the experience of song was in early modern Italy. Thus any account of it must deal with a conglomeration of historical traces, traces which become even fainter when dealing with women since men produced the vast majority of sources.[2]

"O come sei gentile," a soprano duet from Monteverdi's seventh book of madrigals, serves as a textual and performative account of early modern constructions of the voice. Replete with the diminutions, augmentations, wide ranges, tremolos and poetic turns of phrase that were quickly becoming conventional, this piece is an extreme version of the physical discipline imposed by vocal compositions, how-to manuals, accounts of singers, and singers themselves. The following discussion stands as the book's most concrete example of the ways in which attending to bodily mechanics of singing that would have instantly and unthinkingly

---

[2] For a consideration of some early modern understandings of gender see Constance Jordan, *Renaissance Feminism* (Ithaca: Cornell University Press, 1990).

inflected the early modern experience of it can change our understanding of a piece.

Rather than insisting that this was a piece necessarily sung by women, I position it as an example of the kind of music making that women participated in during the early years of the seventeenth century. Imagining a performance of "O come sei gentile" by women provides an opportunity to reconstruct the physical experience of singing. The prevalent written-out ornaments, around which my reading focuses, resemble closely those composed by Luzzaschi for the *concerto delle donne* and featured in Caccini's *Le nuove musiche*, which we know were sung by women. In addition Monteverdi certainly worked with singing women throughout his career. At Mantua he directed an all-female vocal ensemble in which his wife Claudia Cattaneo most likely sung, and during his tenure there girls were part of the corpus of children between the ages of eleven and fourteen recruited for the court.[3] Adriana Basile sang at Mantua beginning in 1610 and she continued to be one of his favorite sopranos, as indicated by his request in 1617 for her to sing the roles of Venus and one of three ladies in the never-finished *Le nozze di Tetide*.[4]

Taking "O come sei gentile" as an affair of throats allows for a discussion of the ways that throats were imagined to work and the discourses that circumscribed that working. Discussions of this song, interspersed throughout this chapter, highlight the activities of the throat and the musical structures that contain them, bringing to the fore a tension between the ornamental flourishes and the unrelenting harmonic patterns that they encircle. In the piece, ornamentation stands in for both the throat and singing, and the composed harmonic and melodic gestures can be said to represent a musical containment of song that mirrors the disciplining of female voices. Musical structures propel and contain the female voice in a process highly contingent upon larger social meanings.

Rather than the usual musical or poetic reading, I want to illuminate how the activity of singing "O come sei gentile" would have been understood. Reconfiguring singing as an embodied activity highlights the materiality of the female voice. This involves a different kind of listening, one that takes into account the physical activity of singing and inserts the performer's body into a mode of musical analysis that has tended to erase her and that incorporates historical and social contexts as well as the irreducible bodily element. The body becomes the central unit of analysis and the medium for the experience of music. I am

---

[3] For details about who sang at the Mantuan court, see Susan Parisi, "Ducal Patronage of Music in Mantua 1587–1627: An Archival Study" (Ph.D. dissertation, University of Illinois at Urbana, 1989).

[4] For a detailed discussion of this fiasco, see Paolo Fabbri, *Monteverdi* (Cambridge: Cambridge University Press, 1994).

interested in sonority as it might have been experienced corporeally and sensually by the performer and the listener – in the reverberations through throats, mouths, lungs, ears, and heads. Thinking through this corporeal element involves concentrating on process and local events rather than large-scale architectural elements because the relative autonomy of the sensuality of music passes on a moment-to-moment basis that often eludes large-scale structures. Descriptive analysis then comes into the picture as a mechanism for exposing musical details whose significance may lie outside the notes and because it is our disciplinary method for communicating musical process. My interest in the details lies in the larger contexts for their striking effects and the body parts that performed them in their discursive and cultural milieus.

Choosing a piece generally associated with Monteverdi's later period consciously avoids the assumption of a radical break in Monteverdi's style between early and late periods and between polyphony and monody. Because the seventh book of madrigals seems so in tune with nascent Baroque harmonic practices, musicologists have tended to assign it a leading role in narratives of historical progress. In contrast, listening to the body-based rhetoric that circumscribes the kind of singing on display in these madrigals suggests that the received understandings of the voice – its substance, its production, and its participation in the complex workings of the body – still reflected Aristotelian and Galenic doctrines that would continue to be read in elite learned circles through the beginning of the next century. Monteverdi's music, in other words, elaborates both emergent and residual cultural forces that pushed against each other throughout the seventeenth century.

"O come sei gentile" opens a window to a decidedly Renaissance understanding of singing as an embodied activity. But it also moves beyond the Renaissance, and thus foreshadows the issues of periodization fleshed out in the book's final chapter, by attending to the counterpoint between cultural and musical forces. Monteverdi straddled more than one kind of worldview, which meant that listeners and performers alike could still imagine new vocal styles according to ways of knowing grounded in an earlier age. Because empirical fact always is conditioned by prevailing structures of knowledge, new truths about the body emerged slowly, so that while the so-called scientific revolution called into question basic tenets of humoral medicine, those same tenets still permeated learned medical thought. For instance, Vesalius's 1543 anatomical treatise claimed to correct over a hundred of Galen's mistakes, but nonetheless remained grounded in Galenic thought. And even after William Harvey posited a theory for the circulation of blood in 1624 that all but invalidated these ancient ideas, it took several more decades for medical and social discourses to cast off their humoral vestiges.

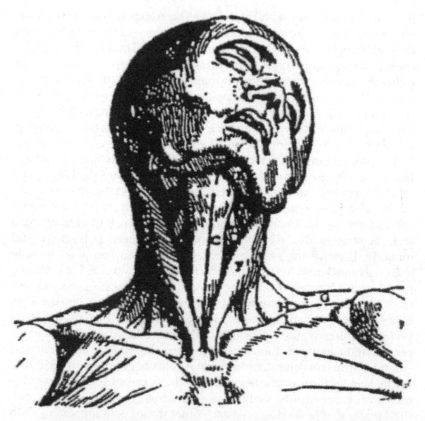

Figure 1.1, Vesalius, drawing of neck muscles. *De Humani Corporis Fabrica* (Basel, 1543)

Representative of the early seventeenth-century penchant for solo and chamber singing over basso continuo, the florid virtuosity of "O come sei gentile" comprises a music making devoted first and foremost to the pleasures and tricks of the voice and in particular to the extreme cultivation of the voice as an instrument of marvel. This "luxuriant style," to borrow Anthony Newcomb's term, characterized by an ability to sing florid passages with great rapidity and accuracy, first appeared in Luzzaschi's madrigals of the 1580s. A number of Monteverdi's madrigals from the fourth, fifth, and sixth books feature two voices singing in counterpoint over a bass part that marks the harmony, perhaps alluding to the presence of the Ferrarese-type *concerto delle donne* at Mantua as early as the 1590s.[5]

---

[5] For a detailed discussion of duets see John Whenham, *Duet and Dialogue in the Age of Monteverdi* (Ann Arbor: UMI Press, 1982).

Monteverdi published "O come sei gentile" as the first of four soprano duets clustered at the beginning of the 1619 *Concerto: settimo libro de madrigali*. The volume, dedicated to sung explorations of love, was compiled during his tenure as maestro di cappella of St. Mark's in Venice. There he trained and maintained the chapel singers, recruiting and cultivating skilled voices and choosing the music they performed. Perhaps his intimate involvement with singers explains the resemblance of this eclectic volume to an aural and poetic dictionary of what was done with the human voice at the time.[6] Reaching both forwards and backwards, the collection appeared almost two decades before public opera was institutionalized in Venice, and two decades after Caccini, Monteverdi, and Peri had each declared himself the father of a new way of composing. This fashion for trained singers inspired an influx of concerto volumes like Monteverdi's that, beginning in the 1620s, flooded Italian print culture and soon all but eliminated the polyphonic madrigal. At this pivotal moment for singing in Italy, trained virtuosi began to dominate musical practice. In terms of style, the luxuriant and florid gestures of the pieces in the seventh book of madrigals retrospectively resemble the duets of the 1607 *Orfeo*, the continuo madrigals from the fifth book of madrigals, and the 1610 Vespers in their free melismas, homophonic declamation, and copious parallel third and sixth passages.[7]

Even without the music, Guarini's poem highlights many of the issues surrounding singing and sensuality that preoccupy this book. The poem's most notable feature may perhaps lie in the ample opportunities it provided Monteverdi to play with some form of the verb *cantare*.

O come sei gentile	How pretty you are,
Caro augellino!	Dear little bird!
O quanto è il mio stato	and how my condition
amoroso al tuo simile!	of love is like yours!
Io prigion, tu prigion;	I am a prisoner, you are a prisoner;
tu canti, io canto;	you sing, I sing;
Tu canti per colei	you sing for her who has bound you,
Che t'ha legato, ed io canto per lei.	And I too sing for her too.

---

[6] For more on Monteverdi's escapades in Venice see Denis Stevens, *Monteverdi in Venice* (London: Associated University Presses, 2001).

[7] Monteverdi dedicated the volume to the Duchess of Mantua, Caterina de' Medici, wife of Ferdinando Gonzaga. Caterina de' Medici had just married Ferdinando Gonzaga, an amateur composer, avid musical patron, and Monteverdi admirer. The proclivities of that court may well have had something to do with dedication. For speculations on the reasons for the dedication see Denis Arnold, "Monteverdi's Necklace," *The Musical Quarterly* 49/3 (July 1973) : 370–381. Arnold suggests that Monteverdi made this dedication because Caterina was the wife of his patron, she was a Medici, and he had missed her recent wedding to Ferdinando Gonzaga.

Ma in questo è differente	But in this my unhappy lot
La mia sorte dolente:	differs in this one way:
Che giova pur a te l'esser canoro;	it serves you well to sing;
Vivi cantando, ed io cantando moro.	Singing you live, but I, singing, die.

The poem contrasts a bird and the speaker who sing for a love object. Singing represents the bird's life, and it sends the speaker to a love-death that highlights the erotic potential of song. Singing brings the speaker to orgasm, which reflects received understandings of the physical activity of singing and body parts that make it possible. At the same time, the linking of love and death and the metaphoric description of orgasm as death draws on the literary and philosophical traditions of Petrarch and the *trattati d'amore* – a set of conventions which had arguably been the central point of Monteverdi's fourth and fifth books of madrigals and had very palpable musical analogues. The conflation in Guarini's final line of singing, love, and death positions singing as an explicitly sexual activity; likewise, it insists on love as dangerous and singing as an activity that, like sexual consummation, can lead to the icy fire of a Neoplatonic love-death. The musical setting makes no textural distinction between the poet and the bird – their interaction is animated by two interlaced high voices.

If women sang the words in Guarini's poem, their overly sexualized bodies, beating throats, and boiling temperatures performed precisely the female allure about which their lips, tongues, and teeth complained. Ventriloquizing male complaints against women, they at once taunted their listeners and exceeded the words they sang. Allowing this possibility reminds us that the gender of the poetic speaking voice, in this case male, does not necessarily correlate with the body that animated it. Again, one thinks of the countless Petrarchan odes to unrequiting ladies sung by women of the *concerto delle donne*, not to mention the frequency with which castrati performed female roles. That female members of the *commedia dell'arte* performed as men, and men in Rome routinely played female roles brings to the fore the very fluid attitude toward the envoicing of masculinity and femininity that pervaded a variety of performance traditions in early modern Italy.

It does not take a well-developed feminist consciousness to see pieces like "O come sei gentile," and the rhetoric that surrounded them, as a reflection of early modern assumptions about gender difference, women's bodies, and musical pleasure. Monteverdi's association of high voices with virtuosity in "O come sei gentile" reflects a fashion for cultivated high voices that can be traced back to the 1580s with the famed *concerto delle donne* of Ferrara and even earlier in court spectacles and that also manifested itself in the presence of castrati. When Monteverdi began his career, singing ladies were most often heard in the open secret of Northern Italian courts and in court-sponsored theatrical entertainments, while by the end of his career they flourished on the vitally public space of the operatic stage.[8] Along the way their voices acquired the status of a commodity as their sounds were slowly separated from the agent of musical and cultural production. In addition to women, the Italians relied on castrati for their high voices, first imported into the Sistine Chapel choir in the 1560s and fully installed as operatic superstars by the end of the seventeenth century.[9]

Despite their surgically altered competitors, female performers quickly rose in status, which in turn inspired numerous artistic celebrations that displayed the female voice and contemplated the immense power of song. In addition to the volumes of poetry dedicated to specific early seventeenth-century virtuose like Adriana Basile, Vittoria Archilei, and Anna Renzi, countless poets and musicians addressed the female voice as an abstract ideal, attempting to capture in words and in music the aesthetic and sensual experience of hearing women sing. Another of Monteverdi's singing madrigals, "Mentre vaga Angioletta," reveals a descriptive process that endeavors to discursively codify, and in effect contain, the unruly force of the female voice. My interest here, however, lies more in the discipline physically enforced upon female singers by the composition of ornaments and vocal training.

The early modern singing body

It is easy to think of the experience of singing a piece like "O come sei gentile" as transhistorical. The performance practice movement has worked to recreate as closely as possible the sounds that filled cathedrals and private chambers four hundred years ago. Moreover, looking at Monteverdi's scores and reading accounts of the piece almost allows the possibility of imagining what it was like to hear this song in an intimate performance: *L'Arianna* at the 1608 festivities, or a madrigal

---

[8] Ann MacNeil highlights the career of the exceptional sixteenth-century actress/singer Virginia Andreini and demonstrates previously unknown ways in which women participated in musical and theatrical life in the sixteenth century: *Music and Women of the Commedia dell'Arte in the Late Sixteenth Century* (New York: Oxford University Press, 2003). Nina Treadwell's dissertation provides a wonderfully complete look at singing women in sixteenth-century court cultures: Nina Treadwell, "Restaging the Sirens: Musical Women in the Performance of Sixteenth-Century Italian Theater" (Ph.D. dissertation, University of Southern California, 2003). Her work builds on and adds to the picture drawn by Anthony Newcomb, *The Madrigal at Ferrara* (Princeton: Princeton University Press, 1980).

[9] For a study of the trajectory of castrati singers see John Rosselli, "The Castrati as a Professional Group and a Social Phenomenon, 1550–1850," *Acta Musicologica* 40/2 (1988): 143–179. For a more recent account, see Roger Freitas, *Un atto d'ingegno: A Castrato in the Seventeenth Century* (New Haven: Yale University Press, 1998).

in the Mirror Room at Mantua. I am most interested in the "almost" of those statements, and thus in positioning the experience of song as ontologically and phenomenologically determined. It is conditioned by the always-constructed experience of inhabiting a body. If the body materializes according to time and place, then I would suggest that the varieties of experience marked by song and sensation exist outside of any biological reality.[10]

To relate these concepts to actual music making, the performance practice movement might productively be seen as an exercise in materializing the body in an early modern way.[11] Performers of early music use their bodies differently than do modern performers. A harpsichordist's fingers use a softer touch than does a pianist. The best singers of early modern music, like Ellen Hargis and Julianne Baird, cultivate a pure, focused tone, a wide dynamic range, resonant vowels, and the ability to soar in the low to mid ranges of their voices, in contrast to coloratura sopranos. Singing more lightly with a forward focused sound, they move air differently and focus their sound in alternative cavities of resonance. They learn to adjust their bodies to execute the rapid opening and closing of the glottis required for the music they sing and control the natural vibratos of their voices. Earlier techniques tend to favor suppleness and agility over power, using lower air pressure and a more relaxed vocal tract. Making the lightning-quick glottal articulation that lost popularity when singers moved out of princely chambers into large public spaces where they became more difficult to hear, involves air percussing against the soft palate like a giggle. They demand that the singer restrain with exquisite control the release of breath, gathering air and releasing it ever so slowly. The ability to control the rapid opening and closing of the glottis, necessary to produce the throat articulations of "O come sei gentile," reflects a decidedly early modern way of using the body and goes against modern vocal techniques which encourage singers to envision the throat as a hollow tube through which air passes.

Though we can not know for sure what it felt like to make music in the early modern world, we can listen intently to the bodily traces in texts about singing that call attention to interactions between the glottis, ear, sound, and song. My interest in the language of descriptions diverges from most music scholars who, when reading singing treatises, tend to focus intently on training methods and ornamentation instructions, since, as one commentator on the philosophical elements of a Renaissance singing text writes, "this homage to Aristotle and Galen has little

---

[10] Judith Butler, *Gender Trouble* (New York: Routledge, 1990).

[11] I am not here trying to engage the many debates around historical performance or enter into a discussion of authenticity. See Nicholas Kenyon, *Authenticity and Early Music: A Symposium* (New York: Oxford University Press, 1988).

value for modern students."[12] On the contrary, these commentaries on ancient thinkers mandate careful scrutiny because they reveal concepts about the body that laid the foundation for early modern understandings of the voice.

I want to think first about what pre-modern societies did know about the voice, about their imaginings of producing sounds like those in "O come sei gentile." Even Galen and Aristotle understood that sound depends on the larynx: "It is evident too why fish have no voice, because they have no larynx. And they do not have this part since they neither take in air nor breathe."[13] But it took a very long time for anatomists to understand exactly how the voice was produced. Leonardo's anatomical study *Quaderni d'Anatomia*, completed around 1500, presented the first drawing of the larynx that resembles what we take as truth today. That document had little impact since it was lost for three hundred years. Fabricius also presented anatomically correct drawings of the voice though his work had a similarly negligible impact. The early eighteenth century witnessed a debate about whether the voice was primarily a wind or string instrument. In 1741 Anton Ferrein finally settled the matter with his acoustical experiments that involved blowing through the vocal organs of a corpse and demonstrating that the vocal cords vibrate in the manner of a viol. He was satirized for this project in Denis Diderot's fable about a talking vagina called *Le bijoux indiscrets*. And, as mentioned earlier, in 1855 Manuel García, a Spanish singing teacher living in London, performed an examination of his own larynx that showed the vocal cords in action.

Because the actual mechanics of the voice remained mysterious to musical practitioners for such a long time, it is crucial to examine the rhetoric used to explain a fundamentally invisible apparatus. Even as late as 1760 the music theorist Rameau wrote that "The larynx, the windpipe, and the glottis are not at our disposal, we cannot see their different positions, transformations, to each sound we wish to give; but we do at least know that they must not be constricted in these differences, that they must be left at liberty to follow their natural movement, that we are only masters of the breath, and that in consequence it is not for us to govern it so well, that nothing can disturb the effect."[14] For Rameau, though, the materials of the voice remained mysterious: they were deeply tied to breath.

At the end of the Italian Renaissance, the physicality of song was derived from an understanding of the body that had begun in ancient

[12] Carol MacClintock, *Readings in the History of Performance* (Bloomington: Indiana University Press, 1979), 35.

[13] Hippocrates G. Apostle, *Aristotle's On the Soul* (Grinnell, Iowa: Peripatetic Press, 1981), 34.

[14] Rameau, *Code de Musique Praticque* (Paris, 1760), 16.

Greece and continued to dominate medical practice and cultural under-standings of the body well into the seventeenth century. During this time, medical scholars participated in the humanist fascination with ancient texts, making translations, commentaries, and indexes of ancient sources.[15] Andrew Wear estimates that between 1500 and 1700 in Western Europe at least 590 different translations of Galen appeared in print.[16] As the foundational texts of Galen, Aristotle, Herophilus, and Plato explained it, and as early modern literati understood it, the health of the humoral body depended on a precarious balance of fluids managed by the ingestion and excretion of matter and the maintenance of an appropriate temperate economy. Fluids contained in the body belonged to one of four humors: blood, phlegm, yellow bile (choler), and black bile (melancholy). Modern English retains vestiges of humoral medicine in phrases like a hot temper or the need to cool down after a fight.

The humoral body functioned via a complicated set of internal pro-cedures in which good health depended on maintaining the proper cor-poreal fluidity. All fluids could be continuously transformed into one another, so that sweat, blood, breast milk, semen, saliva, and tears com-prised, at their base, the same materials. Unbalanced humors resulted in bad fluids, which in turn caused illness and pain. A healthy body required a particular balance of the four qualities that described all mat-ter: heat, cold, moisture, and dryness. It consisted of four elements – fire, earth, water, and air – and was physically continuous with the rest of the material and immaterial world. Vocal exercises contributed to all of these concoctions. The increased heat produced by singing favored digestion in the stomach, which helped with evacuation, and the thin-ning of blood which raising the voice caused guarded against excess phlegm by thinning and drying the humors. In this model, the parallel substances of voice, tears, vomit, and sweat turned into one another and flowed in and out of the porous body through open orifices, purifying, nourishing, and flushing it.

---

[15] This reliance on humoral medicine is part of the Renaissance humanist immersion in ancient texts of all kinds. For comprehensive studies of the impact of ancient medical practice on medieval and Renaissance Europe, see Nancy G. Siraisi, *Medieval and Early Renaissance Medicine: An Introduction to Knowledge and Practice* (Chicago: University of Chicago Press, 1990); Siraisi, *Avicenna in Renaissance Italy: The Canon and Medical Teaching in Italian Universities after 1500* (Princeton: Princeton University Press, 1987); Ian Maclean, *The Renaissance Notion of Woman: A Study in the Fortunes of Scholasticism and Medieval Science in European Intellectual Life* (Cambridge: Cambridge University Press, 1980); Giancarlo Zanier, "Platonic Trends in Renaissance Medicine," *Journal of the History of Ideas* 48 (1987): 509–519.

[16] Andrew Wear, "Medicine in Early Modern Europe 1500–1700," *The Western Medical Tradition 800 BC to AD 1800*, ed. Lawrence Conrad et al. (Cambridge: Cambridge University Press, 1995), 253.

Music, and more particularly singing, could radically alter this delicate system by stimulating the pulse or rebalancing the humors. This alterative ability manifested itself in part through the health benefits and dangers associated with vocal exercises that peppered medical writings from the ancient world through the eighteenth century. In these writings vocal and musical activities could be used to modulate the pulse or the body's fluid balance. In the absence of theories of circulation, pulse remained a mysterious force that was inherently imbued with music and that musical sound could alter. From this perspective, the voice was assimilated into bodily processes through an analogy between the spirit, breath, and voice in which the latter coalesced with the spirit – a vaporous and airy substance or non-substance that animated the body, fusing the live but incorporeal soul with the lifeless corporeal body that it inhabited.[17] Galen explained that the emission of breath was "the materials of voice" and "expiration is generally defined as the specific substance of the voice."[18] Aristotle wrote that "voice is the impact of the air breathed on the so-called windpipe and is caused by the soul in three parts of the body."[19]

Beginning with Aristotle, philosophers had imbued song with an animating force and used it as one of the primary distinctions between humans and animals. Song was crucial to humanness both because it kept the body in motion and because it made communication possible.

For as already stated, not every sound made by an animal is voice (sound can be made also by the tongue and when one is coughing), but that which produces the impact should be animate and do so with some image. For voice is a certain kind of sound with meaning and not any sound of the air breathed like a cough; an animal uses the air breathed to strike the air in the windpipe against the windpipe. A sign of this is that an animal cannot make a vocal sound while inhaling or exhaling but only while holding the breath for it is only with the breath held that an animal can cause the motion, which makes a vocal sound.[20]

In peripatetic philosophy, then, voice implied meaning and, like the material spirits themselves, was animate.

In addition, the voice participated in maintaining an appropriate body temperature. Normal breathing regulated body heat. Singing raised the body temperature and, conversely, cooling down the body damaged the voice. Galen makes explicit the intimate relationship between voice

---

[17] My understanding of the spirit and the organic soul in Renaissance philosophy and the importance of these concepts to music owes much to Gary Tomlinson's work on Renaissance magic and subjectivity. See his *Music in Renaissance Magic: Toward a Historiography of Others* (Chicago: University of Chicago Press, 1993).

[18] Margaret Tallmadge May, *Galen On The Usefulness of the Parts of the Body*, vol. II (Ithaca: Cornell University Press, 1968), 341.

[19] Apostle, *Aristotle's On the Soul*, 34.   [20] Ibid., 34.

and temperature when he writes that "I also know of a patient whose recurrent nerves were so damaged by extreme cooling during surgery of the neck in winter time that his voice was almost lost. But when we understood this we heated the vocal organ with warm drugs and thus restored the natural balance for the nerves."[21] Likewise, Aristotle directly links voice to body temperature:

The heat and cold of their place of habitation is another factor contributing to the fact that the natural construction of some animals is such that they have deep voices, and of others that they have high voices. Breath that is hot produces the deepest heaviest voices, owing to its thickness; breath that is cold produces the opposite result, owing to its thinness. This is plain in the case of musical pipes as well: people who blow comparatively hot breath into the pipe – if they breathe it out as though they were saying "Ah" play a deeper note.[22]

Associating the voice with temperature gave it a special proximity to the heart, which was the core of the sensitive soul. The body's heat was centered in the left ventricle of the heart where air drawn in from the lungs and transmitted to the heart cooled and fortified it. The furnace-like cavity of the heart refined airy spirits into vital spirits. The continued currency of this temperate economy allowed Giulio Strozzi, as late as 1643, to describe Anna Renzi, best known for her performance as Ottavia in Monteverdi's *Poppea*, as having a voice that "varies from the temperament of her chest and throat, for which good voice, much warmth is needed to expand the passages and enough humidity to soften it and make it tender."[23]

In addition to reflecting received understandings of the body, the rhetoric used to describe the voice maps onto, and is mapped by, reigning constructions of sex and gender difference. Less perfect than the deep voice which marked a noble nature, the high soprano voice reflected the imperfections of women who were, as a rule, too cold, too weak, too moist, and generally out of control. Hot breath produced deep voices and colder, weaker breath produced high voices. Galen's explanation that "drier bodies make better sounds" slights wet and leaky women.[24] According to him, the deficiencies of the high voice resulted from a too-cold body propelling a small amount of air at too rapid a speed. Boys, girls, and women had high voices because their small throats contain only a very little bit of air. Aristotle explains that "on account of their debility most animals and most females set but a small amount of air

---

[21] May, *Galen On the Usefulness of the Parts*, 389.

[22] Aristotle, *Generation of Animals*, trans. A. L. Peck (Cambridge, MA: Harvard University Press, 1990), 542.

[23] Strozzi, as cited in Rosand, "The First Opera Diva: Anna Renzi," *Historical Performance* 3/1 (1990): 4.

[24] May, *Galen On the Usefulness of the Parts*, vol. I, 344.

in movement and therefore have high-pitched voices."[25] Galen further illuminates these deficiencies through a discussion of castration. "All animals, including humans, when castrated, turn over to the female state because their sinewy strength is slackened and at their source they emit a female-like voice."[26] Weak voices come from weak muscles. In light of the negative implications of the high voice, it comes as no surprise that most writers cautioned men against using the falsetto – or "feigned" voice – made by speeding up movement of the air, unless, according to Camillo Maffei, "he desires to persuade, to move someone, and to impose his will."[27] The power of a voice emitted under high air pressure literally penetrated and imposed itself on the ear.

The doctor/philosopher/musician Camillo Maffei's 1562 letter on singing provides a guide to the elusive vocabularies that reinforced assumptions considered too self-evident to warrant discussion for over a hundred more years.[28] My reading of this document and others deliberately avoids the twentieth-century tendency to substitute figurative meanings when literal ones would be more appropriate. Though I begin my anatomy of the voice with Maffei, I move freely between treatises, poems, and musical settings written between 1562 and 1640. Rather than attempting to posit a stable concept of the voice over such a long period of time, I want to offer a conglomeration of understandings that were in circulation at the turn of the seventeenth century. Since empirical fact, musical practice, and theoretical knowledge move disjunctly, it is not at all unusual for documents that span a period of half a century or more to reflect similar worldviews and use similar descriptive terms and phrases. Thus treatises from the late seventeenth century are still grounded in ideas that Renaissance thinkers gleaned from their ancient sources. In effect, sixteenth-century writers, relying on ancient sources, created tropes that stayed in fashion well into the seventeenth century. For instance, Maffei's terms pervade vocal manuals and descriptions of singers through the end of the seventeenth century. Memorable descriptions using parallel terms include Monteverdi's many assessments of singers from the first years of the seventeenth century and Giulio Strozzi's descriptions of Anna Renzi in the 1630s and 1640s. These terms remained common well into the eighteenth century and appear in treatises like Pierfrancesco Tosi's (1723) *Opinioni de' cantori antichi e moderni o sieno osservazioni sopra il canto figurato*.

[25] Aristotle, *Generation of Animals*, 543.

[26] May, *Galen On the Usefulness of the Parts*, vol. I, 344.

[27] N. Bridgeman, "Giovanni Camillo Maffei et sa lettre sur le chant," *Revue de Musicologie* 1956: 10–34. Translation modified from MacClintock, *Readings in the History of Performance*.

[28] *Canto figurato* also uses Maffei's vocabularies.

With its juxtaposition of singing instructions, philosophical musings, and medical knowledge, Maffei's letter reflects the author's careers as a doctor of medicine, learned philosopher, and amateur musician, reminding modern readers of the intertwining of these disciplines during the Renaissance. Quoting almost verbatim, sometimes with acknowledgment and sometimes not, from Aristotle's treatise *On the Soul* and Galen's *On the Usefulness of the Parts*, Maffei begins with a detailed description of the anatomy, physiology, and philosophy of the voice, a description that presumes the voice to be a substance in motion. "The voice sounds in the instrument because of the air that is forced from the chest into the throat."[29]

In this model, the voice – or breath – forces air from the chest through the throat and into the mouth where the tongue, lips, and teeth give it articulation and create speech or song. Pitch and volume result from the swiftness with which air moves through the throat. Repeating Aristotle, Maffei compares making a voice to making a brass vase. Brass comprises the materials of the vase, and breath the materials of the voice. This suggests that when Guarini talks about "forming and molding" song in his poem "Gorga di cantatrice," discussed at length in chapter 4, he means literally making sound from air.[30] Controlling sound worked something like molding figures out of clay – an understanding that derives from Aristotle's idea that all bodily processes involved master, material, motive, and instrument. The mind acts as the master, the chest represents the motive, air is the material, and the throat and lungs are the instruments. Singing cultivates with mind and body formless sounds that air coursing through the body produces and eventually pushes out into the world. Considering early modern categorizations of form as related to the male and superior soul and of matter, the amorphous physical stuff that receives shape from form, as feminine suggests that the activity of ornamentation involved the rational control over a feminine, physical, and inferior force. The raw female voice awaited formation by the rational male mind.

Maffei, Monteverdi, and others also followed Aristotle in connecting the ability to perform vocal tricks to the pliability of the materials inside the throat. Their discussions referred to the kinds of glottal ornaments that run through "O come sei gentile," and that appear as standard examples of ornaments in singing treatises of the time. For example, when the poet and the bird begin to sing on the words "Tu canti," Monteverdi captures the juxtaposition between the bird and the man

---

[29] Bridgeman "Maffei," 39.
[30] Claudio Monteverdi, *Madrigali guerrieri et amorosi*, ed. Gian Francesco Malipiero (New York: Dover, 1990), ix.

with a string of ornaments and vocal flourishes that are labeled below. The voices take turns articulating melismatic augmentation until they finally come together again in parallel thirds at the end of the poetic line (Ex. 1.1, mm. 32–54). On the first "Tu canti," the singer embellishes a simple scale that moves in contrary motion with the walking bass. "Io canto" gets an embellishment of dotted rhythms over the same walking bass, which Caccini labels in the preface to *Le nuove musiche* as "beating of the throat." On line 6, "Tu canti per lei," the voices alternate a quick turnover with yet another repetition of the same bass line. The word "legato" brings about a gruppo, or double relish, and "io canto per lei" is set to a dotted rhythmic ornamentation of a simple scale over the same walking bass.

Responding to sounds like these, in his poem "Gorga di cantatrice" Guarini lyrically describes a woman "tempering the flexible voice" by "flexing and pushing it."[31] Known for his ability to judge singers, Monteverdi differentiated flexible good voices from rigid bad voices. His use of the terms flexible and rigid can be traced through Maffei's text, which elaborates on their usage. Maffei explains that "I say that both of these voices are caused by the internal surface of the throat. When the surface is smooth and when it is perfect and properly proportioned, it makes the voice smooth and equal. And, if because of some infection of the surface or lack of proper proportion of the throat, it makes the voice become hoarse, harsh and unequal."[32] Singing embellishments, diminutions, passaggi, and tremolo all required a "flexible" voice. Aristotle states that, "Flexibility depends upon whether the organ is soft or hard."[33] Working with Aristotle's text, Maffei explains that "By the flexible voice you must understand that a pliable voice is one that is varied sweetly, so that the ear is satisfied. By the 'rigid' voice you should understand a hard one that varies in a way so that the ear is disturbed."[34] He leaves out the second elaborating part of his predecessor's sentence, which explains that "The reason for roughness and smoothness of voice and all unevenness of that sort is that the part or organ through which the voice travels is rough or smooth."[35]

This materialistic rhetoric continued well into the seventeenth century. In 1636, Marin Mersenne described vocal talent in terms of substance: "it is necessary for the muscles and the cartilage to be very responsive." [36] He explains the pleasure of a flexible voice in some detail as

---

[31] Battista Guarini, *Opere*, ed. Marziano Guglielmetti (Turin: U.T.E.T., 1971), 301.
[32] MacClintock, *Readings in the History of Performance*, 43.
[33] Aristotle, *On the Generation of Animals*, 553.
[34] MacClintock, *Readings in the History of Performance*, 45.
[35] Aristotle, *Generation of Animals*, 543.
[36] Marin Mersenne, *Harmonie Universelle* (1636–37), "Livre Premier de la Voix," p. 4.

sweetness and a certain harmoniousness, on which depends the charms which ravish the hearers, for voices which are hard do not please, however accurate they may be and possessed of other qualities I have mentioned, for they have too much sharpness and glitter, which hurts sensitive ears, and which hinders their gliding pleasantly enough into their hearers' spirit to win them, and to carry them whither so ever you desire.[37]

For Mersenne the ability of sound to move through the ear depends on the appropriate tactile properties. Expressing similar statements as late as 1645, Giano Nicio Eritreo describes a singer who could "move his voice from highest to lowest, passing it through various turns. He could twist and bend it like the softest wax whenever he wished."[38]

Such an intensely physical vocabulary also permeates written descriptions of vocal training, especially of the most basic ornament, the tremolo. Once a singer trained her throat to make a tremolo – one pitch sung repeatedly – she could in theory make her voice do anything. Caccini describes training his two wives and daughters to sing with an exercise that took them through a gradually accelerating tremolo. He instructed them to "restrike" each note with the throat. Zacconi's pontifications on the nature and importance of tremolo display an equally material tendency. His vocabulary always connotes motion, as in his assertion that the "movement of the voice pushes the movement of the gorgia," which refers to air and breath being slowly and carefully released.[39] He also refers to "velocity of the figures." He describes the tremolo at length:

The tremolo, that is the tremulous voice, is the true portal to the passaggi and the means of mastering the gorgia; just as the ship is made to move more easily when already in motion. This tremolo should be slight and pleasing, for if it is exaggerated and forced, it tires and annoys. Its nature is such that if used at all it should always be used since use converts it into habit, for this motion of the voice helps and spontaneously encourages the movement of the gorgia and miraculously facilitates the undertaking of passaggi. This movement of which I speak should not be undertaken if it cannot be done with just rapidity, vigorously, and vehemently.[40]

Zacconi's theory sounds like Aristotelian physics. Objects have preferred states and they stay in those states unless prompted to do otherwise.

The physicality of singing is further exemplified in both Zacconi and Maffei's insistence that proper singing can be learned only through listening. In describing gestures like those of "O come sei gentile" Zacconi

---

[37] Mersenne, *Harmonie Universelle*, vol. II, vi, 353.

[38] Giano Nicio Eritreo, *Pinacotheca altera* II (Amsterdam, 1645), 217.

[39] Zacconi, *Prattica di musica* (Bologna: Forni, 1592) 60.   [40] Ibid., 63.

writes that "it is of such nature that because of the velocity into which so many notes are compressed, it is much better to learn by hearing it than by written examples, because one cannot write down the measure and tempo in which it has to be delivered without error."[41] He describes a physical transmission from ear to mouth. Gestures like tremolos and trills, by manipulating the throat, tongue, and breath, propel a series of physical and physiological processes.

The implications of these processes are partially illuminated by returning to the notion of flexible voices. Maffei, paraphrasing Aristotle's very material discussion, writes that "since anything that is soft can be controlled and made to assume all sorts of shapes, whereas anything hard cannot. Thus this organ, if it is soft, can utter a small sound or a large one, and therefore a high one or a deep one as well, because it controls the breath easily as it becomes hard and soft itself. Hardness on the other hand cannot be controlled."[42] The key to this quotation lies in his insistence on singing as controlling a physical organ.

Consorted and contorted throats

It may seem that I have wandered far from "O come sei gentile," but I use it as an exemplar of the physical processes enumerated above, of what was thought to happen to singing bodies – especially women's. The piece is an affair of throats: the two imaginary throats of the poet and the bird and the two real throats of the singers. The voice becomes a soundboard for the poem's imaginary throats. The affair begins with the piece's opening imitative ornamental flourishes that project the consort of bird and poet. The shared timbre of the two voices allows for a strikingly consonant sound that the focus of the piece on parallel thirds only intensifies. At times, the effect of two such similar voices singing in an imitative texture gives the impression of one single line, as in the setting of the word "legato." (See Example 1.1.) Such a unified effect expresses the poet's sense that with very different consequences he and the bird metaphorically sing the same song.

The virtuosic scalar exclamation on the syllable "O" creates a decidedly nonlinguistic but emphatically sung gesture. It highlights the consort of throats that propels this piece, in which song and not mere language embodies the attraction of both bird and poet to the love object as well as their transitive connection. It almost sounds as if the piece cannot quite take off, so caught up in sound and love is the speaker. The second soprano imitates the first soprano, and finally in the eighth bar the two voices sing together in parallel thirds. Song, like love, is thus conveyed

<hr>

[41] Ibid., 69.   [42] Apostle, *Aristotle's On the Soul*, 34.

Example 1.1, "O come sei gentile," mm. 32–54

Example 1.2, "O come sei gentile," mm. 1–7

both through and as a transformative experience (Example 1.2, mm. 1–7). The ornamented beginning immediately calls attention to the throat while also associating vocal flourishes with sweetness and with the appeal of the singing bird. The words are simple – "O come sei gentile" ("how sweet you are") – and translate well into musical tricks. At the same time, if one was to think harmonically, this opening sequence emphasizes the complexity of that sweetness by elaborating a melodic motion from G to D that the Eb in the bass quickly renders dissonant. Such a striking sonority creates a dissonance that projects palpable vibrations that mimic the bodily dissonance of an orgasm – the death that leads to life. Such dissonances, with the vibrations between the voices, gesture toward the erotic potential of singing and the close connection between the friction of voices and the friction of bodies.

That the flourishes showcase the singing throat and climax on a moment of friction highlights the sensuality of singing implied in the lyrics. When the singers finally ornament together over a Bb major chord with melodic motion from Bb to an F that is rendered consonant by the bass repetition of Bb, their togetherness breeds consort and allows for motion, felt here in the new sonority and the rising melodic line. The move to a major tonal area and a consonant sonority resolves the physical tension between the voices – between the throats – and projects the lover and bird joined in consonant song. I do not mean to suggest here that Monteverdi thought in such terms, but I do argue that the physical relationship between the singers' throats and the sounds was experienced through a discursive space constructed by the understanding of singing body parts and processes projected through musical moments such as these.

In general the harmonic and melodic motion of this opening is slow, almost tortured, focusing the listeners to dwell on the activities of the singing throats. Lines 2 through 4 sound like ornaments in slow motion that can not quite get going, as in the very protracted D major cadence on the final syllable of "augellino." Their slowness exaggerates the movements of the throat and suggests that the prison of love slows down the poet's bodily motion, here metonymically enacted through singing. The "O" that follows stays in this tonal area with an alternated scalar passage whose motion is cut off by the struck dissonance between the two voices on "quanto," recalling the erotic tension between the voices and literally cutting off the breath of the singers for a moment. Not surprisingly, things finally move when the two begin to really sing at the words "Tu canti" (Example 1.1). Monteverdi only breaks the string of ornamentation on the words "Ma in questo è differente" ("But in this [my unhappy lot] differs"), at which point the sopranos sing a brief recitative-like phrase in parallel thirds. This phrase seems to break from the physical tension of singing, an attempt at regaining control. The respite does not last long. As soon as the text mentions singing, "canoro," the imitative patterned ornaments return, highlighting again the throat. After a strong cadence on "canoro," harmony and melody take off for a stunning life/death juxtaposition of "vivi cantando" and "io cantando," in which each time the bird sings "vivi cantando" Monteverdi augments the short "vivi" motive and stretches out the bass sequence, so that both voices continue their ornamental tryst – the passage takes five and a half measures to complete it the second time. In contrast, the poet's singing of "io cantando moro" involves almost no ornamentation or augmentation for either voice. These more speech-like sounds contrast markedly with the overzealous ornamentation of the bird's singing. The poet's speech-like sounds lead again directly into an ornamented setting of "vivi cantando."

What did the various turns and figures that Monteverdi used to set forms of the verb *cantare* require of the throat and how were they imagined? All of these sounds consist of air moving swiftly through the throat where cartilage molds it into sound in an almost alchemical process that turns air into song. Ornaments and embellishments fell under the term "gorgia," which also meant throat or gullet, a double definition that gestures towards the intense cultivation required of singers' throats. Also known as *dispositione della gorgia* – disposition of the throat – these runs reflect a trained but naturally conditioned throat. The dotted rhythms on the first "io canto" involve what Caccini and others of his era called beating of the throat, the most effective kind of ornament. To make the trill on legato – what Zacconi and Caccini called the gruppo – the singer beat each note with her throat. Because, as with the tremolo these trills

accelerate the voice, they serve as good starting points for other passaggi. It works like winding a yo-yo. Caccini, Zacconi, and Maffei all
instructed students to first learn the tremolo by "beating every note
with the throat on the vowel."[43] These tremolo, passaggi, and other
flourishes that Caccini enumerated remained crucial skills for any virtuosa through the next century, as Giulio Strozzi's description of Anna
Renzi's vocal technique demonstrates:

> She has felicitous passages, a lively trill, both double and rinforzato, and it has
> befallen her to have to bear the full weight of an opera not fewer than twenty-six
> times, repeating it virtually every evening without losing even a single carat of
> her theatrical and most perfect voice.[44]

While the beating throats, active lips, and tongues described by Caccini,
Maffei, Zacconi, and Strozzi may seem innocent enough, the direct link
of these activities to sexual reproduction turned singing into an erotic
activity that must have greatly compromised the reputations of even
the most chaste singers. Acting vocally could be tantamount to acting
sexually. In other words, the activity of singing reinforced the erotic connotations of song implied in the focus of "O come sei gentile," on song as
a symptom of love and as a precursor to love-death. The musical enactment of love in struck dissonances, conjoined voices, and especially
musical acrobatics drew attention to the singer's throat, a body part
consistently associated with sexualized behavior and genitalia. When
women like Anna Renzi, Laura Peverara, or Anna Guarini performed
the fabulous passaggi, moving sighs, and other vocal flourishes of
"O come sei gentile" and any number of other pieces, they demonstrated
a well-developed facility with body parts directly linked by medical
practitioners to sex. The body parts that make speaking and singing
possible effected those that make sex and reproduction possible. Articulated in the throat, gorgia induced the rapid closing and opening of
the glottis, an action that paralleled the opening of the uterus imagined
to accompany orgasm. The clitoris meanwhile was known as a little
tongue.

The sexual connotations of the throat, which so enhanced the experience of singing and hearing a piece like "O come sei gentile," can
be traced back to ancient gynecology. Galen describes the neck of the
uterus as capable of opening and closing and the vagina as the door
to the womb. Renaissance thinkers still endorsed the Hippocratic belief
that intercourse deepens a woman's voice by enlarging her neck, which

---

[43] Giulio Caccini, *Le nuove musiche*, trans. H. Wiley Hitchcock (Madison: A-R Editions Inc.,
1970), 51.
[44] Rosand, "The First Opera Diva: Anna Renzi," 3–7.

"responds in sympathy to the stretching of her lower neck."[45] Ancient literature that circulated widely in the Renaissance reflected these same views. For example, predicting the physical aftermath of Thetis's wedding night based on the changes brought on by sex, Catullus writes that "tomorrow the measure of Thetis's neck will be different, perceptibly enlarged."[46] Highlighting the vocal effects of the changes intercourse wrought on the neck, Nemesianus's story of the shepherdess Donace includes a scene in which her parents discover her deflowering by taking note of the fact that "her voice no longer sounds so slender and pure as before, but is troubled and thickened; her neck is coarsened; she blushes a great deal and her veins swell."[47] The deflowering of the lady manifests itself sonically in the less pure – thus deflowered – voice. Along similar lines a husband who wanted to know if he had impregnated his wife could touch her neck: a hot neck suggested he might have succeeded.[48] Traces of this erotic potential of the throat still exist today. Recall the moment in Madonna's documentary *Truth or Dare* during which Warren Beatty protests the examination of her throat on camera. In fact, a glance at any of a number of videos of the vocal cords in action on the web suggests that the innards of the throat may indeed be overwhelmingly erotic.

The issues extended beyond the throat. Singing changed the temperate balance of the body in ways that mimicked sexual activity. Humoral distinctions between genders in Galenic medicine depended fundamentally on women remaining colder than men, and Galen's explanation of why women are "weaker and less fully developed" hinged on their coolness.[49]

Now just as mankind is the most perfect of all animals, so within mankind the man is more perfect than the woman, and the reason for his perfection is his excess of heat, for heat is Nature's primary instrument. Hence in those animals that have less of it, her workmanship is necessarily more imperfect, and so it is no wonder that the female is less perfect than the male by as much as she is colder than he.[50]

This is particularly important for singers because singing requires a naturally hotter body. Avicenna, author of an Arabic medical text widely

---

[45] As quoted from Hippocratic gynecology in Ann Hanson and David Armstrong, "The Virgin's Voice and Neck: Aeschylus, Agamemnon 245 and Other Texts," *British Institute of Classical Studies* 33 (1986): 99. The authors suggest that ancient Greek ideas about the physical signs of virginity stemmed from folk belief and held sway, along with Galenic medicine, well into the seventeenth century.

[46] Ibid., 97.   [47] Ibid., 98.

[48] Gabriele Fallopius, *Secreti diversi et miracolosi* (Venice: Ghirado Imberti, 1640).

[49] Galen, *On Semen*, trans. Phillip De Lacy (Berlin: Akademie Verlag, 1992), 52.

[50] May, *Galen On the Usefulness of the Parts*, 650.

read in the Renaissance, asserted that people with hot temperaments are "more fluent in speech and have a flair for music."[51] Hotter temperatures in woman could suggest their excessive desire. Ferrand wrote that uterine frenzy, caused by too much desire, results in a burning in the womb that leads to an increased body temperature, which in turn leads "such women to chatter incessantly and speak about sexual matters."[52] Raised body temperatures not only signified too much desire but also directly impacted what came out of a woman's body.

Whatever temperature the body settled on stayed constant through the expulsion of appropriate amounts of energy, and more specifically, through breathing, or the exchange of elements with the surrounding air and water.[53] Normal breathing maintained body heat but singing, which required more energy and released more air than breathing, skewed this precious balance by causing women to raise their own body temperatures.[54] With this temperature-based gender hierarchy underpinning Renaissance understandings of the human body, it appears that by heating up their bodies – creating activity and productivity – female singers eroded the sex/gender system that grounded their inferiority in cold bodies. This brings to the fore one of the primary differences between men and women's singing, which in turns suggests at least one "biological" reason that singing for men did not create the same threat. Since men were always "warm," if their singing raised their body temperature, it made them more of themselves but did not threaten the order of things.

The heat that came from singers' amplified circulation of air and breath mimicked the intense blood flow of sexual activity. Thus Soranus, an ancient gynecologist, could prescribe sexual intercourse as a cure for the circulation problems of virgins because of the parallel substances of sexual secretions, sweating, and speaking. He writes:

For as movement of the whole body is wont to provoke sweating, whereas lack of motion to hold it back and prevent it, and as the performance of the vocal function stimulates to an increased excretion the saliva which by nature

[51] Mazhar H. Shah, *The General Principles of Avicenna's Canon of Medicine* (Karachi: Naveed Clinic, 1966), 343.

[52] Jacques Ferrand, *A Treatise On Lovesickness*, trans. David A. Beecher and Massimo Ciavolella (Syracuse: Syracuse University Press), 263.

[53] David J. Furley and J.S. Wilkie, *Galen: On Respiration and the Arteries* (Princeton: Princeton University Press, 1984).

[54] I began thinking about the importance of the temperate nature of singing as a result of Suzanne Cusick's Spring 1995 talk at the University of Pennsylvania, entitled "On Musical Performances of Gender and Sex." Susan McClary has also discussed these issues in *Feminine Endings: Music, Gender, and Sexuality* (Minneapolis: University of Minnesota Press, 1991).

accompanies the passage of the breath – in the same way, during intercourse the associated movement around the female genitals relaxes the whole body.[55]

For Soranus, the activities of vocal function, presumably speaking and singing, caused an extra production of saliva in a process that mirrors the increased movement and secretion of fluids during sexual activity. Also linking singing and the reproductive tract, Soranus recommended vocal exercises during pregnancy to control cravings for unnatural food and after birth for improving the flow and quality of breast milk. Medieval doctors had argued that listening to music helped women in labor with digestion.[56]

Within humoral understandings of sexual and vocal processes, both vocal and sexual reproduction required a rise in body temperature. Conception required mutual orgasm reached via erotic friction, which heated both men and women up to their boiling point – ejaculation.[57] The sixteenth-century French doctor Ambroise Paré's oft-quoted pre-scription for how husbands can entice their frigid wives tells them that to turn up the furnace, they must

entertain her with all kind of dalliance, wanton behavior and allurement to venery. If he finds her to be slow, and more cold, he must cherish, embrace and tickle her, should creep into the field of nature, intermix wanton kisses with wanton words and speeches, and caress her safest parts and dugs until she is afire and enflamed.[58]

Paré's prescription implies that the wife sits still and silent while her husband coaxes her chilly sexuality into activity. Female desire exists only as it responds to male desire and leads to propagation. In con-trast to Paré's quasi-scientific ideological ideal, representative of dom-inant strains of Renaissance thought, women who sang were anything but passive. Rather than being acted upon by men in the interest of sexual reproduction, they did the acting themselves, taking control of their bodies by both raising their temperatures and manipulating their voices. When these women took control of their bodies and enacted movements and sensations that paralleled sexual activity, they mim-icked a non-procreative sexuality that went against sexual and moral

[55] Soranus, *Gynecology*, trans. Owsei Temkin (Baltimore: Johns Hopkins University Press, 1956), 29.

[56] Nancy Siraisi, "The Music of the Pulse in the Writings of Italian Academic Physicians," *Speculum* 50 (1975): 589–610.

[57] Thomas Lacqueur and Stephen Greenblatt have discussed this in detail. See Lacqueur's *Making Sex: Body and Gender from the Greeks to Freud* (Cambridge, MA and London: Harvard University Press, 1990); Stephen Greenblatt, "Fiction and Friction," in *Shake-spearean Negotiations: The Circulation of Social Energy in Renaissance England* (Berkeley: University of California Press, 1988), 66–94.

[58] As cited in Lacqueur, *Making Sex*, 102.

codes. And again, even if singing heated male singers' bodies in a way that mimicked sexual production, that production hardly had the same implications for them.

Vocal disciplines

"O come sei gentile" and other similar pieces contain the female voice. Such a piece also depends on a long and rigorous training process. It functions as a performative analogue to the control exerted on the female throat by the vocal training of, virtuosic compositions for, and discursive treatments concerning the female voice. The raw and natural sounds of talented singers were cultivated, or carefully molded, by composers, singing teachers, and the singers themselves who had to manipulate their throats, breath, and minds. And these training processes were particularly vexed because they demanded skill that surpassed the effortless *sprezzatura* valued in a chaste court lady.

For the acquisition of gorgia, passaggi, and other vocal tricks the *dispositione della gorgia* required rigorous training. Maffei makes a clear distinction between the trained voice and the untrained voice, "since every cultivated singing voice is a sound but not every sound is a cultivated voice."[59] Monteverdi told his son Francesco, an aspiring singer, that "This is the most difficult thing about the gorgia and it needs study and diligence rather than mere desire to put so many figures together."[60] Maffei criticizes those singers who practice only a few times and then complain that Nature has not endowed them with the proper aptitude and disposition, calling them "lazy." He goes on to suggest a harsh training procedure in which singers practice several hours a day in front of mirrors, training their throats to make faster and faster sounds and their mouths and bodies to avoid any jerky or inelegant movements.

Though Maffei's concern lay mainly with men, we know that women underwent similar instruction. Annibale Guasco's letter to his daughter Lavinia stands as one of the most complete accounts of the training of an early modern female virtuosa.[61] Guasco does not discuss in detail the teaching of specific ornaments, but his progression from reading, singing and writing music to learning instruments matches Maffei's program very closely.[62] Throughout the letter, Guasco seems as pleased with himself as a pedagogue as with his daughter's accomplishments. Guasco, like Maffei, kept his pupil unbelievably busy; as he put it: "you,

---

[59] MacClintock, *Readings in the History of Performance*, 44.
[60] Stevens, *Monteverdi's Letters*.
[61] Thanks to Suzanne Cusick to pointing out this source to me and for sharing her translation.
[62] Annibale Guasco, *Ragionamento a D. Lavinia sua figliuola della maniera del governarsi ella in corte; andando per Dama* (Turin: 1586), fol. 4r.

being also engaged in learning to write, hardly had time to breathe, much less to rest."[63] He details the process by which he taught Lavinia first to read at the age of four and then quickly to sing so that she could read music from a part book, which was especially necessary, "In these days when there are so many written musical compositions and the level of difficulty has reached the most difficult possible. You can now handle with ease any song, no matter how weird or hard."[64] He introduced her to instruments starting with the gamba and moving on to the harpsichord. In addition he brought in outside teachers to work with keyboard notation on two staves so that "now you can play on your instrument for at least two hours varying dances, canzonette, madrigals and ricercari."[65] She learned counterpoint and, along the way, mathematical skills. Guasco wanted to ensure that in addition to playing and singing from memory, his daughter could read a variety of music. "For how else could you be the padrona of intabulation, like the music masters themselves?"[66] His motivational tactics involved beating, berating, and screaming. According to Guasco, Lavinia left home a fully trained musician with a memorized repertory and the improvisatory skills to perform for several hours. The letter concludes with an admonishment to continue her daily practice sessions to keep her voice lively, extend the range, and improve her passaggi.

Maffei's methods, though derived for men, seem typical and parallel those used for training women. Caccini trained both of his wives and daughters, and Monteverdi taught a number of female singers, including his daughter Leonora and Caterina Martinelli. Caccini published the exercises he used to train his first and second wives, Lucia and Margherita, and we can assume also his daughters, Francesca and Settimia. He wrote, "I must now demonstrate first how the tremolo and the trill are written by me, and how I teach them to those of my household who are concerned with such matters."[67] Apparently his methods worked. "How excellently the tremolo and the trill were learned by my late wife with the above rule may be adjudged by those who heard her sing during her life, as also I leave to the judgment of those who can now hear in the present wife how exquisitely they are done by her."[68] Angela Zanibelli's account of preparing for her roles in the celebrated 1608 wedding festivities in Mantua depicts a practice regimen that echoes Caccini, Zacconi, and Maffei:

I shall beat my passaggi better than I formerly did even though I never practiced them with sound [instruments]. Then as to singing with sureness [breath

---

[63] Ibid. [64] Ibid., fol. 6v. [65] Ibid., fol. 7r.
[66] Ibid. [67] Caccini, *Le nuove musiche*, 51. [68] Ibid.

control], Your Most Illustrious Lordship is quite well aware that in so few days I cannot have learned it; but as to studying, I am studying.[69]

Just before sending Zanibelli off to serve at the Mantuan court, the Marchesa Bentivoglio alludes to the process of cultivating her raw voice into the tamed voice of a singer:

I am sending you this young woman of ours who sings . . . About the young woman, I must tell Your Highness that it is roughly eighteen months since she became a member of our household and that [when she arrived] she not only was unable to read but did not know so much as a syllable or note of song, possessing no valuable quality other than her voice. Since then, to be sure, we have had her taught to understand written words and musical notation with the result that she is beginning to read a bit and, in a groping fashion, to sight-sing. (So far the pieces she sings have all been learned by rote.) Your Highness accordingly may wish to impart all of this to whomever shall have charge of teaching her. Nor should I neglect to bring to Your Highness' attention that it takes hard work and great endurance for her own teacher to get his teaching into her head . . ."[70]

The matter of Angela's training continued to preoccupy her handlers even after she arrived in Mantua. An officer of the Mantuan court wrote that the Highnesses liked her voice enough that they "agreed to have Rasi or some other virtuoso keep her in training but when His Lordship the Prince's wedding is over, the Most Serene Madam is thinking of sending her to Florence, to the household of Zazzerino [Jacopo Peri], for at least a year in order that she may better refine that talent which, through judicious guidance, nature aided by study will grant her."[71]

Singers' voices required constant cultivation and surveillance by teachers, most of whom were men. Like the beating throats of *passaggi*, training may have been innocent enough for men, but it could cause big trouble for women, who often entered the professional world of singing at very tender ages. Francesca Caccini and Caterina Martinelli both sang in public by the age of thirteen.[72] The interactions of these women with their male singing teachers carried the same sexual connotations as almost any intimate private interaction between the sexes. Then, as now, what occurred behind closed doors between men in power and women without power was dangerous business. Perhaps for these reasons, young singers like the daughters of Caccini, Guasco, and Adriana Basile received their training in their parents' homes.

---

[69] Stuart Reiner, "La vag'angioletta (and others)," *Studien zur Italienisch-Deutschen Musikgeschichte* 9 (1974): 26–89, 62.

[70] Ibid., 38.   [71] Ibid., 42.

[72] For information about Caccini see Suzanne Cusick, "Thinking from Women's Lives: Francesca Caccini after 1627," in *Rediscovering the Muses*, ed. Kimberly Marshall (Boston: Northeastern University Press, 1993), 206–227.

Some of the anxiety about the training of young women is evoked in a series of letters surrounding the Mantuans' trafficking of Caterina Martinelli, in which her handlers decided that the presence of Monteverdi's wife and daughters made his home a safer haven for the young virtuosa's chastity than Caccini's. Writing to Ambassador Arrigoni in Rome to make final arrangements for Caterina's entrance into the Mantuan court, Duke Vincenzo insisted that she not stop in Florence to study with Caccini – the preeminent vocal trainer of the day.

She should be brought directly to Mantua, where our idea is that for the learning time in exchange of studying with Giulio Romano [Caccini] she will stay in the home of Claudio Monteverdi, who has a wife and other family and where we can keep her under our eyes, until having been taught as planned she can come at once to the house to serve the duchess, where we should have her come now if it were not inconvenient to teach her and have her go in a little room one or more times a day with no benefit and difficult for those responsible for her.[73]

Despite the fact that Caccini had a wife and daughter the court felt that Caterina would be safer in the Monteverdi household, perhaps because they could keep her "under their eyes." Francesco Rasi, in a letter dated July 9, 1603, informed the Duke that Caccini refused to teach Caterina unless she was placed in his house. "He (Caccini) insisted on trying to make me understand that she would be safe, but I closed his mouth with a single word."[74] Perhaps the Duke thought that Caccini paid too much attention to Caterina's safety or mistrusted him owing to his involvement in a sordid situation in which he was assaulted and in his words "almost murdered" by the jealous lover of one of his pupils.[75]

Caterina's father apparently worried about how long his daughter's chastity would last once her tutors got their proverbial hands on her. In a series of letters about the virginity tests required for Caterina, he claimed to want the procedure repeated after she left the home of Conte Sansecondo in Florence.[76] The emissary sent to bring Caterina to Duke Vincenzo was equally concerned with the status of her virginity. He wrote of "insisting to her family that I wanted to send her to Madam as a virgin and that when it is time I will have her looked at by two or three midwives, and if they find her to be as I say she is I will send her. If she is otherwise nothing more will be done with her."[77] There

[73] A. Ademollo, *La bell'Adriana ed altre virtuose del suo tempo alla corte di Mantova* (Città di Castello: S. Lapi Tipografo, 1888), 38 (my translation).

[74] Edmond Strainchamps, "The Life and Death of Caterina Martinelli: New Light on Monteverdi's L'Arianna," *Early Music History* 5 (1985): 160.

[75] Warren Kirkendale, *The Court Musicians in Florence During the Principate of the Medici* (Florence: Leo S. Olschki Editore, 1993).

[76] Ibid., 37.   [77] Ibid., 36.

was, of course, no "scientific" way to test virginity. But tests and ordeals meant to prove the chastity of a woman go back to the ancient world. One fifth-century story that remained current in the Renaissance told of young Libyan women who ritually battled each other with stones and sticks. If the virgin in question endured a fatal wound she was proven unchaste.[78] And the vestal virgins proved their status by carrying water from the Tiber in a sieve – a task easily completed if the sieve is nicely greased.

The Mantuan concern for the young Caterina's virtue was not unfounded. In the early 1600s Pompeo Caccini impregnated his student Ginevra Mazziere, a crime for which he had to pay a fine of 100 lire and a dowry of seventy-five scudi.[79] The two eventually married. Some forty years later these concerns still ran rampant in Venetian society. The Roman singer Leonora Luppi brought charges against her thirteen-year-old daughter Silvia's singing teacher, Giovanni Carlo del Cavalieri, for seducing the young girl.[80] Silvia testified to a not unfamiliar narrative – men making false promises to women in order to get sex.

His intention was to teach me to sing and to play, as both I and my mother are professional musicians. With longer acquaintance he began to show me signs of affection, and said that if I would give in to these desires he would take me for his wife . . . In the end, he made so many promises that now I can only remember half of them. Therefore, enticed by such promises, and without the firm assurance that he would take me for his wife, I consented, allowing myself to give in to his desires.[81]

Luppi thus lost what was considered her most precious possession – her chastity.

Matters of honor were particularly vexed in a society obsessed with maintaining the sexual purity of its women as untouched virgins, faithful wives, and celibate widows. Chastity existed as a moral category and as a physical state, both of which singing implicated. It was understood as a condition of the uterus, which scientific doctrine often assimilated with the throat. The throat, then, acted as the sieve through which chastity leaked out into the world and which rendered singing an activity that could prove the singer anything but chaste. In terms of morality,

---

[78] Kathleen Coyne Kelly, *Performing Virginity and Testing Chastity in the Middle Ages* (London: Routledge, 2000), 64.

[79] Beth Glixon, "Scenes from the Life of Silvia Galiarti Manni, a Seventeenth-Century Virtuoso," *Early Music History* 15 (1996): 102. Timothy J. McGee, "Pompeo Caccini and Euridice: New Bibliographic Notes," *Renaissance and Reformation/Renaissance et Reforme* 14 (1990): 81–90.

[80] For a detailed account of the controversy, see Glixon, "Scenes," 97–147.

[81] Ibid., 102.

Lodovico Dolce's 1545 *Della istitutione delle donne*, one of the most frequently reprinted tracts on noble womanhood, suggests that a woman could hold on to her physical virginity but still fail at moral chastity, which depended on remaining absolutely untouched by intercourse, desire, and all manners of pollution from sex and dancing to spicy food and lascivious texts.[82] Thus young ladies could protect their *castità* with fasting, cleanliness, regulated sleep, and modest clothing. Dolce reminds his readers that in the ancient world the loss of chastity was punishable by death, a punishment he says makes sense given that a woman's sole job was to hold on to her chastity.

The intense vulnerability of a young lady's virtue prompted prescriptive literature that limited reading, writing, and education to only carefully chosen classical and contemporary texts, usually scriptural or moral. Juan Luis Vives, in his classic text *On the Education of a Christian Woman*, warns that "ignorance is safer than education in a wife," and that reading can lead to contrariness and other problems.[83] Taking this statement even further, Giovanni Bruto in his *La istitutione di una fanciulla nata nobilmente* (Antwerp, 1555) warns against the dangers of writing: "The danger is as well that they will learn to be subtle and shameless lovers, as cunning and skillful writers of ditties, sonnets, epigrams and ballads."[84]

The trouble with singing related to the early modern understandings of chastity as an over-determined concept whose presence or absence could be signified by almost any action or inaction. It stood as such a precarious attribute that any slanderous words could permanently delete it. In the words of the Spanish writer Juan Luis Vives, "Call her a naughty baggage and with that one word, thou hast taken all from her and left her bare and foul."[85] An imaginary space – one that was always already lost and that could disappear the moment it achieved recognition – chastity had very real implications for female virtuose. For instance, the Duke of Ferrara maintained a deep commitment to hiring women beyond reproach, arranging their marriages and dictating their private lives. Women who sang during this time period often

---

[82] Lodovico Dolce, *Dialogo: Della istitutione delle donne* (Venice: Giolito, 1560).

[83] Juan Luis Vives, *The Education of a Christian Woman*, ed. and trans. Charles Fantazzi (Chicago: University of Chicago Press). First published in 1523 and translated in 1546, Vives's book, like Dolce's, divides women into three central categories: girlhood, marriage, and widowhood. Giuseppi Zonta suggests that Dolce was an Italian-language rewriting of Vives's popular tract. See *Trattati del Cinquecento sulla donna* (Bari: Laterzo, 1913).

[84] Giovanni Bruto, *The necessarie, fit and convenient education of a young gentlewoman* (Amsterdam: Theatrum Orbis Terrarum, 1969).

[85] Juan Luis Vives, *The Education of a Christian Woman* (Chicago: University of Chicago Press, 2000).

found their virtue debated.[86] Singing involved putting their bodies on display: a self-promotion that, as a result of the male anxiety about their public exposure, was imagined to be unseemly at best. Making matters worse, there existed very real associations of courtesans with singing: the most famous, like Veronica Franco and Tullia d'Aragona, used music as part of their daily performances of self and as an instrument of seduction.[87]

Writing the throat

I turn now to a different kind of discipline, the kind enforced on singers by the composers and the music they wrote. In the late sixteenth century, composers had generally left improvisatory gestures to the discretion of singers. Apparently singers got out of control. This prompted composers like Monteverdi and Caccini to put ornaments in writing, which, in effect, dictated the actions of the singer's throat. Thus, for instance, the strings of ornaments in "O come sei gentile" reflect a style in which singers would have created their own ornamentation. At the same time, dedications to specific singers suggest that publication of virtuosic songs often attempted to capture the sound of a particular performance. In either case, the publication of already-ornamented pieces served as mechanisms for controlling and disciplining potentially unruly singers and their voices.

Such a process is endemic to the construction and performance of "O come sei gentile," especially the ways in which the various settings of the verb *cantare* function. Written-out ornaments and harmonically underpinned virtuosic gestures represent a musical containment of the natural untamed voice that is reiterated in the larger discourses of voice and body elaborated in this chapter. In this piece ornaments become the locus and not an elaboration of something else. The vocal tryst that begins at the words "Tu canti" (see Ex. 1.1) is contained by a repeated rising bass ending consistently on D major leading to a G cadence that does not arrive until much later. Similarly, the gruppo on "legato," and the ornamented scale of "io canto per lei" reflect rising tension through a continuation of the walking bass that finally resolves on G. On the one hand the pattern represents the words in that it moves toward climax but does not end, thus mimicking the unresolved desire that lies beneath the ornamental gestures, which stand in for singing. Perhaps

---

[86] Writing about women who sang on stage in the sixteenth century, Nina Treadwell argues that few actresses escaped censure and those that did had to work especially hard to maintain a public image that was beyond reproach. Treadwell, *Staging the Siren*.

[87] For details of this association see Bonnie Gordon and Martha Feldman, *The Courtesan's Arts* (Oxford: Oxford University Press, forthcoming).

more importantly, this is a moment when the sounds of the singing voice are controlled by the structures in which they are embedded. Reflecting a similar process, the final juxtaposition of "vivi cantando" and "io cantando" features the bird's "vivi" motives occurring over fifth-related bass sequences and the poet's "io cantando" rising above a scalar bass that repeatedly cadences on D major until the final drop to G. This may juxtapose the circling, playful singing of the bird with the finality of the singer's love-death, but it also once again contains the ornaments within harmonic structures and dictates the motion of the singer's throats. The walking bass that lies beneath the ornamental setting of "tu canti" and "io canto," as well as settings of "legato" and "io canto per lei," stand in for the composer's physical control of the singer's throat. Likewise, the sequences underlying "io cantando" and "vivi cantando" harmonically constrain the bird's song and thus the voice's singing.

This piece was part of a larger trend toward writing out and incorporating into a piece's structure ornaments that had once been left to the discretion of the singer. In his preface to *Le nuove musiche*, Caccini makes explicit his endeavor to rein in singers. He writes that, because of the indiscriminate ornamentation of singers, he was forced to have his pieces published:

But now I see many of them circulating tattered and torn, moreover, I see ill-used these single and double roulades – rather, those redoubled and intertwined with each other – developed by me to avoid that old style of passaggi formerly in use ... And I see the vocal crescendos–decrescendos, exclamations, tremolos, and trills and other such embellishments of good singing style used indiscriminately. Thus I have been forced (and also urged by friends) to have these pieces of mine published.[88]

Ornamentation was deemed problematic when it appealed only to passion and not to reason. Degree of ornamentation turned a particular musical performance either into an ethically beneficial venture or into one of degradation – it comprised the difference, in other words, between songs that led to God and those that led toward lascivious desires. Caccini's instructions for acceptable passaggi highlight this fine distinction: "Passaggi were not devised because they are essential to good singing but rather, I believe, as a kind of tickling of the ears of those who hardly understand what affective singing really is. If they did understand, passaggi would doubtless be loathed, there being nothing more inimical to affective expression."[89] His worry about the potential of these sounds to tickle the ear suggests that because song could penetrate the body, it could entice a dangerous physical feeling of pleasure.

---

[88] Caccini, *Le nuove musiche*, 40.   [89] Ibid., 41.

This concern for rampant ornamentation permeates the conservative writings of Artusi, and even those of less conservative thinkers such as Doni, who warned against songs that enticed pleasure but did not move the affections. Doni refers to overly ornamented music as sweet consonances that "give the greatest content to the ears even though the intellect does not receive its due."[90] Describing compositions like those in Monteverdi's seventh book of madrigals, Doni writes that "in this are accepted all kinds of graces or accenti, even very long passaggi, not that they are apt to express the affections, for as Caccini says there is nothing in music more contrary than those who listen less carefully, or else because singers themselves wish to demonstrate their disposition and as one says to go over the top."[91] Here he explicitly attacks gestures associated with vocal performance – ornamentation. Similarly, Bottrigari wrote that the greatest discordance and confusion in modern music results from the unabashed use of passaggi.

From this perspective, the telos of ornamentation was to enhance a musical piece rather than to display the singer's prowess. This was especially true for dramatic works. Marco da Gagliano, in his 1608 preface to *La Dafne*, critiques overzealous ornamentation. "Many people are mistaken about this point, they strive for gruppi, trilli, passaggi, and esclamazioni without bothering to understand what is the purpose and what is proper . . . But when the piece does not require them, all ornaments should be omitted; otherwise one could easily fall into the error of the painter who, knowing well how to paint cypresses, introduced them into every picture."[92]

Like everything else about singing, the nuances of decorous ornamentation had particularly drastic connotations for women, whose voices moved precariously between harmless pleasure and threatening excess. They had to navigate the dissonances between a musical practice that displayed trained women's voices and social mores that demanded silent women whose quieted voices reflected their chasteness and distanced them from inappropriate eroticism. Ornamentation embodied the contradictions of being a woman in early modern society, particularly the mandate to do everything well but not too well. Both Caccini and Zacconi insisted that good singing had to reflect the effortless *sprezzatura* expected of court ladies and courtiers, a concept most famously elaborated by Castiglione in *Il cortegiano*. Music comprised part of a

[90] As quoted in Fabbri, *Monteverdi*, 166.   [91] Ibid., 166.

[92] Marco da Gagliano's preface to *La Dafne* in Angelo Solerti, *Le origini del melodramma* (Turin: Bocca, 1903), 79. "E qui s'ingannano molti, i quali s'affaticano in far gruppi, trilli, passaggi ed esclamazioni, senza aver rigardo per che fine e a che proposito . . . Ma dove la favola non lo ricerca lascisi del tutto ogni ornamento; per non fare come quel pittore, che sapendo ben dipingnere il cipresso, lo dipingneva per tutto."

larger process of achieving grace, but that grace could only be affected with moderate ornamentation.

Sprezzatura is the charm that a song gets from a few short dissonant notes over their bass notes: these relieve the song of a restrained narrowness and dryness and make it pleasant, free, and tuneful, just as in everyday speech eloquence and facility make the matters being spoken of sweet. And to the figures of speech and the rhetorical flourishes in such eloquence correspond the passaggi, tremolos, and other ornaments, which may occasionally be introduced with discretion in the music of any mood.[93]

For Caccini, music had to remain within the boundaries of grace that were circumscribed by degrees of ornamentation. Sung performances mimicked the spoken performances of a court culture that demanded an affectation of effortlessness and subtlety. Zacconi described particular ornaments in similar terms.

This tremolo should be slight and pleasing, for if it is exaggerated and forced, it tires and annoys, its nature is such that if used at all it should always be used since its use converts it into habit, for its motion the voice helps and spontaneously encourages the movement of the gorgia.[94]

Prescriptions for ornamentation were curiously inflected with a rhetoric that re-inscribed the imagined differences between men and women. Words like unruly, discordant, and excessive all resonated with a language used to position women's bodies as permanently out of control. The need to control ornaments stemmed from their associations with women and with empty pleasure. In effect, ornamentation reflected the empty beauty that had long been associated with women, sirens, and Circes. These associations were also present in the literary realm. For example, in *Gerusalemme liberata*, Tasso, like others before him, embodied the dangers of poetry and song in his female characters. In musical practice, the dangers of song were likewise embodied in female singers who performed the ornaments that tempted the ear and blinded rationality.

To return to "O come sei gentile" and to make a very speculative conclusion, this control is also played out in the music itself, in the repeated bass patterns – walking bass and progressions that move by fifths – underlying the string of ornaments. The voice must adhere to externally imposed patterns. Their consistency, brevity, and circular motion frame the voice within a musical logic that operates independently from the body. Such instrumental patterns would eventually dominate Baroque music and circumscribe the voice within a rational system.

[93] Caccini, *Le nuove musiche*, 45.
[94] Zacconi, *Prattica di musica*, 60.

At the same time, vocal writing would become so virtuosic and orna-mented that it would mold the voice into a mechanized process severed from spirit and disconnected from the inner workings of the body.

For instance, "Chiome d'oro," a beautiful soprano duet from the end of Monteverdi's seventh book of madrigals that seems to have been written considerably later than "O come sei gentile," consists almost entirely of repeated vocal and instrumental patterns in which musical logic matters most. A two-part strophic canzonetta on a walking bass, it prefigures Venetian trends of the 1620s. The bass line of the ritor-nello is the same as that of the vocal section, so that both appear as strophic variations on their own basses. The music follows the poetry in basic structure: each phrase of poetry gets a phrase of music. Each section of the poem stands as a musical section concluded by a firm cadence.

Like "O come sei gentile," it features the diminutions, augmentations, trills, and parallel thirds that characterized much soprano writing of the mid-seventeenth century. The repeated bass lines that occurred inter-mittently in the earlier madrigal become the foundations of the later piece, repeating over and over again as the violins and sopranos dance above it. Vocal ornaments are pushed past their breaking point until they become the melody of the violin, which traffics in notes faster than the voice moved at that time – the rhythmic pulse of what Monteverdi would later proclaim the *stile concitato* is given here a melodic impulse. Taken to its most extreme, performers of all kinds become instruments for the composer's imaginings.

Taking the notion of the voice as a trained and manipulated instru-ment one step further, the counterpoint between the sopranos and the violins suggests an almost equal relationship between the two, in which mechanized instruments are as capable of musical expression as the human voice, or rather, both instruments are equally incapable of ani-mating the body and the universe. Perhaps this was the impulse that led also to the hyper-virtuosity of the castrati, whose voices would become the ultimate musical instrument. The piece begins with an extended vio-lin introduction followed by long phrases alternating sopranos and vio-lins. As it progresses, the violin and vocal parts move closer and closer together until they finally sing together for the final two measures. The vocal texture is homophonic, with thirds predominating.

The anonymous canzonetta text itself mechanizes and dissects the female voice and, as such, mirrors the Petrarchan blazon (see p. 140 below). The poem fetishizes the lady's parts in favor of the whole. It catalogues and objectifies each piece of her body with metaphors from the natural world: her hair golden tresses, her teeth bright pearls, her eyes bright stars. Only her curled lips are mentioned by name.

Chiome d'oro, bel tesoro,	Golden tresses, beautiful treasure,
tu mi leghi in mille modi	you bind me in a thousand ways,
se t'annodi, se ti snodi.	whether you are bound or set free.

Candidette perle elette,	Precious white pearls,
se le rose che coprite	when the roses that you cover
discoprite, mi ferite.	are uncovered, you wound me.

Vive stelle, che si belle	Bright stars which shine,
e si vaghe risplendete,	so beautiful and lovely,
se ridete m'ancidete.	when you laugh, you kill me.

Preziose amorose	Precious, loving,
coralline labbra amate,	beloved coral lips,
se parlate, mi beate.	if you speak you give me bliss.

O bel nodo per cui godo,	O fair bond, through which I have joy,
o soave uscir di vita,	o sweet death,
o gradita mia ferita.	o welcome wound.

   This attention to visible details follows the Marinist style of the seventh book of madrigals as a whole.[95] In this piece, form comes from the music itself – not from the text, not from the spirit, and not from the humors. A piece constructed by preconceived sections, phrases, and motives, it does not highlight one poetic ideal or affection. In this it follows Monteverdi's compositional penchant for structured vocal articulations. It puts violins and voices in concert with one another, thereby embodying the contradictions inherent in the word "concerto," which at once signifies a conflict and a coming together. The violins are as much a mediated force as the female voices. As I will argue at the very end of this book, such a technologically mediated song might reflect a mechanized movement of lips and tongue that is as instinctive as walking and talking. It may also gesture towards a post-Harveyan anatomy in which the heart beats all by itself, keeping blood in circulation. Spirit, and thus voice, no longer animates the human body, and temperate economies no longer matter much.

---

[95] See Gary Tomlinson, *Monteverdi and the End of the Renaissance* (Berkeley: University of California Press, 1987), for more on this style.

2

Back talk: the power of female song on the stage

Monteverdi composed *L'Arianna* and *Il ballo delle ingrate* for a ritual celebration honoring the 1608 marriage of Francesco Gonzaga to Margherita
of Savoy. During an action-packed two weeks of nuptial festivities,
guests witnessed a stream of punished and otherwise violated women in
productions that induced tears in the spectators and offered instructions
to the ladies. These productions served as performed versions of texts
that endeavored to mold women into good wives: the conduct books,
medical literature, legal documents, and letters that legislated female
behavior by dictating appropriate sounds and gestures and suggesting punishments for transgressions of those codes. The stories all have
clear plots and morals. Daphne, the unfortunate heroine of Gagliano's
eponymous drama, written for the festivities but actually performed at
carnival a few months earlier, attracts Apollo with her desirable body
but then escapes his rape only when her father turns her into a laurel
tree. Her transformation into a static figure permanently and harshly
chastens her sexually appealing female body – being sexy is bad.[1]
Meanwhile, two of the *intermedi* to Guarini's *L'Idropica* dramatize the
rapes of Proserpina and Europa, both of which lead to some kind of
cosmic harmony. These two rapes and others also appeared in fres-
coes in the Palazzo del Tè in Mantua. In the final *ballo*, *Il sacrificio
d'Ifigenia*, Agamemnon follows an oracle who commands him to sac-
rifice his lovely daughter for the good of his fleet of ships, forcing him
to choose duty over flesh and blood.[2] Follino describes ladies being
brought in after one of the large feasts to see this production, in which
Iphigenia's sacrificial altar becomes the wedding altar on which the
princess is served up to Achilles. Removed from her father's care, Iphigenia laments her destiny and ultimately ends up as the well-protected

---

[1] My quick interpretation here reads Daphne's fate as punishment since she is forever
condemned to eternity in the form of a tree, deprived of body and voice.

[2] This story is taken from Euripides' *Iphigenia in Aulis*.

chattel of her husband.[3] *Il ballo delle ingrate*, an exemplary tale showing what happens to women who refuse their lovers, seems a fitting end to a set of entertainments so curiously invested in women.

While musicologists have tended to spend most of their energy on *L'Arianna*, I will direct attention toward the nuptial circumstances of Monteverdi and Rinuccini's other, less famous contribution to the Mantuan celebrations – *Il ballo delle ingrate*.[4] Considering this piece in conjunction with literary, medical, and social understandings of the female body circulating in early modern culture suggests that even works created by men sometimes opened up a space for the female voice to resist patriarchal constraints. This discussion moves from the material components of the voice explored in the first chapter of this book toward a more discursive reading of the voice as symbolic of female expressiveness or its lack. While the first chapter concentrated on the effects singing had on real living singers, this chapter presents perhaps the most confusing conglomeration of female figures in the book. It focuses on tensions between literary and sung representations of women and the live singers who envoiced them while imagining some of the intended effects on women as historical subjects.

L'Arianna and *Il ballo delle ingrate* send contradictory messages that at first seem to leave women little room to move. Ariadne is punished because she loves too much and the *ingrate* because they do not love enough. The problem with all of these women lies in their claiming of sexual agency: Ariadne does so by choosing her own mate and the *ingrate* by denying male pleasure. Formerly beautiful women, the *ingrate*, now bodiless souls, reside in the dark underworld because they scorned their suitors. In the ballo proper, Pluto leads the pathetic souls out in pairs through a fire-belching *bocca d'inferno* in order to demonstrate for the lovely ladies of Mantua "a qual martir cruda beltà si serba" [to what torture cruel beauty devotes itself]. Punished for their lack of passion, the hard-hearted ladies dance but do not sing until the ballo's last moment. Then, as the king of the underworld orders the wailing souls back to his

---

[3] There are several complete studies of the 1608 festivities. Most are based on Federico Follino, the master of the revels, who compiled the official accounts entitled the *Compendio delle sontuose feste fatto l'anno MDCVIII nella città di Mantova, per le reali nozze del serenissimo principe d. Francesco Gonzaga con la serenissima infante Margherita di Savoia*, which is found in Angelo Solerti's *Gli albori del melodramma*, 3 vols. (Turin: Bocca, 1903). Also see A. M. Nagler, *Theatre Festivals of the Medici* (New Haven: Yale University Press, 1964); Susan Parisi, "Ducal Patronage of Music in Mantua 1587–1627: An Archival Study" (Ph.D. dissertation, University of Illinois at Urbana, 1989); and Jessica Gordon, "Entertainments For The Marriages of the Princesses of Savoy in 1608," in *Italian Renaissance Festivals and their European Influence*, ed. J. R. Mulryne and Margaret Shewring (Lewiston: The Edwin Mellen Press, 1992), 119–141.

[4] For enlightening discussions of both of these works see Tim Carter, *Monteverdi's Musical Theatre* (New Haven: Yale University Press, 2002).

murky and airless caverns, one *ingrata* remains on stage to sing a brief lament. Singing farewell to the light and air of the mortal world, she urges the ladies listening to her to learn compassion. Then the voices of four *ingrate* sing from the depths of hell, echoing her final plea for "pietà"[pity]. The solo lamenter and her echoes use their voices for a moment to resist confinement and defy the silencing impulses of early modern discourses.[5] Despite the seeming constraining impulse of the work as a whole, Monteverdi and Rinuccini gave women the last word.

Il ballo delle ingrate rehearses early modern struggles over the female voice in which constraints were defied and then redoubled. Through the power of sung performance, women continually asserted the unsettling force of their voices, despite discursive and social pressures for them to mime passive, closed-mouth reflections of patriarchal ideals. In *Il ballo delle ingrate*, the solo *ingrata* interrupts the silence of dance and breaks out of the anonymous mass of *ingrate*, claiming a voice and a body. The ballo's contrast between singing and silent dancing and its culminating display of the female voice strikes dissonances between mandates for female silence and the pleasurable and potent sounds of female voices, and between social demands for chastity and the biological necessity of women's desire in Galenic medicine. These dissonances also permeate the intertwined literary traditions of Ovid and Petrarch, which underpinned the cultural expressions of the late Renaissance elite, including most court music dramas. The tensions inherent in *Il ballo delle ingrate* point out the internal conflicts of mythological stories, which at once quell the excessive potential of women's bodies and feature female voices that talk back.

Given these messages and the prominence of *L'Arianna*, it is hardly surprising that in the last decade Ariadne's surviving lament has become something of a springboard for musicologists working on gender issues in early modern Europe. Suzanne Cusick has argued that the musical processes of Monteverdi's *Lamento d'Arianna* purge Ariadne of passion and desire in order symbolically to make her a good wife.[6] According to this model the lament reflects Renaissance marriage and gender ideologies that silenced women and put them in their place. Ariadne has dared to choose her own mate and therefore must suffer. Her fate is dramatized by her uncharacteristically long lament, which enacts the transformation women experienced as they gave up their own desires

---

[5] This fits in with Lawrence Lipking's argument that abandoned women also abandon convention, decorum, and control, thereby subverting authority and propriety. See *Abandoned Women and Poetic Tradition* (Chicago: University of Chicago Press, 1988).

[6] Earlier versions of this chapter were read at the 1996 meeting of the American Musicological Society and the 1997 meeting of the International Musicological Society. An earlier version was published as "Talking Back: The Female Voice in *Il ballo delle ingrate*," *Cambridge Opera Journal* 11/1 (1999): 1–30.

to the constraining institution of marriage.[7] Cusick's argument follows recent critical tendencies to read early modern culture in terms of the opposition between passive female silence and active male desire. [8] This chapter makes this somewhat easy and general dichotomy more dynamic and specific by listening to the resistant sounds of the female voice in a particular performance context.

Disciplining women

Especially when viewed in conjunction with the other pieces commissioned for the mammoth 1608 Mantuan festivities, *Il ballo delle ingrate* appears as something like a live conduct book, a performed version of the countless treatises and tracts published from the fifteenth through the seventeenth centuries that endeavored to mold women into compliant wives.[9] As a dramatic ballo employing a wide variety of musical and dramatic techniques including recitative, arioso, arias, marvelous stage machinery, and dance techniques of the French *ballet de cour* probably gleaned from the francophile Florentines, the piece must have had a visceral effect on its audience.[10] As Iain Fenlon has suggested, the conglomerate elements of spectacle-oriented pieces like *Il ballo delle ingrate*

---

[7] Suzanne Cusick, "'There Was Not One Lady Who Failed to Shed a Tear': Arianna's Lament and the Construction of Modern Womanhood," *Early Music* 22/1 (February 1994): 21–45.

[8] Ann MacNeil, Tim Carter, and Suzanne Cusick have all recently done very interesting work on the artistic and cultural context of *L'Arianna* which have added to my interpretation of the events. See the special issue of the journal *Early Music*, "Laments," 17/3 (August 1999).

[9] The primary and secondary source literature on marriage manuals and conduct books is vast. One oft-quoted source is Francesco Barbaro's "On Wifely Duties," in *The Earthly Republic* (Philadelphia: University of Pennsylvania Press, 1978). For critical studies of this literature, see Ruth Kelso, *Doctrine for the Lady of the Renaissance* (Urbana: University of Illinois Press, 1956), and Pamela Joseph Benson, *The Invention of the Renaissance Woman: The Challenge of Female Independence in the Literature and Thought of Italy and England* (University Park: Penn State Press, 1992). For a discussion of the relationship between conduct books and Venetian opera see Wendy Heller, "Chastity, Heroism, and Allure: Women in Opera of Seventeenth-Century Venice" (Ph.D. dissertation, Brandeis University, 1995).

[10] *L'Arianna* was likely a much more controlled production. Of the court music dramas written at the end of the Renaissance to imitate ancient theatre, only Rinuccini went so far as to call his tragedy an attempt to recreate the generic traits of a classical tragedy. In contrast, as a court ballet, *Il ballo delle ingrate* does not follow strict generic rules or model ancient precedents. Tim Carter and Bojan Bujić have investigated the generic categorization of *L'Arianna* as a tragedy, suggesting that it may have been retrospective categorization and not necessarily an intended gesture on the part of Rinuccini. See Tim Carter, "New Light on Monteverdi's *Il ballo delle ingrate* (Mantua, 1608)," *Il saggiatore musicale* 6 (1999): 63–90, and B. Bujić, "Rinuccini the Craftsman: A View of his *L'Arianna*," *Early Music* 18 (1999): 75–117.

that mobilized the wondrous effects of the *intermedi* may have made them even more popular than elevated compositions like *L'Arianna*.[11]

Deciphering the surface message of *Il ballo delle ingrate*'s simple plot hardly poses a challenge. Venus, upset because Cupid's arrows have ceased to work, journeys to the edge of the underworld. There she asks Pluto to make a spectacular example of hardhearted women in order to show the women in the audience the perils of refusing male desire or enticing love they will not requite. The piece opens with Venus and Cupid singing a duet that describes the unhappy fate of the *ingrate*. Venus begs Pluto to lead the *ingrate* out to the mortal world of Mantua to show the ladies what can happen if they refuse their suitors.[12] In the process she describes an impressive array of male efforts that failed to impress the *ingrate*. The women have laughed in the face of Cupid's arrows, immortal poetry, heroic actions, and even the tears and blood of their lovers.

> No, non de' più fidi amanti
> odon le voci e i pianti.
> Amor, costanza e fede
> non pur ombra trova trovar può di mercede.
> Questa gli altri martiri
> narra ridendo, e quella
> sol gode d'esser bella
> quanto tragge d'un cor pianti e sospiri.

[No, they do not hear the words and laments of even the most faithful lovers. Love, constancy, and fidelity cannot find even a shadow of mercy. This one tells with laughter the torments of others, and that one only delights in being beautiful when she draws tears and sighs from the hearts of men.]

Pluto, agreeing with Venus, exclaims the piece's moral in no uncertain terms. "Mal si sprezza d'Amor la face e 'l telo sallo la terra e 'l mar, l'inferno e 'l cielo" (It is wrong to scorn the torch and weapon of love, and this is known on earth and sea, in hell and heaven).[13] Venus finally

---

[11] Iain Fenlon, "The Origins of the Staged Ballo," in *Con che soavità: Studies in Italian Opera, Song and Dance, 1580–1740*, ed. Tim Carter and Iain Fenlon (Oxford: Clarendon Press, 1995), 24.

[12] Eric Chafe calls attention to the G minor tonality of Venus's plea in which the goddess of love reminds Pluto of her role in his conquest of Proserpina. This emphasis on G minor also recalls Proserpina's sympathy for Orpheus in Act 4 of *L'Orfeo*. See *Monteverdi's Tonal Language* (New York: Schirmer Books, 1992).

[13] Pamela Jones argues that in Cesare Negri's early seventeenth-century treatises on dance the "entrata" separates social dance from that of the dramatic ballo. See "Spectacle in Milan: Cesare Negri's Torch Dances," *Early Music* 14 (1986): 182–198. Iain Fenlon has suggested that *Il ballo delle ingrate*'s ballet music – six distinct sections with contrasting rhythms – is based on a model for seventeenth-century large-scale dance spectacles first developed by Cavalieri. See "The Origins of the Staged Ballo."

convinces him to bring the *ingrate* up from hell when she reminds him of her role in "wooing" Proserpina. Then they enter two by two in an *entrata*, while Pluto stands in the middle, walking with "passi naturali e gravi" (natural and slow steps).

Il ballo delle ingrate follows a long tradition of holding up negative exemplars for the purpose of showing women what not to do, by demonstrating what befalls those who break the rules. The women in the audience were meant to identify with the punished women, an identification that would mold them into ideal female figures fabricated by and for the patriarchy. To this end, dramatic productions like *Il ballo delle ingrate* that spoke directly to the audience could surpass the reading of conduct books to visceral effect.

The text highlights the piece's didactic purposes by addressing the audience. Court chronicler Federico Follino wrote that Pluto moved "with great gravity toward the princesses who were in view facing the stage; once he had approached them, full of horrid majesty, he began to sing."[14] Within the ballo's text, characters periodically sang to the listening nobles, making sure that the ladies in particular got the moralizing message. After an introductory dialogue with Venus, Cupid journeys to the underworld to ask Pluto to bring the *ingrate* up to Mantua as an example for the ladies of what will befall them should they become hardhearted. At this moment, Venus calls the women in the audience to attention by singing her invective in a strophic variation aria with a sinfonia.

> Udite, donne, udite
> i saggi detti di celeste parlar nel cor serbate:
> Chi nemica d'amor ne' crudi affetti
> armerà il cor nella fiorita etate,
> sentirà come poscia arde a saetta

[Listen, ladies, listen and keep the wise sayings of heavenly speech in your heart: She who, an enemy of love, shall blunt her feeling and harden her heart in her youth, will feel how it later burns like an arrow.][15]

Pluto too addresses the ladies in the audience halfway through the ballo. The ashen ladies stop dancing and Pluto delivers the story's moral in a long arioso with intermittent instrumental ritornelli. Monteverdi's notes to the 1638 edition instruct Pluto to "stop in mid-course and address the princesses and ladies present in the fashion described in

---

[14] Translation modified from Paolo Fabbri, *Monteverdi*, trans. Tim Carter (Cambridge: Cambridge University Press, 1994), 91.

[15] Claudio Monteverdi, *Madrigali guerrieri e amorosi*, ed. Gian Francesco Malipiero, trans. Stanley Appelbaum (New York: Dover, 1990), xxx.

the text." Notations in the score read, "They dance the ballet up to the halfway point. Pluto assumes a noble stance and, turning to the princesses and ladies, says . . ." Here he sends a twofold message: first setting up an ideal to which the viewing ladies should aspire and second showing what befalls those who fail to conform. He begins by extolling the virtues of the bride, painting a perfect picture of the ideal Renaissance wife – good, chaste, free of ornament and a mirror of her husband.

> Fugga, Donna, il timor dal molle seno.
> Arso di nova fiamma al ciel sereno
> donna o donzella per rapir non vegno.
> E quando pur da vostri rai nel petto
> languisce immortalmente il cor ferito,
> non fora disturbar Plutone ardito
> di cotanta regina il lieto aspetto:
> donna al cui nobil crin non bassi fregi
> sol pon del cielo ordir gli eterni lumi,
> di cui l'alma virtù, gli aurei costumi
> farsi speglio dovrian monarchi e regi.

> Madam, let terror flee from your soft breast.
> I do not come to this serene heaven
> ablaze and scorched, to abduct a lady or maiden.
> And even though, smitten by your light
> my heart languishes eternally,
> Pluto would not forcefully disturb
> the happy countenance of so prized a queen:
> a lady for whose noble hair
> only the eternal lights of heaven can compose worthy ornaments
> whose kindly virtue and golden morals
> monarchs and kings should adapt as their mirror

He then moves on to making clear that these poor souls were meant to be a negative exemplar.

> Sceso pur dianzi Amor nel regno oscuro
> preghi mi fè, ch'io vi scorgessi avanti
> queste infelici ch'in perpetui pianti
> dolgonsi invan, che non ben sagge furo.
> Antro è là giù di luce e d'aer privo
> ove torbido fumo ogni hor s'aggira.
> Ivi del folle ardir tardi sospira
> alma ch'ingrata hebbe ogni amante a schivo.
> Indi le traggo, e ve l'addito e mostro
> pallido il volto e lagrimoso il ciglio
> perchè cangiando homai voglie e consiglio

non piangete ancor voi nel negro chiostro.
Vaglia timor di sempiterni affanni
se forza in voi non han sospiri e prieghi.

A moment ago, Love, descending to the dark world
asked me to bring before you
these unfortunate women who in perpetual plaints
weep in vain, for they were far from wise.
There is a cave down there without light or air,
where turbid smoke always swirls.
There the hardhearted soul that shunned every lover
sighs too late over her foolish recklessness.
From there I bring them out and demonstrate to you
their pale faces and tearful eyes
so that, now, changing your wishes and intentions,
you too will not weep in the black cloister.
Let the fear of eternal sufferings avail
if sighs and prayers have no effects on you.

Both Ovid and Boccaccio had used this tactic of discouraging women from denying their lovers through stories that involved the display of *ingrate* tortured for their cold hearts.[16] Their tales, like *Il ballo delle ingrate*, relied on a powerful identification between the protagonist and the viewer, threatening the female reader in order to coerce her into the roles prescribed by patriarchal ideals. In the *Metamorphoses*, for example, Pomona, a beautiful maiden, loves nature more than she could ever love a man. Caring only for the trees and flowers, she summarily rejected countless suitors. Then one cunning lad disguises himself as an old lady and tells Pomona a story that frightens her into submission. He tells of Anaxarete and her devoted suitor Iphis, whose rejection prompts Iphis to kill himself. When the selfish maiden sees him dangling from a tree, she turns to stone. The freezing of her body punishes and mimics the previous coldness of her heart. After telling the story, Pomona's suitor turns from an ugly old lady back to a beautiful man, and she immediately acquiesces to his wishes. "He was all ready to force her will, but no force was necessary; and the nymph, smitten by the beauty of the god, felt an answering passion."[17] She had learned her lesson.

Boccaccio presents a similar scene in his *Decameron*, a work widely circulated in the Renaissance and described by the sixteenth-century humanist Lodovico Dolce in a Boccaccio biography as an improving work of literature for young ladies in the throes of love or, one imagines,

[16] I discussed the literary roots of this production in my article "Talking Back." Since then Tim Carter has also raised similar issues in " New Light on Monteverdi's *Il ballo delle ingrate*."

[17] Ovid, *Metamorphoses*, Books IX–XV, trans. Frank Justus Miller, rev. G. P. Goold (Cambridge, MA: Harvard University Press, 1977), 335.

on the brink of marriage.[18] As in the related story from the *Metamorphoses*, Boccaccio incorporates a tale within a tale through which ladies identify with a punished woman and learn through a powerful negative example how not to behave. The narrator Filomena introduces this episode, saying to the lady readers that

our cruelty is severely punished by divine justice. And in order to prove this to you, as well as to give you an incentive for banishing all cruelty from your hearts, I should like to tell you a story as delightful as it is full of pathos.[19]

The story that Filomena tells is as follows. Nastagio degli Onesti encounters the ghosts of a knight and lady who repeatedly act out an infernal punishment. Like Pomona and Iphis, the cold lady had refused her suitor, which prompted him to kill himself. His ghost eternally hunts the lady, cuts out her cruel and cold heart with a huge knife, and feeds it to his dogs. She, of course, faces eternal torture. Creating a theatrical space in the forest, Nastagio invites all the village ladies to watch this grisly scene. Predictably, his own hardhearted maiden consents to marriage in the story's moralistic conclusion:

So great was the fear engendered within her by this episode, that in order to avoid a similar fate she converted her enmity into love . . . On the following Sunday Nastagio married her, and after celebrating their nuptials they settled down to a long and happy life together. Their marriage was by no means the only good effect to be produced by this horrible apparition, for from that day forth the ladies of Ravenna in general were so frightened by it that they became much more tractable to men's pleasures than they had ever been in the past.[20]

The story's finalizing conceit celebrates a victory of the "piaceri degli uomini." This at once acknowledges the structure of domination underpinning marriage and posits the institution of marriage as a mechanism for making women amenable to male desire.

Violent and punishing scenes like this often made their way into the commemorative art and dramas of wedding festivities in which pervasive stories of rape and violence against women serve as mechanisms for collective disciplining. *Il ballo delle ingrate* sent the same kind of message as Boccaccio's story, but through a more powerful medium. Where in the *Decameron* ladies read of women who were frightened into yielding to male desires, the audience of *Il ballo delle ingrate* actually saw a horrible

---

[18] For the classic discussion of Boccaccio's reception in the Renaissance, and in particular for Dolce's biographical sketch that introduced his edition of Boccaccio, see Angelo Solerti, *Le vite di Dante, Petrarca e Boccaccio scritte fino al secolo decimosesto* (Milan: Vallardi, 1904), 720–722.

[19] Giovanni Boccaccio, *The Decameron* (Toronto: Penguin Books, 1972), 419.

[20] Ibid., 424.

sight that taught them, like Nastagio's bride, always to acquiesce to the pleasure of men.[21]

The visceral effects of *Il ballo delle ingrate* would have exceeded the written text. The audience of *Il ballo delle ingrate* actually watched, and in effect participated, in a dreadful vision. The ladies in Mantua did not read about women who heard horror stories, but instead viewed the horror themselves and lived for at least a short time inside the performance. The production blurred boundaries between the worlds of the court and the stage; the ballo occurred in a ballroom, involved the participation of nobles, addressed the audience, and was followed immediately by a ball. At the same time the production mobilized the powerful force of song which, with its special physical force and kinesthetic energy, could move emotions and humors of listeners.

The music literally compels the audience to respond to the fate of the *ingrate*. When the *ingrate* climb up from hell, Venus and Cupid express their mournful shock at the miserable women in a duet whose D minor tonality contrasts with Pluto's C major and Venus's preceding G minor. The duet begins with "Ahi vista troppo scura, o miserelle." Their song embodies the women's suffering. Cupid begins with halting speech on a repeated E♭. The range finally expands on his first sigh of "O miserelle" which stops the flow of speech with a leap up of an augmented fifth rendered dissonant by the struck dissonance in the bass and a downward leap of a sixth. The empathetic "Miserelle" continues to break the rhythmic flow of speech, halting the deities as it is meant to halt the viewing ladies. Venus too emphasizes the word this time with another leap from C♯ to A leading immediately to a dissonant B♭, a minor ninth above the bass. Venus's "O" again stops the flow of speech which halts one more time with a rest before her falling a fourth on "miserelle." Just as Venus and Cupid seem to have broken out of their sorrow at a flourish on the "O" after "troppo scura" the misery returns. This exclamation returns to close the duet (Example 2.1). Such music translated the depths of passion into sound and propelled those passions in listeners.

While the fate of the *ingrate*, coupled with the moralizing commentary of the gods, shows what can befall those who do not love enough, Ariadne's story demonstrates the perils of loving too much. She

---

[21] Boccaccio's gory rendition of Nastagio degli Onesti appears on a set of Botticelli wedding panels from the mid-1480s depicting the knight chasing a naked lady. They were commissioned in 1483 for the marriage of Lucrezia di Piero Bini and Giannozzo Pucci, a cousin of the Medici. For a discussion of these panels see Susan L. Wofford, "The Social Aesthetics of Rape: Closural Violence in Boccaccio and Botticelli," in *Creative Imitation: New Essays on Renaissance Literature in Honor of Thomas M. Greene*, ed. Margaret W. Ferguson, G. W. Pigman III, Wayne A. Rebborn, and David Quint (Binghamton: Medieval and Renaissance Text Studies, 1992), 191–229.

Example 2.1, Venus and Cupid, duet from *Il ballo delle ingrate*

acquiesces to Theseus's seduction and lets sexual desire get the better of her, thus defying duty, propriety, and her father's wishes.[22] Monteverdi and Rinuccini's version of the story also serves as a warning to women who might succumb to the seductions of bad men. Cusick argues that the "ravishing" musico-poetic rhetoric that they created for Ariadne embodies her excessive desire. Ariadne's outburst, which brings together musical sound and speech to embody anger, sadness, and despair, marks her as lascivious, representing "a woman whose willfulness and autonomy must be purged through suffering before she is worthy to be taken as a wife."[23] Rendering her passions audible marks Ariadne as seductive, because such a lengthy effusion metaphorically displays her active sexuality in front of the on-stage fishermen as well as the off-stage audience.[24] In light of late Renaissance musico-dramatic conventions, Cusick suggests that the lament's musical process acts out "the eventual triumph in Arianna's character of female piety over promiscuous speech." This triumph effectively constitutes a public musical chastening of the incautious woman who dared to choose her own mate.[25] Making a slightly different point about the lament, Ann MacNeil has argued that *L'Arianna*

---

[22] Positioning Ariadne's plight as a cautionary tale for other similarly tempted women, Giovanni Andrea dell'Anguillara's Italian version of the *Metamorphoses* includes a telling introduction by Giuseppe Orologgi: "Let the story of Arianna be a document to incautious women that they should not wish to believe the promises of those who appear to love them, because they run the risk of throwing themselves into the arms of faithless and ungrateful young men, by whom they are, with greatest infamy, often ruined." Cusick suggests that the ladies would have known Ariadne's story through Orologgi. I have quoted Orologgi from Cusick's "'There was not one lady who failed to shed a tear,'" 24. In addition, Fabbri suggests that Rinuccini probably drew most heavily on the same source, since it includes a long extension of Ariadne's abandonment. Anguillara's 1561 edition, entitled *Metamorfosi di Ovidio*, was reprinted sixteen times between 1561 and 1607.

[23] Cusick, "There Was Not One Lady," 23.

[24] Sixteenth- and seventeenth-century musical productions tend to make musico-rhetorical distinctions between genders and between chaste and lascivious women. For an informative discussion of the kinds of musico-rhetorical distinctions between genders in Monteverdi's music, see Susan McClary, "Constructions of Gender in Monteverdi's Dramatic Music," in *Feminine Endings: Music, Gender, and Sexuality*, (Minneapolis: Minnesota University Press, 1991). For a discussion of the ways that song was deployed by female characters in Venetian opera, see Ellen Rosand, "Monteverdi's *Il ritorno d'Ulisse in patria* and the Power of Music," *Cambridge Opera Journal* 7 (1995): 179–183, and Tim Carter, "In Love's Harmonious Consort? Penelope and the Interpretation of *Il ritorno d'Ulisse in patria*," *Cambridge Opera Journal* 5 (1993): 1–16. See also Linda Phyllis Austern's "Alluring the Auditorie to Effeminacie: Music and the Idea of the Feminine in Early Modern England," *Music and Letters* 74 (1993): 343–354.

[25] Cusick, "There Was Not One Lady," 30. Cusick argues that Ariadne's passionate self and her disciplined self are represented in the internal conflicts of the lament's opening phrase. For her, the musical processes of that phrase represent the purging of Ariadne's passion.

and the *intermedi* to *L'Idropica* functioned as theatrical representations of the marriage rite itself. She reads the dramas in terms of Aristotelian catharsis and focuses on the importance of death and mourning in wedding rituals.[26]

In something close to a mirror reversal of Ariadne's drama, the *ingrate* find themselves punished for the double transgression of enticing male desire and then not returning it.[27] The contrasting messages sent by *L'Arianna* and *Il ballo delle ingrate* are reflected in the different positions that the two concluding laments give to singing. The "cold-heartedness" – a loaded term in Renaissance sex lingo – of the *ingrate* manifests itself in their inability to sing but is overturned in the piece's final moments. In both pieces song embodies female desire, but for Ariadne the desire needs to be crushed and for the hard-hearted ladies it requires coaxing. Monteverdi's conflation of song and desire follows late Renaissance understandings of singing. Recall the musico-poetic linking of song and sensuality that I suggested in relation to "O come sei gentile," and the erotic potential of the physical process of singing as it was understood in early modern cosmologies.

At the same time, in each work song embodies a distinct version of the tug-of-war between female force and the powers attempting to constrain it. Put another way, the presence of Virginia Ramponi's singing voice counteracted the message of the words she sang. Ariadne's words project desperation but that despair, evoked through the mouth of Ramponi, rendered Ariadne and the woman who envoiced her, more musically and rhetorically potent than early modern conventions would otherwise allow. The *ingrata*'s final lament allows her to momentarily reanimate herself and escape the confines of Pluto's hell, derailing the piece's didactic purposes. When she for an instant refuses to go back to "tornar a lagrimar ne l'antro oscuro" [weep in the dark cave] Ramponi's act of singing pushes the dramatic trajectory of the piece away from its goal and ensures that the production, seemingly aimed at silencing the female voice, ends at a different point.

Echoing Ovid/remembering Petrarch

In creating *Il ballo delle ingrate* Rinuccini made use of themes, characters, and descriptive rhetorics that pervaded the texts of Ovid and Petrarch. For instance, Renaissance audiences would have known Venus and Cupid for their habits of stirring up sexual appetites and stealing

---

[26] Ann MacNeil, "Weeping at the Water's Edge," *Early Music* 27 (1999): 406–418.

[27] I want to thank Suzanne Cusick for pointing out in her response to the version of this paper delivered at the fall 1996 meeting of the American Musicological Society that all the women in these productions sin against patriarchy.

virtue. In the ballo, Venus directs her anger at the *ingrate* on behalf of her son's now failing arrows. The punishing physical transformation of the beautiful but cold-hearted women, along with their refusal of male desire that led up to it, recalls the fate of women in Ovid's stories whose incitement of unrequited love leads to metamorphosis. Refusing male desire, the *ingrate* privilege their own bodies over those of their lovers, an act by which they claim a sexual agency that metamorphosis stifles.

Ovid's stories consistently dramatize the complicated relationship between women's voices and sexual transgression. Taken at their most surface level, they seem to narrate the violent and permanent silencing of women who break sexual rules and challenge accepted power dynamics. However, reading between Ovid's lines suggests that women's voices work a powerful but vexed magic, one that is inextricably intertwined with eroticism, sexual transgression, transformation, and communication despite some enforced silence. In other words, women struggle against the restrictive conditions within which they represent themselves, and by doing so produce a powerful cultural expression which in turn inspires patriarchal restraint. Even with their unfortunate ends, these stories do not simply deliver a litany of silenced and raped women but rather present women who talk, or ultimately sing, back.

When infused with a heavy dose of Christian morality, Ovid's stories proved useful to Renaissance artists and writers for perpetuating patriarchal ideals and dictating female behavior. Monteverdi and Rinuccini's appropriation of familiar mythological tropes and whole Ovidian stories in their productions commissioned for the 1608 wedding festivities follows the contemporary literary practice of rewriting episodes from the *Metamorphoses* to perpetuate dominant ideologies and uphold the ruling powers. More specifically, Renaissance wedding festivities typically reenacted mythological tales of all-powerful universal love in ritual celebrations that sat at the intersections of art and life, aesthetics and politics.[28] Almost every nuptial celebration from the period featured at least one of Ovid's tales of love and death, and many appear to draw on Orologgi's conduct-mandating edition of the *Metamorphoses*. By merging the world of the gods with that of mortals, such reconstructions validated existing social structures and mores. At the same time, they could imbue universal messages with local specificity, as in the Mantuan text of *Il ballo delle ingrate*, which apparently refers to a well-known cruel local beauty. According to Paolo Fabbri, the lines "O barbara fierezza, / una

---

[28] For a discussion of the mythological rhetoric of the 1608 festivities see my "Singing the Female Body: Monteverdi, Subjectivity, Sensuality" (Ph.D. dissertation, University of Pennsylvania, 1998). For the classic discussion of Renaissance readings of mythology see Jean Seznec, *The Survival of the Pagan Gods: The Mythological Tradition and Its Place in Renaissance Humanism and Arts*, trans. Barbara F. Sessions (Princeton: Princeton University Press, 1961), 229–262.

io ne vidi (e potre dir il nome)" (O barbarous pride, / (only one I saw and I could say her name), allude to Barbara Sanseverino, Countess of Sala.[29]

Following this tradition of basing nuptial entertainments on mythological stories, *L'Arianna* repeats Ovid's plot, though in the original version the title character makes only a very small and mostly silent appearance. Her abandonment is a postscript to the main event, which is Theseus's winding journey through the labyrinth.

To her, deserted and wailing bitterly, Bacchus brought love and help. And, that she might shine among the deathless stars, he sent the crown she wore up to the skies. Through the thin air it flew; and as it flew its gems were changed to gleaming fires and, still keeping the appearance of a crown, it took its place between the Kneeler (the constellation Hercules) and the Serpent-holder (Ophiuchus).[30]

In Ovid's *Heroides*, a collection of plaints by women who suffer from love, Ariadne's lamentations take center stage as she narrates in graphic detail the emotional experience of her abandonment, from the moment she reached for Theseus's warm body and, not finding him there, "tore at my hair, all disarrayed as it was from sleep."[31]

While Rinuccini based *L'Arianna* on a particular segment of the *Metamorphoses*, for *Il ballo delle ingrate* he drew on a more general narrative that plays out several times in famous episodes from the *Metamorphoses*, especially in the first book which presents a series of women who are transformed because their beauty entices a love they later reject.[32] Again and again, women take control of their bodies by refusing male sexual advances but then lose those bodies through transformation.[33] Daphne's beauty attracts Apollo, but her vow of chastity thwarts his desire.[34] She escapes rape only when her father freezes her in the shape of a tree; she then serves as an inspiration for great poetry but can never again

---

[29] *Il ballo delle ingrate* was printed in Monteverdi's eighth book of madrigals, published in 1638. Fabbri, *Monteverdi*, 99.

[30] Ovid, *Metamorphoses*, Books I–VIII, 419.

[31] Ovid, *Heroides and Amores*, trans. Grant Showerman, ed. E. H. Warmington (Cambridge, MA: Harvard University Press, 1914), 123.

[32] In a devious version of this paradigm, Jove turns his illicit love object Io into a glorious white heifer when his wife approaches the site of their liaison. Unlike the other women, she is ultimately returned to her human form.

[33] The position that I take in this section reflects the influence of Lynn Enterline's "'You speak a language that I understand not': The Rhetoric of Animation in *The Winter's Tale*," *Shakespeare Quarterly* 48 (1 1997): 17–45. Reading Shakespeare's *The Winter's Tale* as a rewriting of the Pygmalion myth, she argues that the play follows Ovid and Petrarch in ascribing to the female voice an unsettling power. She also discusses the Ovidian roots of Petrarchan conventions. For a detailed discussion of Petrarch's complicated relationship to Ovid see Giuseppe Mazzotta, *The Worlds of Petrarch* (Durham, NC: Duke University Press, 1993).

[34] Ovid, *Metamorphoses*, Books I–VIII, 41.

express herself. Similarly, Pan falls in love with the nymph Syrinx, but rather than return his affection, she gives up her human shape. Pan finds himself holding not his lover but marsh reeds, "and while he sighed in disappointment, the soft air stirring in the reeds gave forth a low and complaining sound. Touched by this wonder and charmed by the sweet tones, the god exclaimed: 'This converse shall I have with thee,' and so the pipes . . . took and kept the name of the maiden."[35]

Like Ovid's nymphs and shepherdesses, the women of *Il ballo delle ingrate* inhabit female forms that inspire male lust, but they refuse to satisfy that lust. For this denial, they are transformed into souls without individual bodies. Follino described their new form:

These condemned souls were dressed with garments in a very extravagant and beautiful style, which draped to the ground, and were made of a rich cloth that was woven precisely for this effect. It was gray in color, mixed with most subtle threads of silver and gold with such artifice that to look upon it, it seemed to be ashes mixed with flashing sparks, and thus one saw the dresses, and likewise the cloaks (which hung from their shoulder in a very bizarre manner), embroidered with many flames made of silk and gold, so well arranged that everyone judged that they were burning, and between the said flames, there could be seen scattered in most beautiful order garnets, rubies and other jewels which resembled glowing coals. Their hair, also seen to be woven with these jewels, with part cut short and part spread around with wondrous art, seemed destroyed and burned; and although it was all covered with ashes, nonetheless it showed between the ash and the smoke a certain splendor, from which one could well recognize that at another time they were blondest of blondes like gold thread; and their faces, showing signs of a former beauty, were changed and pallid in such a way that they brought terror and compassion together on looking upon them.[36]

Cloth, hair, and fire merge in Follino's description of the *ingrate*.[37] Once alluring and perfect in appearance, they had hair that was "blondest of blondes." But now, the wondrous arrangement of jewels and flames distorts their bodies. Artificial gems substitute for natural beauty. Follino describes an arrangement of misconstrued man-made parts. The audience never sees a unified beautiful body.

The *ingrate* occupy a space between life and death. This permanent liminality mimics the liminality of sex and death – two experiences that in early modern terms involved a physical transformation and flux

---

[35] Ibid., 53.

[36] Translation modified from Fabbri, *Monteverdi*, 91. Original Italian in Solerti, *Gli albori del melodramma*, vol. III, 255–256.

[37] Costumes carried enormous symbolic power in early modern theatre. See Peter Stallybrass, "Worn Worlds: Clothes and identity on the Renaissance Stage," in *Subject and Object in Renaissance Culture*, ed. Maureen Quilligan, Peter Stallybrass, and Margreta de Grazia (Cambridge: Cambridge University Press, 1996), 289–337.

that threatened the unity of the body. Death was understood as a state in which the soul leaves the body en route to a higher existence, just as orgasm was thought to cause the soul to disappear and reappear in the heart of the beloved. Thus as souls without bodies, confined to the subterranean regions, the *ingrate* are condemned to a permanent liminality that mirrors the very sexual ecstasy they refused in life.[38] In Ovidian terms transformation also substitutes for sex, suggesting that in the end the *ingrate* get precisely what they denied.[39]

Along with their bodies, the *ingrate*, like Daphne, lose their voices and their access to intelligible language. They also lack individual emotions which, combined with their lack of voice, denies them subjectivities. They can convey feelings only through choreographed emblems of generic passions which Monteverdi calls "pitiful gestures."

They did a *balletto* so beautiful and delightful, with steps, movements, and actions now of grief and now of desperation, and now with gestures of pity and now of scorn, sometimes embracing each other as if they had tears of tenderness in their eyes, now striking each other with rage and fury. They were seen from time to time to abhor each other's sight and to flee each other in frightened manners, and then to follow each other with threatening looks, coming to blows with each other, asking pardon, and a thousand other movements, represented with such affect and with such naturalness that the hearts of the onlookers were left so impressed that there was not one in that theatre who did not feel his heart move and be disturbed in a thousand ways at the changing of their passions.[40]

For most of the production, the *ingrate* probably could not be distinguished from one another. First, it is more than likely that Italian balli used choreographed set dances of the variety described by Fabrini Caroso and Cesare Negri.[41] Second, the materials surrounding this event give no indication that the *ingrate* were differentiated from one another or that any one of them stood out – until the very end. Their group movement and amorphous materiality characterized by draped extremities likely blurred physical distinctions and the spaces between

---

[38] Ariadne also undergoes transformation. Her betrothal to Bacchus moves her to the heavens where she lights up the sky and presumably enters a life of excess as the wife of Bacchus. For an interesting discussion of Renaissance understandings of the process of death and its similarities to orgasm, see Jonathan Sawday, *The Body Emblazoned: Dissection and the Human Body in Renaissance Culture* (New York: Routledge, 1996).

[39] Lynn Enterline and Leonard Barkan have made this argument for Ovid as a whole. Lynn Enterline, "'You speak a language that I understand not'"; Leonard Barkan, *The Gods Made Flesh: Metamorphosis and the Pursuit of Paganism* (New Haven: Yale University Press, 1986).

[40] Follino, translation modified from Fabbri, *Monteverdi*, 91.

[41] For a detailed argument of this point see Fenlon, "The Origins of the Staged Ballo."

them.[42] With this lack of distinction between the *ingrate* and absence of individual subjectivity the piece seems, until the lament, determined to rob women of their individuality.

The effective dis-individuation of women by *Il ballo delle ingrate* harks back to Ovid's stories. Episodes in the *Metamorphoses* culminate not in sex but in transformations that preserve a silent female love object for the exclusive use of her male admirer. The female figure stimulates him to creative rather than sexual production. Thus, Daphne's leaves provide Apollo's crown and poetic talents, but he can never realize his physical desire; Pan's breath becomes music as he sighs through the now inert body of Syrinx. And of course, as musicologists well know, Orpheus makes beautiful music mourning Euridice's death. Moreover the desire of men for perfect beauty sometimes eschewed real women, as in the cases of Narcissus and Pygmalion. When his own image overpowers everything else Narcissus is deprived of female flesh, while the disappointingly inanimate object that Pygmalion creates prevents him from loving women.

In the tradition of Ovid's women and Petrarch's Laura, for most of the production the *ingrate* possess an idealized beauty only visible through the words of others. As distorted images of once-perfect female forms, their former beauty exists in the descriptions of Pluto, Venus, and Cupid. When Renaissance artists like Rinuccini and Monteverdi represented female beauty they drew on the descriptive habits of Petrarch, who replaces Laura with poetic representations of a series of details without a unified voice or body.[43] The poet depicts her surfaces as

[42] Fenlon suggests that *Il ballo delle ingrate* marks the high point of seventeenth-century spectacle dance performances, which he says acquired their generic form with Cavalieri's final ballet for the 1589 wedding production of *La Pellegrina*. For more on the court ballet as a genre and especially on its French influences, see James M. Saslow, *The Medici Wedding of 1589: Florentine Festival as Theatrum Mundi* (New Haven: Yale University Press, 1996) and Iain Fenlon, *Music and Patronage in Sixteenth-Century Mantua* (New York: Cambridge University Press, 1980). Anthony Newcomb suggests that the French ballet de cour influenced the development of the Dancing Duchesses of Ferrara. Considering the artistic cross-pollination between Italian courts, it is more than likely that ballets at Mantua also carried traces of French dance. See Anthony Newcomb, *The Madrigal at Ferrara* (Princeton: Princeton University Press, 1980). For information on European dance in general, see Meredith Elias Little, "Recent Research in European Dance, 1400–1800," *Early Music* 14 (1986): 331–340; Mark Franco, *Dance As Text: Ideologies of the Baroque Body* (New York: Cambridge University Press, 1993), and Jennifer Neville, "The Italian Ballo as Described in Fifteenth-century Dance Treatises," *Studies in Music, Australia* 18 (1984): 38–51.

[43] Nancy Vickers has most famously made this argument. See Nancy Vickers, "Diana Described: Scattered Women and Scattered Rhyme," *Critical Inquiry* 8 (1981): 265–279. Ovid also dismembers his women. For example, Apollo's erotic glance at Daphne effectively takes apart his love object by objectifying each part as an individual entity: hair, eyes gleaming like stars, and a sensuous mouth.

composites of dissociated objects, precious metals and stones.[44] As a collection of inanimate jewels and articles "scattered like the objects of fetish worship," she is represented metonymically, taking on a unified form only as the reader imbues each idealized but isolated part with the status of the whole.[45] Rinuccini's portrayal of the *ingrate* follows in this tradition. Their hair and features now literally appear as gems and stones.

Lacking an audible voice, the *ingrate* remain silent in the face of everyone else describing them. This silence reflects the opposition between male creative expression and female silence displayed in Ovid's stories and reified by Petrarchan poetry. In these connected traditions, female figures serve as mute projections of male ideals and vehicles for male creative expression. Petrarch's descriptive dismembering techniques, like Ovid's transformations, turn the love object into a safely distant and disembodied form that perpetuates poetic fascination.[46] Male subjects are plagued by a riveting attention to an object that leads to an indefinite deferral of desire. As Catherine Belsey says of English lyrics written in the Petrarchan tradition, "these texts of absence, like desire itself, seek an impossible, a metaphysical presence, which is the inscription of love. In each case the figure deflects what it sets out to define, paradoxically re-enacting the precise process of deferment, which constitutes desire sustained."[47] The subject's utter captivation of his object creates an absence or at least a ubiquitous postponement that constitutes the subject.[48]

The *ingrate* represent the ultimate impossible objects. By adamantly refusing to be wooed they make desire an end in and of itself. Such a privileging of desire parallels Petrarch's poetry, which positions desire as a generative and descriptive force that takes aim at something other than the original love object; Laura's absence necessarily precedes the poet's

[44] Vickers, "Diana Described."

[45] John Freccero, "The Fig Tree and the Laurel," in *Literary Theory/Renaissance Texts*, ed. Patricia Parker andDavid Quint (Baltimore: Johns Hopkins University Press, 1986), 29.

[46] Elucidating the Ovidian roots of Petrarch's representational strategies, Vickers examines Rime 23, a poem in which Petrarch takes on Actaeon's voice. She argues that the poet's anxiety about seeing Laura's whole body emerges because he associates himself with Actaeon, whose forbidden encounter with Diana led to dismemberment and immobilization. Vickers, "Diana Described," 273.

[47] Catherine Belsey, "Desire's Excess and the English Renaissance Theatre: Edward II, Troilus and Cressida, Othello," in *Erotic Politics: Desire on The Renaissance Stage*, ed. Susan Zimmerman (New York: Routledge, 1992), 66.

[48] For a similar argument also see Lynn Enterline, "Embodied Voices: Petrarch Reading (Himself Reading) Ovid," in *Desire in the Renaissance: Psychoanalysis and Literature*, ed. Valeria Finucci and Regina Schwartz (Princeton: Princeton University Press, 1994), 124.

writing voice and serves as desire's only realization.[49] As Petrarch turns his attraction to Laura into a poetic rhetoric of love, metaphors of winter, darkness, death, and sickness signify desire, turning it into an endless series of postponements and ensuring that the constitutive power of absence eclipses the actual woman in question.[50] In other words, the loss of Laura's body constitutes an intolerable absence, which in turn creates a reason to speak and finally an entire poetic corpus. Though the *ingrate*, in the tradition of Petrarch's Laura and Ovid's women, seem to be essentially impossible objects, the performative nature of *Il ballo delle ingrate* renders them palpably possible.

A different tune

Though informed by Petrarchan representations of the female body and by Ovid's stories, early modern music dramas were by no means compelled to endlessly repeat the dependence of male creative expression on violence against women, or to advocate the association of female silence with male rhetorical prowess. After all, women kept singing and men kept writing music that depended on female voices. The force of women's song consistently opposed constraints on their bodies, creating an endless tug-of-war between female utterance and the powers trying to stifle it.

The final moments of *Il ballo delle ingrate* mark this defiance and complicate oppositions drawn by scholars between male agency and female passivity. When the lone lamenter refuses to return to hell, she momentarily reverses her metamorphosis, taking on a verbal and vocal agency that reunites her soul literally and figuratively with an articulate voice and whole body.[51] Because song partakes of the same material as breath – the animating force of life – the physical activity of singing pushes her spirit and soul back into her body. Metaphorically, she escapes the amorphous mass of bodiless *ingrate* who make up Pluto's troupe by

---

[49] Vickers, "Diana Described." Also see Elizabeth Cropper, "The Beauty of Woman: Problems in the Rhetoric of Renaissance Portraiture, " in *Rewriting the Renaissance: The Discourses of Sexual Difference in Early Modern Europe*, ed. Maureen Quilligan, Nancy J. Vickers, and Margaret W. Ferguson (Chicago: University of Chicago Press, 1986), 175–191.

[50] The literature exploring the influences on and of Petrarch's representational strategies is vast. For discussions with a similar theoretical stance as this one, see Enterline, "Embodied Voices: Petrarch Reading (Himself Reading) Ovid," and Mazzotta, *The Worlds of Petrarch*. Both of these scholars also discuss the influence of Augustine on Petrarch, particularly with respect to the origin of language in desire.

[51] Within Neoplatonic cosmologies, song and the spirit had a special magnetic affinity for one another, turning song almost into a living thing. See Gary Tomlinson, *Music in Renaissance Magic: Toward a Historiography of Others* (Chicago: University of Chicago Press, 1993).

reclaiming for an instant the expressive potential of her human form. She uses those expressive capabilities to talk back to her punishment.

> Ahi, troppo è duro
> crudel sentenza e vie più cruda pena,
> tornar a lagrimar nell'antro oscuro.
> Aer sereno e puro,
> addio per sempre, addio o cielo, o sole,
> addio lucide stelle,
> apprendete pietà donne e donzelle
> [last line repeated by four *ingrate*]
>
> Al fumo, a' gridi, a' pianti,
> a sempiterno affanno!
> Ahi dove son le pompe, ove gli amanti,
> dove sen vanno
> donne che sì pregiate al mondo furo?
> [repeat from "Aer sereno" through "donne e donzelle"]

[Ah, it is too hard, a cruel sentence and an even crueler punishment, to return and weep in the dark cave. Clear and pure air, farewell forever, farewell, sun; farewell shining stars; ladies and maidens learn to show pity. To the smoke, to the cries, to the tears; to the eternal suffering! Ah where is the pomp, where are the lovers, where are those ladies going who were so prized in the world?]

Taking over a musico-poetic style reminiscent of Ariadne's much-analyzed lament, the solo *ingrata* refashions her capacity for expression, which releases her from the confines of dance. Because such rhetorically heightened language signals individuality in the world of late Renaissance music dramas, this musico-poetic rhetoric separates the lamenting *ingrata* from the mute, dancing, shapeless bodies of her comrades. Here we need only recall Monteverdi's famous letter to Alessandro Striggio in response to Scipione Agnelli's fable *Le Nozze di Tetide*: "How, dear Sir, can I imitate the speech of the winds, if they do not speak? And how can I, by such means, move the passions? Ariadne moved us because she was a woman."[52] Reading this statement in conjunction with the writings of Neoplatonic philosophers and music theorists who understood song to be the most powerful imitator of all things suggests that, by singing in the style of Ariadne, the *ingrata* would have moved listeners because she temporarily reclaimed the power of her voice and its female form. The Ariadne-like rhetorical effectiveness allows the *ingrata* for a moment to reclaim a subject and a body.

To set the ballo apart from Pluto's warning which precedes it, Monteverdi turns to G minor from the A minor music that accompanies her companions as they process back to the underworld and the

---

[52] Denis Stevens, *The Letters of Claudio Monteverdi* (Cambridge: Cambridge University Press, 1980), 117.

Example 2.2a, Final section of *Il ballo delle ingrate*, opening bars

Example 2.2b, *Lamento d'Arianna*, opening

Example 2.2c, *Lamento d'Arianna*, second part, beginning

C major of Pluto's invectives. The *ingrata* articulates her despair at reentering the infernal caverns with affective repetitions and gestures that structurally parallel Ariadne's lament (Example 2.2a–c). The melody moves largely in disjunct motion and begins with a vocal sigh on "Ahi troppo" with which she introduces first a minor seventh and then a minor ninth above the bass, leading to the melodic peak of her opening. The high E♭ is accentuated by the following downward leap of a diminished fifth through a passing B♭. The dissonance of the *ingrata*'s opening – especially the setting of "Ahi troppo è duro" – recalls

Ariadne's famous opening cry of "Lasciatemi morire." Like Ariadne's lament, this shorter plaint is characterized by an intensely controlled musico/rhetorical structure which highlights the communicative abilities of the solo lamenter. The octave descent between "Ahi troppo" and "sentenza" is followed in the second half of the sentence by an ascent back to the C of the first "Ahi troppo." All of this occurs over a C held in the bass for five measures which allows her melody, with its frequent return to the dissonant F♯, to make the harmony unstable and thus in turn renders her melody unruly. She, in other words, destabilizes the bass line.

Her next line reverses her punishment more dramatically. There she turns Pluto's orders "Tornar a lagrimar" ("return and weep"), uttered just before the lament, into a repeated affective exclamation. Not only does she refuse his command but she also throws the words and music back at him and at the audience. By taking over and extending Pluto's imperative in words and music, the *ingrata* momentarily gains access to and exceeds the patriarchal rhetoric used to constrain her. This moment also recalls Ariadne's repeated exclamation of "O Teseo mio." The melodic sequence begins with a falling third on the first "tornar," and increases in vehemence as the rising pitches of the next two cries are highlighted with falling fourths – the final one rises to a high F, the highest pitch in the brief lament. Each falling cry lands on a dissonance. Throughout the lament, such structural devices give the *ingrata* rhetorical control even as she seems to weep. The lines that begin with "Aer sereno" through "Addio per sempre" are repeated, giving it a refrain-like feel. The setting of fourth- and fifth-related progressions, recalling in its harmonic progression the opening to "Sì ch'io vorei morire" from Monteverdi's fourth book of madrigals, provides rhetorical structure and imbues the lament with rising tension. In the madrigal these harmonies embody a prelude to sexual ecstasy; here they thwart her transformation back to soulless woman clad in smoke and ash.

The *ingrate* have until this moment been confined to dancing generalized passions. Now the soloist's voice overturns the imposed silence and articulates the pain of her "sempiterno affanno" (eternal suffering). Her song of farewell to the mortal world cries out the harshness and cruelty of her sentence. Monteverdi and Rinuccini gave four off-stage *ingrate* the last word. They echo the lamenting *ingrata*, repeating the line "apprendete pietà donne e donzelle," without basso continuo but with a pungent dissonance between a B♭ in the melody and a B♮ in the bass on the word "donne." This dissonance, suggesting pain, emphasizes the prescriptive warning that underlies the lament. Such dissonances, which effect pain, pepper even the final cadential measure, which has a C against a B♭ in one part and an A against a B♮ in another.

This four-voiced echo underscores the sympathetic effect of the lament, suggesting both identification with the suffering and a collective refusal of silence. This effect highlights, and in fact compels, the empathy that the production was meant to inspire in the viewing ladies. At the same time the refrain-like structure of the repeated "addio per sempre" and "apprendete pietà," which allows the grinding Bb/B dissonance to recur twice, underscores this empathetic effect. Even though these women all envoice words written by men, the palpable presence of their voices on the stage works against the silencing impulses of *Il ballo delle ingrate* and the Petrarchan and Ovidian traditions upon which it drew. Here the real live singing women sound against the representations of women.

Even the Ovidian and Petrarchan models for the *ingrata*'s persistent song do not silence the female voice in any simple way. Ovid's women sing quite frequently and pervasively, and Laura, though silent for most of Petrarch's canzonieri, wields an arresting power when she occasionally speaks. Ovid and Petrarch imbue the female voice with a disturbing residual potency while ostensibly granting the male voice dominance. In many Ovidian stories, men's voices fail while women's succeed. Recall that women silence Orpheus, for although his songs move the underworld, he meets his demise when the drums and chanting of the Bacchantes drown out his lyre, and the dancing women, angry because he has scorned their kind, tear him to bits. Orpheus's plaintive verse does not prevent his destruction and dismemberment.[53] While Orpheus enthralled beasts and trees, the crazed women of Cicones remained completely unmoved by the man who, like the *ingrate*, scorned the opposite sex. "Then one of these, her tresses streaming in the gentle breeze, cried out 'See, see the man who scorns us,' and hurled her spear straight at the tuneful mouth of Apollo's bard . . ."[54] The failure of his voice at this moment flies in the face of early modern fantasies of an animating and controlling male voice exemplified by the Petrarchan and Ovidian tendencies to present creative men and silent, described women.

In contrast to this male failure, women's voices work. Diana's invective against Actaeon's description of her naked body turns him into a stag that cannot speak.

No more than this she spoke; but on the head which she had sprinkled she caused to grow the horns of a long lived stag, stretched out his neck, sharpened his ear tips . . . And last of all she planted fear within his heart . . . But when he sees his features and his horns in a clear pool, "Oh, woe is me!" he tries to say; but no words come. He groans – the only speech he has – and tears course down his changeling cheeks.[55]

---

[53] Ovid *Metamorphoses*, Book XI, 121.   [54] Ibid.   [55] Ibid., Book III, 139.

Although Apollo cannot coax Daphne out of her virginity, her prayer to lose her beauty prompts her father to transform her. Ariadne's wailing entices Bacchus to wed her, a fate that includes a metamorphosis from mortal to god as she joins him in the heavens. Altering more than just her own form, Ceres brings winter to all the lands by crying over her daughter Proserpina's rape and abduction.

Recalling Ovid's women, when Petrarch describes Laura's voice, he imbues it with a disarming potency. Her sounds wield a troubling force that chains the poet's senses:

> Ma 'l suon che di dolcezza i sensi lega
> col gran desir d'udendo esser beata
> l'anima al dipartir presta raffrena.

[but the sound that binds my senses with its sweetness, reins in my soul, though ready to depart, with the great desire for the blessedness of listening.][56]

Angelic, divine, seductive, and dazzling, the magic of love turns her breath into a beautiful voice. Petrarch goes on to say that her hand gathers

> e i vaghi spirti in un sospiro accoglie
> co le sue mani, et poi in voce gli scioglie
> chiara, soave, angelica, divina

[her wandering breath into a sigh with her hands, and then looses it in a clear, soft, angelic, divine voice].[57]

Her voice penetrates Petrarch's heart like "sirene al suono" (siren's song) and wields "e 'l cantar che ne l'anima si sente" (strange charm and singing that is felt in the soul).[58] She fills his heart with sweet poison.

Like her body, Laura's voice functions as an invisible and often inaudible object of desire. When poetic description replaces Laura's body and voice, Petrarch follows Ovid's Pygmalion, who in his longing to hear his statue craves the sounds of his beloved. In the Pygmalion-inspired Sonnet 78, he cries out "se risponder s'avesse a' detti miei!" (if only she could reply to my words).[59] Fantasizing about her voice attains the power of actually hearing it. He imagines her voice as a whole, functional and powerful force that commands his attention even in its absence. This contrasts markedly with her body, which he imagines only in bits and pieces.

At the rare moments when Petrarch does refer to Laura's actual voice, it comes at him with disconcerting force. This is especially evident in

---

[56] Petrarch, "Canzone 167," 312.   [57] Ibid.
[58] Ibid., "Canzone 207," 360 and "Canzone 213," 367.   [59] Ibid., "Canzone 78," 178.

71

Canzone 23, the so-called Canzone of the Metamorphoses. Petrarch's echoing song angers Laura:

> Ella parlava sì turbata in vista
> che tremar mi fea dentro a quella petra

[She spoke, so angry to see that she made me tremble within that stone].

Taking on Diana's voice, Laura commands him to be silent and thus freezes him into stone with the words, "Di ciò non far parola" (make no word of this).[60] Laura's voice, in its presence, both real and imagined, drowns out and counters Petrarch's own, reducing him like Echo to a repetitive voice, transforming him like Actaeon into a silent stag, and turning him like Pygmalion's statue into mute stone.

Women do not lack voice or rhetorical prowess. On the contrary, their voices have too much power. Thus Ovid's stories transform female characters because, not in spite, of the force of their voices. Daphne's answered prayer, Echo's repetitive voice, and Philomela's severed tongue all mark women whose expressive power leads to their transformation and sometimes violent containment. Women's voices maintain a destructive and disturbing potential that contrasts markedly with feeble male voices. Our notion of a silencing male domination over women is too simplistic. The female voice embodied in the *ingrata*'s final song, even when it ventriloquizes the words of men, can resist the collusion between male expression and violence to the female body.

Early modern mouth anxiety

In the published version of *Il ballo delle ingrate*, Monteverdi wrote that "First there is a scene in which the setting represents a mouth of hell, with four paths, each side of which is to emit flames."[61] From Follino's accounts of the original Mantuan performance we know that the stage did indeed take the shape of a gaping mouth exuding fire and smoke, which apparently gave the audience the feeling of standing dangerously close to the edge of Hell:

In the middle of the stage one saw the large mouth of a wide and deep cavern, which, stretching beyond the confines of the scene, seemed that it went so far beyond it that the human eye could not reach to discern its end. That cavern was surrounded within and around by burning fire and in its darkest depths, in a part very deep and distant from its mouth, one saw a great abyss behind which there rotated balls of flames burning most brightly and within which there were countless monsters of the inferno so horrible and frightening that many did not

---

[60] Robert Durling, ed., *Petrarch's Lyric Poems: The Rime sparse and Other Lyrics* (Cambridge, MA: Harvard University Press, 1976). "Canzone 23," 63–65.

[61] Monteverdi, *Madrigali guerrieri e amorosi*, xviii.

have the courage to look upon it. It seemed a horrifying and monstrous thing to see that infernal abyss full of such fire and such monstrous images.[62]

Through the entire production, this orifice swallowed and spat out various *ingrate* and deities, including Cupid and the infernal shades, all of whom spent a great deal of time moving in and out of the entrance to hell. In closing, Follino describes the final moment of the piece as a swallowing one:

At the end of so beautiful a plaint they again entered the cave, but in such a manner that they seemed pushed by a lively force; no sooner were they swallowed up by it than, closing its great mouth, the scene remained with a beautiful and delightful view.[63]

An interpretation of this particularly voracious *bocca d'inferno* in relation to the story of the ballo and to the final lament must account for the fact that at the end of the Renaissance social mores, informed by Galenic medicine, understood the female mouth and the sounds emanating from it as primary sites of threatening female sexuality. This understanding came largely from the interchangeability of both orifices and suggests some of the reasons why women's voices were more sexualized and more unruly then men's. Put quite simply, men do not have wombs or vaginas. For women, mouths provided access to the inside of their bodies. At the same time, silence, for women but not for men, was metaphorically conflated with chastity and speech with wantonness, while for men eloquence was a virtue. These associations permeate contemporary conduct books as well as in the authoritative medical literature handed down from the ancient world.

Endeavors to shut women's mouths by commanding them to silence reflected early modern assumptions that women could not sufficiently control their own bodies or souls. In Aristotle's words, quoted through the Renaissance, "The female appears to be the product of nature's deficiency."[64] This assumed inferiority also underpinned prescriptive literature. For example, the most misogynistic character in Castiglione's *Il cortegiano*, Gaspare, echoes Aristotle when saying, "when a woman is born this is a mistake or defect, and contrary to Nature's wishes."[65] In

---

[62] Follino, as quoted in Fabbri, *Monteverdi*. 89. Original Italian in Solerti, *Gli albori del melodramma*, 256.

[63] Fabbri, *Monteverdi*, 92., original in Solerti, *Gli albori del melodramma*, 258.

[64] Jacques Ferrand, a French medical philosopher writing in the mid-seventeenth century, is here drawing on Aristotle's famous dictum. See *A Treatise On Lovesickness*, trans. David A. Beecher and Massimo Ciavolella (Syracuse: Syracuse University Press, 1990), 311 and Aristotle's *Generation of Animals*, trans. A. L. Peck (Cambridge, MA: Harvard University Press, 1990), Bk. 1, Ch. 20, 103.

[65] Baldesar [Baldassare] Castiglione, *The Book of the Courtier (1528)*, trans. George Bull (New York: Penguin Classics, 1986), 217.

the world of elite court culture, in which self-fashioning involved count-less daily performances and in which the categories of courtesan and lady pushed up against each other, conduct books wielded a formative discursive force.[66]

In light of beliefs that ladies should speak only rarely and that their responsible comportment depended on rigid disciplining, it comes as no surprise that Francesco Barbaro, in his 1555 treatise dedicated to wifely duties composed for the wedding of Lorenzo de' Medici, writes that "Loquacity cannot be sufficiently reproached in women, as many very learned and wise men have stated, nor can silence be sufficiently applauded."[67] Later, still endorsing quiet women, he claims that nature advocates silence because "She has with good reason furnished us with two ears but only one tongue and this she has guarded with the double defense of lips and teeth."[68] He anecdotally equates women's speech with the exposure of their bodies:

When a certain young man saw the noblewoman stretch her arm out of her mantle that had been drawn back he said to his companion: "How handsome is her arm." To this she replied: "It is not a public one." It is proper, however, that not only arms but indeed also the speech of women never be made public, for the speech of a noblewoman can be no less dangerous than the nakedness of her limbs.[69]

In this representative story, the conflation of speech and promiscu-ity turns a closed mouth into a sign of chastity and silence into a cardinal virtue. Along similar lines, a fictional character in Stefano Guazzo's 1574 treatise on civil conversation highlights the lascivious and sexual undertones of talking with women.[70] Lodovico Dolce writes

---

[66] Here I refer to the many conduct books and debates on women that appeared from the fourteenth through the seventeenth centuries. Castiglione's famous *Il cortegiano* is just one representative work among many. Much work has already been done on these discursive battles over women's bodies. For accounts that take these "eti-quette books" as mostly didactic, see Ian Maclean, *The Renaissance Notion of Woman: A Study in the Fortunes of Scholasticism and Medieval Science in European Intellectual Life* (Cambridge: Cambridge University Press, 1980). For accounts that treat conduct books more as literature and look closely at cultural contexts, see Constance Jordan, *Renais-sance Feminism: Literary Text and Political Models* (Ithaca: Cornell University Press, 1990) and Ann Rosalind Jones, "Nets and Bridles: Early Modern Conduct Books and Sixteenth-century Women's Lyrics," in *The Ideology of Conduct: Essays on Literature and the History of Sexuality*, ed. Nancy Armstrong and Leonard Tennenhouse (New York: Methuen, 1987).

[67] Francesco Barbaro, "On Wifely Duties" (1555), 204.

[68] Ibid., 205.   [69] Ibid., 205.

[70] Stefano Guazzo, *La Civil Conversatione* (1575), ed. Amadeo Quondam (Modena: Panini, 1993), 211–233.

that "The most beautifully praised song of a young woman is her silence."[71]

Though the dangers associated with female speech and singing were many, social practices such as courtly repartee, music dramas, and madrigals required that at least some women speak and sing. Voicing a more nuanced prescription than Barbaro, Castiglione instructs women to maintain the impossible combination of conversational skill and chastity. In the third book of *Il cortegiano*, which is dedicated to defining an ideal court lady, Castiglione's character Giuliano de' Medici states that:

The lady who is at Court should properly have, before all else, a certain pleasing affability, whereby she will know how to entertain graciously every kind of man with charming and honest conversation, suited to the time and the place and the rank of the person with whom she is talking. And her serene and modest behavior, and the candour that ought to inform all her actions, should be accompanied by a quick and vivacious spirit by which she shows her freedom from boorishness; but with such a virtuous manner that she makes herself thought no less chaste, prudent and benign than she is pleasing, witty and discreet. Thus she must observe a certain difficult mean, composed as it were of contrasting qualities, and take care not to stray beyond certain fixed limits. Nor in her desire to be thought chaste and virtuous, should she appear withdrawn or run off if she dislikes the company she finds herself in or thinks the conversation improper.[72]

The court lady had to walk a tightrope: to talk, but not too much; to appear chaste, but not priggish. In dictating to ladies the practical ramifications of these ideals, Castiglione says that they must elicit good conversation without actually participating freely in it. They should entertain men with singing and dancing, but because overzealous activity of any kind corroded their honor, they must never exhibit eagerness or excessive proficiency in either arena. According to the character Giuliano de' Medici, "when she is about to dance or make music of any kind, she should first have to be coaxed a little, and should begin with a certain shyness, suggesting the dignified modesty that brazen women cannot understand."[73] Here the lady's stance parallels the demure shyness that begins nearly every poetic description of an amorous encounter in the early modern period.

As with courtly repartee and sex itself, music making required female participation even as social mores turned that participation into a sign of

---

[71] "Il saper danzare, sonare, e cantare a una Giovane non è il silentio." Dolce, cited in Solerti, *Le vite*, 31.
[72] Castiglione, *The Book of the Courtier*, 212.   [73] Ibid., 215.

lasciviousness.[74] Though he depicted virtuous singing women in his dialogues, Pietro Bembo did not want his daughter to make music. Thinking her too interested in music and not enough concerned with domesticity, he wrote her the following letter:

Playing music is for a woman a vain and frivolous thing. And I would wish you to be the most serious and chaste woman alive. Beyond this, if you do not play well your playing will give you little pleasure and not a little embarrassment. And you will not be able to play well unless you spend ten or twelve years in this pursuit without thinking of anything else. What this would mean you can imagine yourself without saying more. Therefore set aside thoughts of this frivolity and work to be humble and good and wise and obedient. Don't let yourself be carried away by these desires, indeed resist them with a strong will.[75]

For Bembo, music making, presumably playing an instrument or singing, works against more appropriate domestic pursuits like "writing and cooking" and threatens his daughter's chaste reputation. Yet, somewhat paradoxically, his own dialogues take the songs of women as starting points. Pietro Aretino, a satirist writing in the late sixteenth century, made explicit the inverse relationship between music and virtue that Bembo only suggested, when he wrote that "the sounds, songs, and letters that women know are the keys that open the doors to their chastity."[76]

The presumed lasciviousness of women's song held sway well into the seventeenth century. As late as 1630 the Roman lawyer Grazioso Uberti included in his dialogue about local musical culture an interlocutor who repeatedly informs readers of the benefits of silent women. In stating the views of music patrons around the holy city, he insists that singing puts a woman too much in the public eye and makes her vulnerable to desire – which would then of course be her fault. The character Severo says that "Many say that nothing should be appreciated in women but honesty, that women should rather avoid dealing with men, than hold them in conversation and charm them with song."[77] He goes on to write of other

[74] Laura Macy suggests that late sixteenth-century madrigals, especially as depicted in Doni's dialogues, imitated good conversation. Laura Macy, "Speaking of Sex: Metaphor and Performance in the Italian Madrigal," *Journal of Musicology* 14/1 (1996): 1–45.

[75] As translated in Gary Tomlinson, *Strunk's Source Readings in Music History*, vol. III (New York: Norton, 1998). Of course Bembo was very conscious of a public readership and was overly preoccupied with Helena's illegitimacy. He tried and failed repeatedly to establish her in Venetian society.

[76] Pietro Aretino, *Lettere*, ed. Paolo Procaccioli (Rome: Salerno Editrice, 1992), 204 Letter to Messer Ambrogio De Gli Eusebi, "Take a woman for a mistress but poetry for a wife." Venice, June 1, 1537.

[77] Grazioso Uberto, *Il Contrasto musico, opera dilettevole*, Pt. 2, ed. Giancarlo Rostirolla (Lucca: Libreria Musicale Italiana, 1991), 68.

men who say that the music of dishonest women should be condemned and avoided. But since singing can make a dishonest woman of anyone, it would seem that all music performed by women has a dangerous potential.

When inflected with a characteristically early modern dread of the female body and female appetites, these anxieties about women's voices took on an undeniable sexual charge that was peculiar to women. Many historians have pointed out that both medical discourses and cultural expressions collapsed the mouth and female sex organs into one another, positioning them both as signs of female unruliness and wantonness. Particularly relevant to the staging of *Il ballo delle ingrate* are two intersecting associations that connect threatening female sexuality with the horrors of the underworld, death, and destruction. Because both mouths and sex organs could "swallow" and "consume," medical texts make the two orifices analogous to one another. At the same time, artistic representations conflate mouths with the damning abyss of hell and recall the medical associations by emphasizing the entrance to this dark and dangerous place.

As I have already discussed, early modern assimilation of voice and reproductive body parts linked the throat to the neck of the uterus, the mouth to female genitals, and the diaphragm to the womb. Galen asserted a sympathetic relationship between mouths and wombs, whereby actions at one end of the body exerted a direct influence on the other. In explaining this conflation, he cited Herophilus, who "likens the nature of the uterus to the upper part of the windpipe."[78] The generative capacity of the womb, reached through the vagina, and the digestive capacity of the stomach, reached through the mouth, were analogous. Both cavities could hold onto and process matter: the womb turned a seed into a baby, which it then expelled, while the stomach turned food into the humoral materials that permeated the body and were expelled in the form of blood, breath, saliva, and other matter. Comparing the cavities of the womb and stomach, Galen wrote, "those parts of the animal which are especially hollow and large are the stomach and the organ which is called the womb or uterus . . . For the stomach retains the food until it has quite digested it, and the uterus retains the embryo until it brings it to completion."[79] In short, the vagina consumes sexually as the mouth consumes by eating. Suggesting a more direct connection, a favorite Hippocratic method for determining a woman's fertility

[78] Herophilus supposedly discovered the ovaries in the third century. Hippocrates, *The Medical Works of Hippocrates*, ed. John Chadwick and W. N. Mann (Oxford: Oxford University Press, 1950), 217.

[79] Galen, *On The Natural Faculties*, trans. Arthur John Brock (Cambridge, MA: Harvard University Press, 1991), 227 and 229.

that I discussed in the last chapter involved sitting her over something smelly, often garlic, and then seeing if it could be smelled in her mouth. If it could, things were working properly; if not she was deemed infertile.[80] And Jacques Ferrand in his 1624 treatise on lovesickness says that chapped and dry lips indicate a "dry womb."[81] To be sure, this association between stomach and voice existed even for men; Camillo Maffei repeats the story of Nero putting a lead plate on his stomach in order to strengthen his diaphragm and thus to build a better voice. But this all had vastly different connotations for women – connotations that related to the early modern womb/mouth anxiety.

Moreover, though Galen had disproved Plato's description of the womb as a hungry animal which, without enough sex, might wander through and even out of a woman's body, medical and social discourses still imagined this wayward organ as always on the verge of overpowering women's senses and thereby threatening the outside world. They routinely diagnosed women who did not get enough sex with uterine frenzy, a disease that Ferrand described as

a raging or madness that comes from an excessive burning desire in the womb, or from a hot temperature communicated to the brain and to the rest of the body through the channels in the spine, or from the biting vapors arising from the corrupted seed lying stagnant around the uterus.[82]

Especially common in widows and engaged girls, this disease struck women not bound by marriage, women whose voracious sexualities were on the loose. Possessing a seemingly independent psychological agency, the womb harbored concentrated powers of intimidating female sexuality. As a mysterious site of consumption, expulsion, and pleasure, the womb led to the unknowable and thus threatening interior of the female body.

Renaissance anatomies that highlighted the swallowing potential of the mouth and of the vagina made their way into popular and literary representations of dangerous gaping orifices like the *bocca d'inferno*. Monteverdi's flaming stage represents a tamer and less aggressive version of the hungry swallowing mouths that Mikhail Bakhtin found so intriguing in Rabelais and other popular literature of the sixteenth and seventeenth centuries. For Bakhtin those orifices stand in for the grotesque body, which in turn stands in for female excess.[83] In this

---

[80] Hippocrates, *The Medical Works of Hippocrates*, 262.

[81] Ferrand, *A Treatise On Lovesickness*, 294.   [82] Ibid., 263.

[83] Bakhtin connects grotesque figures to the social body by suggesting that they are universal representations of all the people. While the parallels between the mouth of hell and Bakhtin's grotesque orifices are clear, it is crucial to move beyond Bakhtin's gender-blind fascination with the mouth. Bakhtin erases the gendered implications of this imagery, and then proceeds categorically to ignore women by positing the grotesque

context the stage of *Il ballo delle ingrate* becomes a burning symbol of female desire, making it possible to see the whole production as a metaphoric consumption of the *ingrate* by their own excessive bodies. In life they seduced and then rejected lovers; consequently their sexuality devours them. Cupid describes them as they enter:

> Fuor de l'atra caverna
> ove piangono invan

[out from the murky cavern where they weep in vain]

Their residence in the caverns of hell binds them to the threatening nature of female mouths.

The perpetual crying of the *ingrate* reflects another way in which the Galenic heritage differentiated women's bodies from men's and construed them as fundamentally out of control and thus differentiated the effects of female singing from those of male singing. Gail Paster has suggested that representations of women as overly effusive made them into "leaky vessels." Humoral medicine and social discourse "isolate one element of the female body's material expressiveness – its production of fluids – as excessive, hence either disturbing or shameful."[84] Because female bodies produced breast milk and menstrual blood, they contained more liquid than men's bodies. Soranus, a third-century Greek gynecologist well read by Renaissance doctors, described menstruation as a purging of unnecessary fluids, "since, as some people say, excreting blood from the body like excessive matter, it effects a purgation of the body."[85] In this understanding, menstruation is analogous to other forms of feminine incontinence – sexual, linguistic, and urinary. All of these served as potent signs of a woman's inability to control her body and thus everything else about her.[86] Extra fluids rendered women always incontinent and found a discursive corollary in their predisposition to speak, emote, and exude too much, all of which made inhabiting a female body something of a biological and social hazard.

Hazardous in and of themselves, the fluids that emerged from the female body could wreak havoc in the world. Isidore of Seville, a sixth-century thinker cited well into the seventeenth century, says of menstrual blood that

body as implicitly female. Mikhail Bakhtin, *Rabelais and his World*, trans. Helene Iswolsky (Bloomington: Indiana University Press, 1984).

[84] Gail Kern Paster, *The Body Embarrassed: Drama and The Disciplines of Shame in Early Modern England* (Ithaca: Cornell University Press, 1993), 25.

[85] Soranus, *Gynecology*, trans. Owsei Temkin (Baltimore: Johns Hopkins University Press, 1956), 17.

[86] See Paster, *The Body Embarrassed*, 83.

From contact with this blood, fruits fail to germinate, grape-must goes sour, plants die, trees lose their fruit, metal is corroded with rust, and bronze objects go black. Any dogs which consume it contract rabies. The glue of bitumen, which resists both metal and water, dissolves spontaneously when polluted with that blood.[87]

It was also believed that conception during menstruation caused leprosy and other deformities, because the unborn child took its nourishment from blood that was, in the words of the sixteenth-century physician Ambroise Paré, "contaminated, dirty and corrupt."[88]

Philosophers expressed a similar dread of female leakiness and the escaping humors. Girolamo Cardano, a Milanese doctor and philosopher writing in the mid-sixteenth century, described these dangers by saying "When a woman menstruates, she will tarnish a metallic mirror, it will become rusty, and she will damage the crops through which she walks. Furthermore, the firstborn son can contract leprosy if such blood gets into his bath, as I have myself witnessed."[89] Exhibiting a similar fear, Ficino claims that a menstruating woman can bewitch a boy.[90] In keeping with the humanist reliance on the classics, both men found in Aristotle a convenient source for their menstrual anxiety. Ficino quotes Aristotle's view that "women, when the menstrual blood flows down, often soil a mirror with bloody drops by their own gaze."[91]

Since all bodily fluids were transformed into one another and since the mouth and womb were thought to be interconnected, Ficino's remarks might easily enough suggest that the dangerous forces contained within menstrual blood, flowing from the womb, also corrupted fluids and sounds emanating from the mouth. Singing in particular had suggested such a relationship in the ancient world. Soranus, a second-century doctor who wrote a treatise on gynecology, asserted that the amount of menstrual flow is less in "teachers of singing."[92] In a tract about menstrual disorders, he claimed that some women do not menstruate "because they are pregnant, or mannish, or barren singers and athletes in whom nothing is left over for menstruation, everything being consumed by the exercise or changed into tissue."[93] Soranus's assertion suggests both that singing affects the flow of blood from the womb and that it derails the natural processes of the female body.

---

[87] Isidore of Seville, *Isidori Hispanensis Episcopi, Etymologiarum sive Originum*, trans. W. W. Lindsay (Oxford: Clarendon Press, 1962), 102.

[88] Ambroise Paré, *Of Monsters and Marvels* (1573), trans. Janis L. Pallister (Chicago: University of Chicago Press, 1982), 5.

[89] Markus Fiertz, *Girolamo Cardano*, trans. Helya Niman (Boston: Burkhauser, 1983), 99.

[90] Marsilio Ficino, *Commentary on Plato's Symposium on Love*, trans. Sears Jayne (Dallas: Spring Publications, Inc., 1985), 161.

[91] Ibid., 160.   [92] Soranus, *Gynecology*, 19.   [93] Ibid., 133.

They sang anyway

The final moments of *Il ballo delle ingrate* highlight the powerful unruliness of the female voice as a force emanating from the mouth of the singer. The solo lamenter and echoing *ingrate* sung from the *bocca d'inferno*, exuding sound from the mouth that consumed them. Just as hazardous fluids that emanated from the vagina and the womb escaped the body, encroaching on the outside world, so too did their voices escape their mouths and thus for a moment resist confinement.

By bringing to life these punished but not passive female figures, the singers asserted the very agency that the productions attempted thematically to suppress.[94] To be sure, these are not female-authored moments of resistance. The text remains the work of men. But through the act of singing, women could enact something that posed as feminine resistance. Counteracting the conduct book-like prescriptions of their words, the performative force of the female voices undoes the dramas and defies their constraining messages. Of course, the story of female resistance does not end here. Like the fictional characters, singers suffered discursive and physical quelling. Think of the virginity test that Caterina Martinelli had to undergo before she was deemed fit to sing for the Duke of Mantua. Less dramatically, for propriety's sake Settimia Caccini sang only music composed by her husband.[95]

The imagined over-sexed nature of singers even infiltrates writings meant to denigrate new music. Artusi's well-known vituperative assaults on the *seconda pratica* leveled complaints against the overzealous and over-sexualized body language of nameless madrigal singers who may have included some of the *concerto delle donne*:[96]

[94] Recent studies have argued that Follino and generations of Monteverdi scholars have slighted two very powerful women in the genesis of the most lasting of the wedding celebration productions, *L'Arianna* – a slight which might suggest a different kind of reading. See Tim Carter's "Lamenting Ariadne." The addition of Ariadne's lament could have been written in an attempt to assuage the proto-diva Virginia Ramponi, hired in the final moments after the untimely death of Catarina Martinelli, and the civically powerful Duchess Leonora Medici-Gonzaga. This lament allowed the former to show off her dramatic virtues and might have combated the dryness that the latter complained of upon first seeing the tragedy (Carter, "Lamenting Ariadne," 398). The festivities' supposedly most disciplining moment – Ariadne's lament – may carry with it traces of specifically female modalities of power.

[95] Ellen Rosand, "Barbara Strozzi, virtuosissima cantatrice: The Composer's Voice," *Journal of the American Musicological Society* 31/2 (1978): 241–282.

[96] Suzanne Cusick has argued that Artusi uses the singers' overly sexualized bodies to denigrate Monteverdi's music. She suggests that this rhetoric strengthened the inherently feminizing power of its sounds. See "Gendering Modern Music: Thoughts on the Artusi Controversy," *Journal of the American Musicological Society* 46 (1993): 10–26.

those [effects] which the singers themselves produce while they sing those songs, who slowly turn the head, arch their eyebrows, roll their eyes, twist their shoulders, let themselves go about in such a way that it seems that they wish to die, and they produce many other transformations, which Ovid would never have dreamt of. And they produce these grimaces precisely when they arrive at those dissonances that offend the sense, to demonstrate that which they do, others should likewise do. But those who listen, instead of being moved, are ruffled by its roughness and its poor satisfaction and going off their heads they leave poorly satisfied.[97]

Artusi's contention that these singers employed unseemly body language implicitly faults both the music and its singers for excessive sexuality and for an exaggerated and overdramatic rendition of the words. Whether Artusi's remarks are directed at men or women matters less than the bodily connotations he ascribes to singing. The erotic charge of "transformations which Ovid would never have dreamt of" and rolling eyes and twisting shoulders that look like a "wish to die" is clear especially in light of the commonplace Renaissance usage of death as a metaphor for orgasm and Ovid's substitution of transformation for sex.[98]

By insisting that these singers displayed too many gestures, Artusi denigrated music that he had already faulted for including too many unnatural dissonances.[99] This mapping of the threat to harmonic order in the music of the *seconda pratica* onto the destabilizing of gender orders acted out by female singers implies that just as extra dissonances altered the natural order of the music, extra motion altered the natural order of the body.[100] In addition, the aural seduction of the music mimicked the wantonness of its practitioners. In a world in which bodily excess, imperfection, and the domination of senses over reason marked women as different from men, Artusi's attacks ascribed lascivious tendencies to the singers – accusations that were particularly damaging if directed at women.

The resistance of female song to discursive constraints repeats itself over and over again and works its way into the performance structure of dramatic productions. These works challenge the prevailing Petrarchan and Ovidian predilections for passive female anti-subjects. The live presence of the *ingrate*, and in particular the lamenting soul, renders the

---

[97] Translation modified from Fabbri, *Monteverdi*, 47.

[98] See Macy, "Speaking of Sex: Metaphor and Performance in the Italian Madrigal," for a discussion of madrigalian uses of this metaphor.

[99] See Cusick, "Gendering Modern Music," for the gendered implications of those dissonances.

[100] The literature on the *seconda pratica* is large. See for example Denis Arnold, "Seconda Pratica: A Background to Monteverdi's Madrigals," *Music and Letters* 38 (1957): 341–352.

love object palpably present. The *ingrate* hold onto a disturbing force that prevents male creative expression from substituting fully for the female love object and the possibility of sex. These once beautiful women do not represent mute vessels to be filled up with and appropriated by male expression. Not the invisible objects of desire prevalent in non-dramatic representations, they stand as audible subjects. As such, they thwart the idealization promoted by lyric poetry, and thus reassert their agency, blocking the constitutive power of the male subjects who desire them. Escaping from their lovers' minds turns the *ingrate* from mirrors of male desire into independent forces, which causes the impossible love object whose absence makes her safe to become frighteningly possible.[101]

In the end, the subversive force of the *ingrata*'s voice sings against the grain, transcending the conventions that represent her. Even the ideologically complicit Ariadne challenges her constraints, for though she may ultimately be pushed into wedded, lasting silence, Virginia Ramponi's performance of that transition defies its end result. Accounts of the production do not stress moral lessons but instead again and again remark on the incredible power of Ramponi's song, a power imagined and conceived by Rinuccini and Monteverdi but realized by the singer.

Of course, my reading cannot end here, since even in performance the female voice never truly triumphs. In response to the self-assertion of *Il ballo delle ingrate*'s final lament, commentators followed Monteverdi and Rinuccini's lead by positioning the collective female body as a mass of fluids. Follino's representative description of the empathetic weeping of the ladies in the audience reaffirms early modern essentialized conceptions of women as physically unruly and therefore deserving of social control. In other words, even as the *ingrate* and Ariadne sang, the language men used to talk about them together with the ladies in the audience replaced individual subjectivities with a collective excessive body, which then pushed them all back into received understandings of women as out of control. Within the text of *Il ballo delle ingrate*, Pluto describes the *ingrate* souls as constantly weeping:

> queste infelici ch'in perpetui pianti
> dolgonsi invan, che non ben sagge furo

[these unhappy women, who in perpetual laments / grieve in vain, for they were far from wise]

---

[101] Barbara Johnson makes an interesting psychoanalytic argument about an aesthetic of female silence that allows male authors to appropriate female muteness as an aesthetic trope. She suggests that female silence about pleasure and violation collapses the two into one another. See "Muteness Envy," in *Human, All Too Human*, ed. Diana Fuss (New York: Routledge, 1996), 131–148.

In light of gender differences reflected in distinct constitutions of body fluids, Follino's portrayal of the incessant weeping and unbridled passions of the ladies both on and off the stage seems as much revealing social commentary as innocent description of courtly spectacle. His accounts of the 1608 wedding festivities display a concern with crying ladies – one so pervasive as to seem almost an obsession. Every production featured a lamenting woman whose fate elicited tears from female audience members. What strikes musicologists as remarkable about Ariadne's lament – that, according to Follino, "there was not one lady who failed to shed a tear" – is just the tip of the iceberg.[102] Follino also tells us that the ladies cried with Europa and Proserpina during their laments during the intermedi to Guarini's *L'Idropica*, and that they wept once more with the lamenting *ingrate*, whom he describes in characteristically watery terms: "one of the Ingrates, who had stayed on the stage when the others descended to dance, burst forth in such tear-filled accents accompanied by sighs and sobs, that there was no woman's heart in that theater which did not let loose from their eyes some pitying tear."[103] For Follino, the *ingrata's* song merges with her tears – a fusion that suggests that the ladies on and off the stage exude connected and excessive secretions: tears and song.

From a twenty-first-century vantage point, Follino's effusive prose seems quaintly exaggerated if not ludicrous. To read his accounts, one would think that the ladies cried for the entire two weeks. Because these words do not capture contemporary experiences of inhabiting our bodies, we anachronistically discount and neglect the dynamic, almost violent processes endemic to the early modern humoral body. However, viewed through a Galenic lens, the weeping of the ladies on and off the stage illustrates a pervasive conception of women's incontinence. This was an age in which Ferrand could write that women cried more because of their "humidity."[104] Textually enacting a profound essentialization of women's bodies as excessive and unruly, Follino's account puts women back into the discursive space constructed for them by men. Follino's preoccupation with tears gestures toward an entire network of discourse that denigrated women because of their inherent lack of self-control.

In other words, whether or not the women actually cried for two weeks, or whether or not the music was so rhetorically proficient that it always elicited tears matters less than Follino's seeming need to represent the ladies in the audience as perpetually leaking. In this way, Follino's accounts have some of the exaggerating tendencies of court propaganda, intending to manifest the morals and marvels of the performances for those not in attendance, disseminating in blunt terms the

---

[102] Fabbri, *Monteverdi*, 86.   [103] Ibid., 92.
[104] Ferrand, *A Treatise On Lovesickness*, 278.

messages embedded in the productions. Rather than taking Follino's chronicles as a record of the ladies' reaction to seeing their own lives portrayed on stage, I read his descriptions as a representation – a construction within male-dominated discourse – of female incontinence. His remarks reflect a conditioned response to the idea of the female body, not necessarily a report of its activities. By insisting that women on stage and off produce excess fluid, he instantiates their inability to control their bodies and souls. Thus, even at the moment when it resists constraints, the female voice is already being constrained again.[105]

And still women continued to sing and to escape even the enclosure implied by the works they sang. Despite the fact that public performance undermined their reputations, talented vocalists took to the stage and brought to life the music that delighted, moved, astounded, and fascinated audiences. *Il ballo delle ingrate* is certainly a visceral mechanism for disciplining the collective female body. But because it exists as a performance, the means of delivering the message exceed the message itself, so that even though the hardhearted woman ultimately ends up in Hell, her song defies social injunctions to silence, as it was likely meant to do. The constant tug-of-war between female force and patriarchal power allowed the female voice more play than we might sometimes think.

---

[105] My discussion here differs from – but does not disagree with – Cusick's opinion that "It was the recognition that the self-transformations enacted by Ariadne's lament constituted their own life stories that caused the women in the first Mantuan audience to weep . . ." Cusick, "There Was Not One Lady," 22. And it also differs from Ann MacNeil's assertion that Follino's tears invoke "a studied refrain that had signified an empathetic response to the recitation of the lament since Augustine." MacNeil, "Weeping at the Water's Edge," 408.

3

Madrigalian desire: the convergence of love and sex in madrigals

The pieces in Monteverdi's 1603 *Il quarto libro de madrigali a cinque voci* sing of desire and, to a large extent, its unfulfillment. Conventional explorations of the lover's inner psychology depict amorous scenes, unrequited love, and tortured souls. To take just a few examples: the speaker of Rinuccini's "Sfogava con le stelle," struck with erotic melancholy, pours forth his sorrows to the stars while calling to mind "O imagini belle" (O lovely images). The lover of "Luci serene e chiare" sets the speaker's world on fire with eyes and words, and upon exchanging souls with his lover "si strugg'e non si duol, muor e non langue" (perishes without pain, dies without languishing). And in Guarini's "A un giro sol de' begli occhi lucenti," the lady's single glance moves winds and sea as "e 'l mar s'acquieta e i venti" (the winds and sea grow calm).

A tribute to lovers' malaise, the texts of this volume tend to depict the spiritual, disembodied, and virtuous love of Petrarchan and Neoplatonic fame – with the notable exception of the explicitly erotic "Sì ch'io vorei morire," which presents a graphic description of physical pleasure. The poetic text, probably by Maurizio Moro, enumerates the pleasure of touching tongues, breasts, mouths, and, finally, of exchanging humors. Though the seventh book of madrigals abounds with *baci*, this is the only piece in the earlier collection where the lovers actually kiss. Monteverdi enhances such linguistic licentiousness with a surfeit of conventional gestures, including suspensions, rising melodies, and long chains of dissonances that leave little to listeners' imaginations. Despite this seeming excess, the piece is not entirely anomalous. The sensations it expresses also lurk beneath the elegant and spiritualized surface of "Cor mio, mentre vi miro," an otherwise textbook statement of Neoplatonic love. Taking these two pieces as documents of early modern Italian understandings of the relations between love and sex and focusing on the sung projection of desire and love, this chapter moves away from the physical mechanics and literary representations of the voice toward the ways in which late Renaissance understandings of sensation implicated the experience of music. It once again explores musical presentations of female objects of desire and thinks through the implications for women of singing explicitly about sex. The model of sensation illuminated here is a materialist one in which passions, often carried by the voice, worked on a body. This was a model that would shift dramatically by the end of Monteverdi's career.

These two pieces, so strikingly different at first glance, offer a framework for understanding the libidinal economy of madrigalian performance at the end of the Italian Renaissance. This chapter explores the ways in which the performance of polyphonic madrigals could blur social, moral, and philosophical boundaries. In particular, such pieces purposefully simulated and stimulated the humoral motions of sensuous experiences that could be characterized as either virtuous or vulgar, but were, in effect, identical. The texts of "Cor mio, mentre vi miro" and "Sì ch'io vorei morire" approach love and sex from opposite directions. The former appropriates the optic of Neoplatonic spiritual love, most clearly articulated by Florentine humanists like Marsilio Ficino and Pietro Bembo, whereas the latter highlights physical pleasure. Though composed before Monteverdi moved to Venice, the celebration of the body in "Sì ch'io vorei morire" resonates with the work of the Venetian painter Titian. Moreover, its eroticization of humanist discourse purposefully exceeds decorum in the style of such Venetians as the erotic satirist Pietro Aretino and the famed courtesans Veronica Franco and Tullia d'Aragona.

But in performance these pieces do not oppose one another. Rather, they produce a dynamic tension that contains within it assertions of similarity and difference. Madrigal poetry separates spiritual from vulgar love, but its sung performance blurs that distinction, exploiting the close proximity of rhetorical eloquence and licentious excess and highlighting the similarities of their humoral experiences. The performance of madrigals rearranged boundaries between the human exterior and interior, subject and world, the virtuous and vulgar, men and women. It could mimic and incite humoral motions, propelling interior sensations in listeners and performers and setting in motion a series of physiological and psychological processes. Using the human voice as a medium, madrigal singing transformed the physical effects of sensations into musical utterances by translating inner feelings into sound and sending the materials of the body into the world. The conventional musical and poetic depictions of love and desire familiar to modern scholars carried in their original context the physical embodiments of physiological conditions like erotomania, the sluggish humors of frustrated desire, and the icy fire of sexual ecstasy.[1] To be sure, taking note of the association between

---

[1] Susan McClary has also done extensive work on issues of eroticism in the madrigal. See "Constructions of Gender in Monteverdi's Dramatic Music," in *Feminine Endings: Music,*

lovemaking and music making is not an altogether new endeavor. But investigating the specific manner in which that association might have occurred in the culture of early modern Italy simultaneously makes it more precise and defamiliarizes it.

This chapter paints a broad discursive picture that necessarily draws on sources from a wide variety of times and spaces. These sources reflect the wide ideological and material circulation of *Il quarto libro de madrigali*, written mostly during Monteverdi's tenure at Mantua, printed in Venice and circulated within a variety of Italian courts.[2] Thanks to a vigorous print culture, this volume, like other madrigal books, philosophical treatises, and erotica, traveled well beyond its point of origin. Thus its ideological context must reflect a broad geographic area and intellectual community. And, coming at the end of a tradition, this collection articulated ideas that had long been current in a number of courts.

The contextualized description of the music concluding the chapter unpacks the humoral motion of these performances and the sensuousness that would have been obvious to, but mostly unacknowledged by, their listeners. I have purposefully saved this detailed treatment of the music for the end of the chapter, not to make the reader wait, but because I think the vocabulary I use depends on the picture painted in the preceding pages. Unfortunately, we have no documents that preserve a vocabulary or method for discussing sung performances in this way: no map of humors, no medical analysis of singing, and nothing like the astrological/modal treatises that connected music to the spheres. Thus any explanation of the humoral motion of madrigal singing can consider only the general musical motion.

Loving the soul

Though philosophical explorations of love were common as far back as the ancient world, the end of the Renaissance witnessed an explosion of interest – philosophical, artistic, and medical – in the mysteries of human

---

Gender, and Sexuality (Minneapolis: University of Minnesota Press, 1991), 35–53, and "Music, the Pythagoreans, and the Body," in *Choreographing History*, ed. Susan Leigh Foster (Bloomington: Indiana University Press, 1995), 82–105. Ellen Rosand's wonderful article, "Monteverdi's Mimetic Art: L'incoronazione di Poppea," *Cambridge Opera Journal* 1/2 (1989): 113–137 touches on musical enactments of the body. Her discussion of Ottone's opening to Act 2 scene 11 points out the importance of understanding singing as a physiological act and highlights musical embodiments of the changes in breathing effected by heightened emotion (126–128).

[2] I draw on sources from the Renaissance and ancient world that were in circulation during this period and that made up the discursive context for Monteverdi's madrigals. Thus Ficino, Plato, and Aretino – all still circulating widely at the beginning of the seventeenth century – made up the textual universe for these madrigals.

attraction. This fascination with love comprises the philosophical context for most of the poetry Monteverdi set in his early compositions. It was a fascination set off largely by Marsilio Ficino's commentaries on Plato's *Symposium*. The first translation of the commentaries into Italian in 1474 was followed quickly by a number of derivative vernacular dialogues – the *trattati d'amore*. Neoplatonism flourished at the courts and, owing to the rise of print culture, its treatises published in Italian centers circulated widely. Pietro Bembo and Castiglione published in Venice, Mario Equicola in Mantua, and Tullia d'Aragona in Florence.[3] The immense popularity of the *trattati* reflects the attempt by a large elite reading public to resolve tensions between Christianity and pagan classical literature, moral and spiritual discipline, and the vulnerable lines between rational and sensual experiences.

Love and sex were bound together in a dynamic relationship that depended on upholding differences and maintaining crucial elements of similarity. Greatly invested in emphasizing the differences, the *trattati* sought to cultivate the restrained and conventional discourses of courtly love while simultaneously attempting to erase any attendant erotic activities. The very fact of such a vast literature devoted to separating love from sex, however, suggests an anxiety about their proximity and, hence, the potential of even the most divine and spiritual experiences to devolve into what was considered excessive erotic pleasure. Recognizing that spiritual and erotic love could in practice easily collapse into one another, writers of the *trattati* attempted to construct rhetorical barriers. Creating a discourse of restraint, they endeavored to produce a safe space of philosophical discussion and decorum that, in theory, kept the body under the rational and virtuous control of the mind and spirit. Love, thus separated from sex, could become a vehicle for the display of rhetorical eloquence.

Giambattista Guarini's "Cor mio, mentre vi miro" captures in a pithy epigrammatic madrigal the essence of the spiritual love propagated by these thinkers. The poem explores the inner psychological ramifications of transformation, finding a love object outside the body and incorporating it within the heart and soul.

---

[3] The literature on sixteenth-century Neoplatonic theories of love is vast. See, for example, Ioan Couliano, *Eros and Magic in the Renaissance* (Chicago: University of Chicago Press, 1987). For a classic summary, see Nesca Robb, *Neoplatonism of the Italian Renaissance* (London: Allen and Unwin, 1935). For studies of English music that draw on similar literatures see Linda Phyllis Austern, "Nature, Culture, Myth and Musician in Early Modern England," *Journal of the American Musicological Society* 51/1 (1998): 1–49, and "'No women are indeed': The Boy Actor as Vocal Seductress in Late Sixteenth- and Early Seventeenth-century English Drama," in *Embodied Voices: Representing Female Vocality in Western Culture*, ed. Leslie C. Dunn and Nancy A. Jones (Cambridge: Cambridge University Press, 1994), 83–102.

Cor mio, mentre vi miro
visibilmente mi trasform'in voi,
e trasformato poi,
in un solo sospir l'anima spiro.
O bellezza mortale,
O bellezza vitale,
poi chè sì tosto un core
per te rinasce, e per te nato, more.

My darling, while I gaze on you,
I am visibly transformed into you
and transformed, then,
in one single sigh my soul expires.
O deadly beauty!
O life-giving beauty!
Since at once a heart
is reborn for you, and for you born, it dies.[4]

Purely spiritual, not physical, love passes through the eyes to the inner soul as seeing the love object transforms the gazing subject: "I am visibly transformed into you." Abandoning himself, the lover carves his own image in the soul of the beloved and is reborn. As such, the beloved serves as a reflective mirror. Guarini's exclamations "O bellezza mortale" and "O bellezza vitale," as well as the line "solo sospir l'anima spiro," gesture toward the Neoplatonic love/death paradigm in which spiritual consummation leads to death and then life again. But these clichés cannot remain cloistered in the realm of the spiritual, for they also reflect the widespread conflation of orgasm and death through opposing sensations – icy fire, life and death. Though Guarini seems studiously to avoid the body, the final moment nevertheless marks love as an experience of transformation, an exchange that here involved spirit and in the case of sex would have involved seed.

Guarini's poem reflects prevailing medical, philosophical, and artistic understandings of love as an obsessive impulse, an assault on reason. As late as 1624, these theories, which had been circulating in Italian courts since the rediscovery of Plato, were summarized by the French medical philosopher Jacques Ferrand. Providing a convenient bibliography and notes for the later-day reader, Ferrand cites a dizzying array of sources including, from the ancients, Galen, Hippocrates, and Ovid, and among the early moderns, Boccaccio, Ficino, and Bembo. His source choices reflect the intellectual dependencies of his era on ancient and Renaissance classics and the intimate relation of medical, literary, and philosophical texts. For Ferrand, as for most of his contemporaries, the

---

[4] This translation is modified from Gary Tomlinson, *Monteverdi and the End of the Renaissance* (Berkeley: University of California Press, 1987), 84.

painful experience of love caused all kinds of inner and outer turmoil, as it "attacks reason, making it her slave." It could lead to divine bliss or to a panoply of physical symptoms, including a "pale and wan complexion . . . slow fever, rapid pulse, swelling of the face, decreased appetite, raging thirst . . . sighing, causeless tears . . . insomnia, headaches, madness, uterine fury, and other pernicious symptoms."[5]

The almost violent consequences of love were thought to arise from desire, which caused a radical imbalance of humors – an excess of blood originating in semen – which, when frustrated, led to erotomania or lovesickness. Ficino's commentaries, still current in the early seventeenth century, explained the physical symptoms: "They are also alternately hot and cold, like those whom a certain fever attacks. They are cold rightly, because they are deserted by their own warmth, and they are also hot, since they are enflamed by the splendors of the celestial ray.[6] " Though the lover of "Cor mio" professes to experience a primarily spiritual love, his sensations are also necessarily eminently physical.

The beauty that Guarini exalted in clichés like "O bellezza mortale, O bellezza vitale" resides in divine truth. Working from Plato's authority, writers of the *trattati d'amore* imagined love as a many-headed desire that, even in its most inappropriate and indulgent form of sexual attraction, ultimately desires divine light – God. Love is the desire for true beauty, and true beauty is God. True beauty does not inspire physical desire, and, likewise, interior goodness supersedes corporeal attractiveness. Pietro Bembo's *Gli Asolani* directly links Neoplatonic love and music.[7] His dialogue stages a conversation during the wedding of the ex-Cypriot Queen Caterina Cornara at Asolo in which the Queen's ladies entertain and charm guests during debates about Ficino's Neoplatonic theories. Love is the desire for beauty and beauty is the grace that results from harmony. Hearing provides access to the soul, as sight to the body, rendering music a vehicle for divine love. Bembo peppers his dialogue with musical metaphors. For instance, if two well-tuned lutes are placed next to each other and one is plucked, the other will sound also. He likens this sympathetic response to two loving souls making harmonious music even when separated.

Stopping just short of denying altogether the existence of bodily desires and pleasures, Neoplatonic thought separated sex from spiritual matters. Like Plato before him, Ficino insists that physical desire, contrary to virtuous love but one with the search for the divine, arose

---

[5] Ibid., 229.

[6] Marsilio Ficino, *Commentary on Plato's Symposium*, trans. Sears Jayne (Dallas: Spring Publications, 1985), 52.

[7] Pietro Bembo, *Gli Asolani* (Venice, 1535; reprinted Ridgewood: The Gregg Press Incorporated, 1965). Also available in a modern translation as *Pietro Bembo's Gli Asolani*, trans. Rudolf B. Gottfried (Bloomington: Indiana University Press,) 1954.

from irrational urges and only found resolution in the senses. It is nothing more than love's necessary corollary, or perhaps its evil twin. This bifurcation made corporeal pleasure and spiritual yearning entirely different. "The desires for coitus and love are shown to be not only not the same motions but the opposites."[8] When this notion of physical pleasure as a deplorable instrument of something better met the Christian concept of sin, physical attraction turned into something profane.

Students of Monteverdi recognize this radical distinction between spiritual and sexual love, as well as the attendant characteristic of love as necessarily unfulfilled, from the composer's settings of *ottave* from *Gerusalemme liberata* in *Il combattimento di Tancredi e Clorinda*. Forever limited and unresolved, the love relationships in Tasso's epic exist in the realm of sensuality and loss and revolve around frustration, denial, and control. At the conclusion of the *ottave* chosen by Monteverdi, Tancredi plunges his sword into Clorinda's chest, penetrating her. As she lies dying he baptizes her with his water, granting her soul a new divine life. Converted to his faith, she praises both him and his beliefs as liberating her soul from her doubly abject female and Arab body. At the moment of death, Clorinda sings of spiritual salvation and conversion in what is the piece's most sung moment – forever tangling the love-death with the female voice. Her musical death, to which I will return in this book's epilogue, makes explicitly Christianized Neoplatonic links between sex, death and transformation.

> Non morì già che sue virtuti accolse
> tutte in quel punto e in guardia al cor le mise;
> e premendo il suo affanno a dar si volse
> vita con l'acqua a chi col ferro uccise.

> He had not died yet, that he summoned up all his powers
> for the moment and set them to guard his heart
> and, repressing his grief, he turned to give
> life with water to her whom with the sword he killed.

Her death simultaneously keeps their chaste attraction separate from lascivious sex and enacts the fantasy of divine love wielding a life-giving force. Tancredi finds in Clorinda's soul divine illumination, taking the Neoplatonic obfuscation of the female body to new heights.

Moving to prescriptive literature, the final book of Castiglione's *Il cortegiano* presents one of the clearest and most widely circulated elaborations on the distinctions between spiritual love and carnal pleasure. The fictional Bembo, parroting the real Pietro Bembo, outlines a progression from love of earthly beauty to love of God in which male admiration of a woman leads to heaven.

[8] Ficino, *Commentary on Plato's Symposium*, 41.

So let us direct all the thoughts and powers of our soul towards this most sacred light which shows us the path that leads to heaven; and following after it and divesting ourselves of the human passions in which we were clothed when we fell, let us ascend by the ladder whose lowest rung bears the image of sensual beauty to the sublime mansion where dwells the celestial, adorable, and true beauty.[9]

Practiced with the proper virtue, the desire for beauty can approach the divine and thus fulfill the quest of human existence.

Though parts of the book read like a how-to manual on Neoplatonic love, *Il cortegiano* reveals the precariousness of the concepts it enacts and inadvertently intertwines erotic pleasure and spiritual love. The following speech, again given by Bembo, translates all aspects of love and sensual experience, including erotic pleasure, into spiritual terms. It begins by outlining how an encounter with true beauty leads to perfect love.

So instead of directing his thoughts to the outward world, as those must do who wish to consider bodily beauty, let him turn within himself to contemplate what he sees with the eyes of the mind, which begin to be penetrating and clear-sighted. . . . The soul turns to contemplate its own substance, and as if awakened from deepest sleep it opens the eyes which all men possess but few use and perceives in itself a ray of that light which is the true image of the angelic beauty that has been transmitted to it, and of which in turn it transmits a faint impression to the body.[10]

Eschewing the body, this ideal lover enjoys beauty through his eyes, which allows him to encounter the ray of universal truth. But in describing the soul's escape from the body, Castiglione shifts into an extraordinarily corporeal vocabulary:

Thus, when it has become blind to earthly things, the soul opens its eyes wide to those of heaven; and sometimes when the faculties of the body are totally absorbed by assiduous contemplation, or bound to sleep, no longer hindered by their influence the soul tastes a certain savour of the true angelic beauty, and ravished by the loveliness of that light it begins to burn and to pursue the beauty it sees so avidly that it seems almost drunk and beside itself in its desire to unite with it. For the soul then believes that it has discovered the traces of God, in the contemplation of which it seeks its final repose and bliss.[11]

Lovers partake of their senses as they taste the intoxication of each other, their drunkenness marring the pernicious madness of profane love.

---

[9] Baldassare Castiglione, *The Book of the Courtier* (1528), trans. George Bull (New York: Penguin Classics, 1986), 341; original in *Il libro del cortegiano*, ed. Giulio Carnazzi (Milan: Biblioteca Universale Rizzoli, 1987), 298.

[10] Castiglione, *The Book of the Courtier*, 339; *Il libro del cortegiano*, 304 .

[11] Ibid., 339–40.

"Ravished by the loveliness of that light," the soul can "taste" angelic beauty. Like erotic pleasure, divine love escalates as "It begins to burn and to pursue the beauty it sees so avidly." Ultimately, to discover the traces of God means to seek a post-coital "repose and bliss."

Some Neoplatonists vindicated sexual activity for its own sake. Agostino Ninfo's *On Beauty and Love* (1531) presents love as a condition induced by sensual appetite and fulfilled by sex. In Sperone Speroni's *Dialogues on Love* (1542), inspired by the salon in the home of the Roman courtesan Tullia d'Aragona, the fictional speaker Grazia insists that love starts in the senses and then reason shapes it to the satisfaction of both the body and the mind.[12] Ninfo presents lovers who, tired of only seeing and hearing one another, seek tactile pleasure. Enumerating those pleasures, the character impersonating Tullia d'Aragona satirizes the Bembian view of love and presents what amounts almost to a practical guide to erotic behavior.

The real Tullia d'Aragona, both lusted after and respected in her own right, offered an alternative to the well-rehearsed dualisms of Neoplatonic love. Her dialogue on love, like the performance of madrigals, recognized no distinction between spiritual and physical love – in fact she called those distinctions "unnatural." Aragona's refusal reverses received oppositions and talks back to Neoplatonist authorities.[13] For her, true love balances physical and spiritual fulfillment. Thus, sex can enhance the spiritual union of lovers, as "carnal pleasure" may cause love to "grow in intensity."[14] In a particularly pithy passage she writes, "Is anyone ignorant of the fact that the whole body and soul taken together are more noble and more perfect than the soul by itself?"[15] Aragona suggests that spiritual and carnal love transform into one another:

What is more, its [sex's] acolytes become still more intemperate in their longing for carnal intercourse; they want to enjoy the thrill one more time, and still one more time after that, and so on. . . so that this vulgar and lascivious stain of love can, at times and in some individuals, give rise to a chaste and virtuous love, just as a moral and virtuous love, because of some fault in either the lover or beloved, may turn into one of the vulgar and lascivious variety.[16]

Aragona's causal connection of vulgar and virtuous love points up the precariousness of reigning distinctions between love and sex, reminding

---

[12] Sperone Speroni, "Dialogo d'amore," in *Trattatisti del Cinquecento*, ed. Mario Pozzi (Milan–Naples: Ricciardi, 1978), vol. I, 511–563.

[13] Aragona acquired her reputation as a supreme intellectual courtesan during a brief sojourn in Venice beginning in 1535. For more biographical information and an analysis of her text, see Tullia d'Aragona, *Dialogue on the Infinity of Love*, ed. and trans. Rinaldina Russell and Bruce Merry (Chicago: University of Chicago Press, 1997).

[14] Ibid., 102.   [15] Ibid., 165.   [16] Ibid., 104.

us once again to consider these terms not as opposites but rather as forces in dynamic tension with one another.

Artists of all sorts played in the muddy ground between sex and love. For instance, Titian's painting *Sacred and Profane Love* visually suggests that the widely trafficked opposition between sacred and profane love contains within it insurmountable elements of similarity. The painting presents two figures: one pure and chaste, the other erotic and sexual. But both figures have the same face, suggesting that at a basic level they represent the same woman. Titian portrays her as an ideal classical figure and a sixteenth-century bride (Figure 3.1).[17] The classical nude represents an ideal of spiritual beauty and ancient purity. She chastely covers her genitals and avoids the viewer's gaze.[18] In contrast, Titian associates the clothed bride with sex by making her an erotically charged figure. The folds of her skirt acknowledge her sexuality and she stares directly at the viewer, her gaze defying Renaissance imperatives for chaste women always to divert their glances.

Contemporary responses to Titian's works reveal the precariousness of the physical and spiritual dualism. Lodovico Dolce found in the Venus of *Venus and Adonis* both a divine spirit and a beautiful body. He uses his own visual sexual response to suggest that the painting effects an almost animate image.

She displays by all this certain gentle and lively emotions, and such that one sees expressed only in her; where there is again a wonderful judiciousness in this divine spirit [Titian] for in the hips one recognizes the puckering of the skin caused by sitting . . . One can with truth say that every brushstroke is one of those strokes that only Nature knows how to make with her hand. The expression is likewise that which one must believe would have been Venus's had she ever existed.[19]

Venus's intense verisimilitude makes her particularly dangerous. As a stand-in for beauty itself, she represents the quintessential Neoplatonic life-giving force. But she also embodies an erotic charge, sending the mesmerized viewer's blood coursing through his veins and warming even the coldest man. Dolce goes on to explain the power of the painting to incite physical sensations.

[17] Though Titian's paintings are unmistakably erotic, I would argue that they are not pornographic in the modern sense. Pornography is a modern concept that is dependent on a different set of boundaries between licit and illicit art and culture.

[18] Rona Goffen has made this argument, and much of my discussion of Titian is indebted to her. See *Titian's Women* (New Haven: Yale University Press, 1997).

[19] Translation modified from ibid., 246. This quotation is taken from a well-known letter from Dolce to Alessandro Contarini, dating from 1554 or 1555, which contains an exhaustive description of the *Venus and Adonis* for Philip of Spain. The letter is not included in the original edition of Dolce's letters, "Lettere di diversi eccellentiss", Venice 1554, but is contained in the very rare second edition.

Figure 3.1, Titian, *Sacred and Profane Love*. Galleria Borghese, Rome, Italy. Reproduced by permission of the Bridgeman Art Gallery

I swear to you my lord that one cannot find a man so acute of vision, and of judgment, who seeing her does not believe her to be alive, none so chilled by years nor so hard of complexion that he does not feel himself warmed, softened, and all of the blood stirring in his veins. Nor is it any wonder that a statue of marble could somehow with the stimuli of its beauty so penetrate the marrow of a youth that he leaves a stain – then, what must this painting do, which is of flesh, which is beauty itself, which seems to breathe?[20]

Titian paints Venus so well that she becomes a Neoplatonic love object. Looking at her gives the subject a sexual thrill. Like the subject of "Cor mio," the viewer's eyes serve as vehicles for love. But she is paint on canvas and not flesh and blood.

The body talks back

During the sixteenth century, there emerged a counter-culture of writers and artists like Aretino and Giulio Romano who threw their energies into recuperating the lustier pagan classics, emphasizing physical beauty, carnal desire, and playful amorousness.[21] Aretino, for instance, apparently drew on Ovid for much of his material, and his dialogues probably reflect knowledge of translations of Lucian's *Dialogues of the Courtesans*.[22] As with the *trattati d'amore*, a vibrant print culture enabled the wide circulation of these works, at least within literate circles. Rather than positioning vulgar and virtuous love as opposites, this spicier literature presented the two experiences as variations of one another. Replicating the ability of ancient works of art to incite desire, artists, writers, and musicians aimed for the effects of an infamous statue that inspired enough lust to make women copulate with it. By twisting ideas, methods, and styles against themselves in satirical and erotic productions, artists deliberately blurred boundaries between love and sex, sacred and profane, and high and low culture. At the same time they played with class and gender hierarchies. Pietro Aretino in particular epitomizes the ways in which erotic art and literature threatened humanist elite culture by breaking down social, moral, gender, and linguistic boundaries, thus exposing the radical instability of received hierarchies and oppositions. His works were socially suspect not only because of their content but

---

[20] Goffen, *Titian's Women*, 65.

[21] For a classic discussion of the circulation of mythology in Renaissance Europe, see Jean Seznec, *The Survival of the Pagan Gods*, trans. Barbara A. Sessions (Princeton: Princeton University Press, 1953).

[22] Paula Findlen traces Aretino's classical roots in "Humanism, Politics and Pornography in Renaissance Italy," in *The Invention of Pornography: Obscenity and the Origins of Modernity*, ed. Lynn Hunt (New York: Zone Books, 1993). For a comprehensive work on the erotic elements of Renaissance culture see Bette Talvacchia, *Taking Positions: On the Erotic in Renaissance Culture* (Princeton: Princeton University Press, 1999).

because they made that content public. With the emergence of print culture, anyone could take voyeuristic pleasure in creations that had previously been accessible only in very elite circles.

In spite of, or perhaps to spite, the Neoplatonic reign over Italian court culture, writers, artists, and musicians developed a detailed visual and verbal currency for representing sexual pleasure, which they merged with language and ideals from courtly dialogues in order to whet the sexual appetites of their consumers. Like Ficino and Bembo, writers, largely based in Venice, glossed ancient sources and constructed elaborate debates, but instead of focusing on spiritualized disembodied love, they chronicled the details of carnal pleasure. Written literature in circulation among the elite demonstrated a new sensitivity to the arousing powers of language. Meanwhile, paintings and sculptures presented evidently tactile experiences even when they included spiritual elements. In the 1520s, Raphael, Giulio Romano, Titian, and Carracci, among others, began to create paintings that depicted the sexual exploits of gods and humans. Prints of drawings, like Carracci's *Loves of the gods*, that display both female and male sex organs and portray gods of Ovidian fame engaged in sexual intercourse brought to the fore the erotics of ancient sources. Put perhaps anachronistically, Renaissance artists and writers, like well-trained poststructuralists, knew that history is always subjective – you get what you look for.

Erotic art and literature pushed consumers into a realm where the body dominated the rational mind – the realm so studiously avoided by authors of the *trattati d'amore*. For instance, Aretino described writing his series of sonnets to accompany Giulio Romano's *I modi* (The Sixteen Pleasures) – a visual guide to sexual positions – as a channeling of erotic sensation and desire into artistic inspiration. In a letter to the surgeon Battista Zatti, he describes looking at the sketches as a peculiar kind of poetic fervor.

Having seen them, I was filled with the same spirit that had moved Giulio Romano to design them. And since ancient and modern poets and sculptors, in order to exercise their virtuosity, sometimes engaged in carving and writing lascivious works, such as the marble satyr in Palazzo Chigi attempting to violate a little boy, I tossed out the sonnets which stand below. With all due respect to hypocrites, I dedicate these lustful pieces to you. I despair of the fake prudishness and damnable habits that forbid the eyes to gaze at the things they most delight to see.[23]

---

[23] For the full Italian text of the letter see Pietro Aretino, *Lettere*, ed. Francesco Erspamer (Parma: Fondazione Pietro Bembo/Ugo Guanda Editore, 1995), 654–656: "mi venne volontà di veder le figure, cagione che le querele Gilbertin esclamavano che il buon vertuoso si crocifigesse; e vistele, fui tocca da lo spirito che mosse Giulio Romano a disegnarle. E perchè i poeti e gli scultori antichi e moderni soglion scrivere e scolpire

Images led to artistic energy, which produced arousing literature.[24]

That erotic and not-so-erotic art pushed its consumers to sexual activity suggests that the works straddled the weak divide between art and life. One of Girolamo Morlini's almost pornographic *Novelle* (1520) describes a woman who was so moved by a statue with an erect penis that she had to kiss and have sex with it.[25] In a bizarre real-life parallel to this story, a group of Venetian patricians stood trial in the 1630s for copulating with a statue of Christ.[26]

Not surprisingly, the church, steeped in the prohibitions of St. Augustine, took offense at anything remotely erotic. A crackdown ensued, beginning with the Index of Forbidden Books established by Paul IV in 1559, which outlawed "Books that professedly deal with, narrate or teach things lascivious or obscene."[27] The mandate by the Council of Trent in 1563 that images remain devoid of "seductive charm" set off a systematic censorship of pagan imagery and nudity. Rather than stopping the spread of "obscene" literature, church restrictions gave it a special currency by making it more difficult to acquire and thus raising its market value.[28]

The fate of Aretino and Romano's *I modi*, probably the most famous example of Renaissance erotica, demonstrates the high currency – both positive and negative – of erotica. This multimedia production provides a visual and verbal panoply of erotic activity. Following an ancient tradition of producing catalogues of lovemaking positions, the pictures capture men and women in the midst of erotic gymnastics while Aretino's words allow the reader to eavesdrop on the lovemaking (Figure 3.2).[29] Disseminated by a leading engraver, Marcantonio Raimondi, the prints circulated in Roman elite circles until an outraged Pope Clement VII

alcuna volta per trastullo de l'ingegno cose lascive, come nel palazzo Chisio fa fede il satiro di marmo che tenta di violare un fanciullo, ci sciorinai sopra i sonetti che ci si veggono ai piedi. La cui lusuriosa memoria vi intitolo con pace degli ipocriti, disperandomi del giudizio ladro e de la consuetudine porca che proibisce agli occhi quel che più gli diletta . . ."

[24] This seems to be an erotic twisting of the Neoplatonic concept of poetic furor.

[25] Girolamo Morlini, *Novelle e favole* (Rome: Salerno, 1983.)

[26] For details of this case, see Guido Ruggiero, *The Boundaries of Eros: Sex Crimes and Sexuality in Renaissance Venice* (New York: Oxford University Press, 1985), 110–123.

[27] "Canons and Decrees of the Council of Trent," in Robert Klein and Henri Zerner, *Italian Art, 1500–1600* (Evanston: Northwestern University Press, 1966), 121.

[28] Thriving on those restrictions, an illicit culture emerged, especially in late sixteenth- and early seventeenth-century Venice, in which manuscript copies of works like Lorenzo Venier's *La puttana errante* (1531) and Pietro Aretino's many productions drew high market prices.

[29] Lynne Lawner makes this point in her introduction to *I modi, the Sixteen Pleasures: An Erotic Album of the Italian Renaissance* (Evanston: Northwestern University Press, 1988), 12.

Figure 3.2, "Posture 1" from Lynne Lawner, *I Modi, the Sixteen Pleasures: An Erotic Album of the Italian Renaissance*. Evanston: Northwestern University Press, 1988. Reprinted by permission of Georges Borchardt, Inc., for the author

attempted to erase them by burning the first edition, throwing the artist in jail, banishing the poet from Rome, and threatening to execute anyone involved in its distribution. Despite papal efforts, a second edition of *The Sixteen Pleasures*, accompanied by Aretino's sonnets, appeared and was followed shortly by a number of counterfeit versions lacking place of publication, date, and name of typographer. (The Pope, for his part, managed a thorough-enough purging that the prints disappeared from circulation for 400 years.)

The prints and sonnets of *I modi* reverse the ideals perpetuated by Neoplatonic and Petrarchan love. Sex replaces love and genitals replace the divine as the mysterious seat of all power. Whereas the subjects of "Cor mio" see themselves inscribed in one another's eyes, the subjects of Aretino's sonnets and Romano's pictures find reflections in each other's genitals. The erotic gaze turns a heaven-directed, spiritual

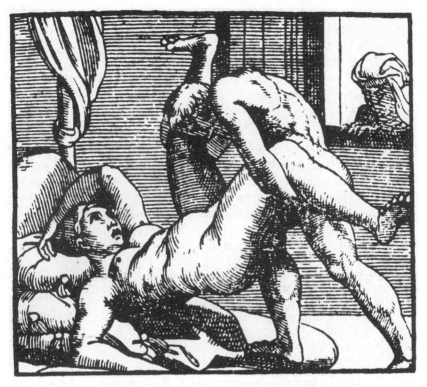

Figure 3.3, "Posture 11" from Lynne Lawner, *I Modi, the Sixteen Pleasures: An Erotic Album of the Italian Renaissance*. Evanston: Northwestern University Press, 1988. Reprinted by permission of Georges Borchardt, Inc., for the author

transcendence into a self-centered sexual pleasure grounded in bodily exchange. Love, a phenomenon of touch and taste with little to do with the higher senses of hearing and seeing, inspires physical pleasure but rejects divine truth and goodness. For example, the sonnet that accompanies Posture 11 debases the lover's gaze (Figure 3.3):

> Apri le cosci, accio ch'io veggia bene
> Il tuo bel culo, e la tua potta in viso,
> Culo da compire un pare un paradiso,
> Potta, ch'i cori stilla per le rene
>
> Mentre ch'io vagheggio, egli mi viene
> Capriccio di basciarvi a l'improviso,
> E mi par esser piu bel, che Narciso
> Nel specchio, che 'l mio cazzo allegro tiene;

101

Open your thighs so I can look straight
At your beautiful *culo* and *potta* in face,
An ass that leads to paradise
A cunt that melts hearts through the kidneys

As I gaze longingly,
Suddenly I long to kiss you,
And I seem to myself more handsome than Narcissus
In the mirror that keeps my prick erect.[30]

This poem and picture position seeing as an explicitly self-reflexive and sexual activity, highlighting the voyeuristic pleasure of watching sex. No longer Neoplatonic windows to the soul or reflections of the divine, the eyes here open windows to the genitals and to bodily pleasure. Aretino continues to play with the mirror imagery so prevalent in Neoplatonic philosophy and Petrarchan poetry in the sonnet accompanying the fourteenth posture, in which the man lies uncomfortably on his arms and legs looking with pleasure at her and says:

E se non, ch'io mi specchio nel cul vostro
Stando sospeso in l'uno e 'n l'altro braccio
Mai non si finirebbe il fatto nostro,
   O, cul di latte, e d'ostro
Se non ch'io son per mirarti di vena,
Non mi starebbe il cazzo dritto a penna.

And if I were not looking into your butt as a mirror
propping myself up on both arms,
our business would never be finished.
   Oh milky white and purple ass,
If I were not gazing with such pleasure at you,
my cock would not hold up a measure.[31]

By re-inserting the body into the disembodied Neoplatonic gaze, these rhetorical twists show the precariousness of distinctions between spiritual and erotic love.

After the controversy surrounding this work forced his escape to Venice, Aretino wrote his *Il ragionamento e il dialogo,* comprising an encyclopedia of sexual acts, a list of Renaissance erotic vocabulary, a compendium of folk beliefs about the female body, a shocking portrayal of the hypocrisies of court and church culture, and a fictional tour of Venice's illicit demi-monde. The form of *Il ragionamento* mimics dialogues of the *trattati d'amore* and mocks humanist predilections for abstract debates and the prevailing conduct books of the day. The

---

[30] My translation from Italian contained in ibid., 69.
[31] My translation from ibid., 86.

main speaker, Nanna, orchestrates a debate about whether her grand-daughter ought to live as a wife, courtesan, or nun. In it, evocative tales of Nanna's exploits in all three occupations reveal all three kinds of women to be fundamentally the same. Meanwhile, the work riffs on conduct books like *Il cortegiano*. It stages Nanna's instructions to Pippa on being a good lover and on the manners and sexual practices of the nobility as a dialogue.

This work offers a more direct satire of elite culture than the sonnets of *I modi* by explicitly attacking and exposing the vices of the upper class. Aretino's fictional universe conflates whores, courtiers, clerics, and sodomites – they speak the same language and engage in the same sexual behaviors. At the same time, in the final dialogue his capricious criticism of artists and their motives takes the form of a midwife who challenges the glorification of women by poets, sculptors, and painters claiming it as "just a way of expressing themselves."[32] For her, all painters, poets, and sculptors are crazy because "they take their own privates and bestow them on their paintings and marble statues."[33] Here Aretino gives his female interlocutor a speech that distorts the inwardness of Neoplatonic art into narcissistic pleasure. Not the stuff of divine truth, painting highlights the body and inspires the drunkenness of profane love. Along similar lines, the midwife goes on to describe a poet who, in a poem like "Cor mio," serenades love as the perfect merging of two souls, but then proceeds to indulge in unrestrained intercourse anyway.

After he recited two stanzas, with which he fed the girl's ears, they really got down to it. Already their breasts were joined so fervently together that their hearts were fused in the same emotion. And as they gently drank each other, their souls rush to their lips from sheer delight and they delve deeply into each other, tasting the bliss of heaven. Their spirits gave the supreme signs of happiness with cries: "Oh, my God – oh, Christ – oh, you're killing me, you're killing me!" and moans: "My life – my soul – my heart – I'm dying – wait till I come!" and then they came. After this they slowly fell apart, breathing out their souls into each other's mouth with a long, deep sigh.[34]

Death stands in for an orgasm. Souls expire from the touch of lips. Souls are "drunk," and heavenly bliss is "tasted." Aretino leaves the eyes and ears conspicuously impotent.

Sensual sounds

Song was even more dangerous than the most threatening visual and literary erotica. If a statue could entice a woman to copulate with it, or Dolce could arouse himself to a state of ecstasy from looking at a statue,

---

[32] Aretino, *Dialogues*, trans. Raymond Rosenthal (New York: Marsilio, 1971), 88.
[33] Ibid., 359.   [34] Ibid., 351.

we can hardly imagine what song could do, with its direct access to the body's interior. To understand what the sensuality of this experience might have felt like demands exploring Renaissance notions of how song acted upon listeners, altering mind and body, through reading a variety of texts passed down from the ancient world through Renaissance philosophers and in circulation at the turn of the seventeenth century. Through the medium of the human voice, sung music moved images from the external world through the body, acting as a medium by which pieces of the world were consumed and transformed into subjective networks of meaning. As I argued earlier, the voice or song existed as a kinesthetic entity with physical substance that consisted of air moving from the throat of the singer to the vulnerable ear of the listener where, in keeping with early modern conceptions of sensory perception, it began to radically alter body and soul. Monteverdi's Milanese admirer Aquilino Coppini understood the composer's madrigals to do just this kind of work. He said of the fifth book of madrigals that it is "governed by the natural expression of the human voice in moving the affections, stealing into the ear in sweetest manner, and thereby making itself the most pleasant tyrant of souls."[35]

The physical, physiological, and psychological effects of song rendered it a potentially unruly force that, like love, was a sensuous experience classifiable as either virtuous or vulgar. It thus comes as no surprise that moral authorities worried over the potential dangers of song, and artists and poets continuously conflated song and sex. Like the materialist conception of the voice I outlined in chapter 1, the inextricable connection between the human voice and the body's inner processes, still at work while Monteverdi's madrigals were in circulation, came from the ancient ideas of Galen, Aristotle, and Hippocrates that continued to dominate medical practice and cultural understandings of the body well into the seventeenth century. [36]

---

[35] Aquilino Coppini, *Il secondo libro della musica di Claudo Monteverdi e d'altri autori a cinque voci* (1608).

[36] This reliance on humoral medicine is part of the Renaissance humanist immersion in ancient texts of all kinds. The humanist recovery of ancient texts stimulated the extensive interest of medical scholars, who made many translations, commentaries, and indexes of ancient sources, including Galen, Hippocrates, Soranus, Avicenna, and Herophilus. For comprehensive studies of the impact of ancient medical practice on medieval and Renaissance Europe, see Nancy G. Siraisi, *Medieval and Early Renaissance Medicine: An Introduction to Knowledge and Practice* (Chicago: University of Chicago Press, 1990); Siraisi, *Avicenna in Renaissance Italy: The Canon and Medical Teaching in Italian Universities after 1500* (Princeton: Princeton University Press, 1987); Ian Maclean, *The Renaissance Notion of Woman: A Study in the Fortunes of Scholasticism and Medieval Science in European Intellectual Life* (Cambridge: Cambridge University Press, 1980); and Giancarlo Zanier, "Platonic Trends in Renaissance Medicine," *Journal of the History of Ideas* 48 (1987), 509–519.

The voice coalesced with the spirit, a vaporous and airy substance or non-substance that animated the body, fusing the live but incorporeal soul with the lifeless corporeal body that it inhabited.[37] Under Aristotelian and Galenic sciences, the motions and actions of that spirit – air and heat running through the body – engendered life.[38] This animating motion of the spirit also transmitted perceptions of things in the world.[39] Eyes and ears were imagined as sponge-like sensory receptacles that received sensible forms, images, and sonic motions, which they conveyed through the spirit into the body all the way to the soul. In this way, the sensory receptacles served as a medium between the materials of the world and the effects they inspired in human subjects.

The materiality of the spirit and the potential of immaterial things to affect the body gave emotions and sensations tangible physical effects. Imbued with natural motion, they shot through the body like water in a pipe. Song transmitted by the voice comprised a force that altered body, soul, and spirit and maintained a special affinity to the spirit, because both were airy substances whose mimetic motion crossed fluid boundaries between the material body and the immaterial soul.[40] In a representative statement, Ficino writes:

But musical sound, by the movement of the air, moves the body: by purified air it excites the aerial spirit, which is the bond of body and soul; by emotion it affects the senses and at the same time the soul; by meaning it works on the mind; finally, by the very movement of the subtle air it penetrates strongly.[41]

As air set in motion, song and spirit fused while traveling through the throat of the singer and the ear of the listener. Motion endowed song with the very essence of the human organism, the spirit coursing through the humoral body. This all rendered it the most powerful imitator of things, as Ficino put it. Like the imagination, song was at

[36] Herophilus supposedly discovered the ovaries in the third century. Hippocrates, *The Medical Works of Hippocrates*, ed. John Chadwick and W. N. Mann (Oxford: Oxford University Press, 1950), 217.

[37] My understanding of the spirit and the organic soul in Renaissance philosophy and the importance of these concepts to music owes much to Gary Tomlinson's work on Renaissance magic and subjectivity. See his *Music in Renaissance Magic: Toward a Historiography of Others*.

[38] Gail Kern Paster discusses the materiality of the spirit, as well as understandings of the visceral effects of sensation, in "Nervous Tension: Networks of Blood and Spirit in the Early Modern Body," in *The Body in Parts: Fantasies of Corporeality in Early Modern Europe*, ed. David Hillman and Carla Mazzio (New York: Routledge, 1997), 107–129.

[39] The motion of spirits would continue to be vital for keeping the human organism alive and for sensory perception through the time of René Descartes.

[40] Gary Tomlinson and D.P. Walker have written at length about this. See Tomlinson, *Music in Renaissance Magic*, D. P. Walker, *Music, Spirit and Language*, ed. Penelope Gouk (London: Variorum Reprints, 1985).

[41] As cited in Walker, *Music, Spirit and Language*, 137.

once material and immaterial, coursing through the veins and directly impacting the spirit, the nexus of perception. It propelled and induced the same bodily activities and motions as the emotions, passions, and the other things that it imitated.

Sung performances projected in sound the motions of emotions through the human voice, which in turn inspired those same emotions in listeners. They could alter the body's humoral balance by inducing the effects of what they imitated – the heated blood of desire or the sluggish humors of melancholy. Vincenzo Galilei insisted that music had the power to "induce in another the same passion that one feels oneself."[42] Similarly, Girolamo Mei wrote that "Nature gave a voice to animals and especially to man for the expression of inner states."[43] He goes on to discuss this in some detail:

It is clear that affections are moved in the souls of others by representing as if before them, whether as objects or recollections, those affections that have been previously aroused by these images. Now this cannot be brought about by the voice except with its qualities of low, high, or intermediate pitch, which nature provided for this effect and which is a proper and natural sign of that affection which one wants to arouse in the listener.[44]

According to Mei, sound communicates the passions through its natural qualities: low pitches with slower vibrations reveal the moderate disposition of a person with ambling humors, while very high tones with increased vibrations propel the quick humoral motion of an excited and uplifted spirit. Similarly, tempos that accelerate reveal a spirit "poised" to take off, while slow tempos reflect a "sluggish and lazy" one.

Because it so viscerally imitated and stimulated the passions, song exerted a troubling force, one that could corrupt the soul by setting off in its listeners and performers what were thought to be wanton emotions and actions. Thus, in opposition to Renaissance writings that praised the power of music, there emerged a strain of thought fueled by Christian piety and skepticism that approached song with suspicion and denounced its lascivious effects, focusing on its pernicious potential to wrench the body out of rational control. Such worries stood behind debates about the appropriateness of music in church and about its place in instructing comportment. Both debates circled around the issue of whether music promoted ethical conduct or incited moral degradation.

---

[42] Vincenzo Galilei, "Dialogue on Ancient and Modern Music" (1581) in *Strunk's Source Readings in Music History*, vol. III, rev. edn., ed. Gary Tomlinson (New York: W. W. Norton and Company, 1998), 188.

[43] Girolamo Mei, "Letter to Vincenzo Galilei," in Claude V. Palisca, *The Florentine Camerata: Documentary Studies and Translations* (New Haven: Yale University Press, 1989), 60.

[44] Ibid., 124.

Song had long carried these dueling associations of spiritual inspiration and corporeal delight. Concern for the ethical effects of song arose within the context of church-condoned dichotomies that imagined song as enacting either devilish seductions or divine exaltations. Recall St. Augustine's classic account of the inner conflict between his love of music and his Christian consciousness. Augustine wavers between denigrating the dangers of songs that merely gratify the senses and praising the potential of musical liturgy to instill spirituality in the masses.[45] Following this tradition, Christian fidelity and its incumbent distrust of song tempered late Renaissance explorations of the power of ancient music by exposing the dangers of a force so intimately connected to the spirit and capable of so profoundly moving the emotions.[46]

Reacting to these so-called lascivious tendencies, humanists busily touting the virtues of ancient music also knew that song could quickly escape their control. Gioseffo Zarlino warned against excess in composition, saying that, "If it does not corrupt the sense, it at least corrupts the instrument [the singer]."[47] Similarly, in describing song's affective power, Giovanni dei Bardi reminds his readers that music can embody lascivious forces: "among Moors and Spanish women one may see shameless and wanton customs represented in music and dancing."[48]

Of course song could do immense good. Ferrand writes that song could "pacify the perturbations of the spirit, according to Galen. King Agamemnon . . . would leave no other guardian of his wife's chastity than an excellent Dorian musician who by his harmonies prevented Clytemnestra from falling into base and immodest love."[49] But according to writers on music, song attained to Ferrand's ideal and avoided the dangerous zone only when it worked on the mind and left the body alone. These writers made discursive efforts to govern the dangerous allure of music in ways that bring to mind attempts to control erotic art and literature at the end of the sixteenth century.

---

[45] Despite his reservations, Augustine does ultimately endorse singing in church. He follows his statement that song moves him to "greater religious fervor" than speech and kindles his "ardent flame of piety" with a cautionary note: "But I ought not to allow my mind to be paralyzed by the gratification of my senses, which often leads it astray." As translated in Richard Taruskin and Piero Weiss, eds., *Music in the Western World* (New York: Schirmer Books, 1984), 32.

[46] The church even had something to say about "secular art," as in Cardinal Robert Bellarmine's public insistence in 1603 that *Il pastor fido* was more harmful to Catholic morals than Protestantism itself. As reported in Nicolas J. Perella, *The Critical Fortune of Battista Guarini's "Il Pastor Fido"* (Florence: L. S. Olschki, 1973), 28–29.

[47] Gioseffo Zarlino, "Gli istituzioni armoniche," in *Source Readings in Music History: The Renaissance*, ed. Oliver Strunk (New York: W. W. Norton and Company, 1965), 59.

[48] Ibid., 108.

[49] Ferrand, *A Treatise On Lovesickness*, trans. David A. Beecher and Massimo Ciavolella (Syracuse: Syracuse University Press, 1990), 348.

Though discourses of music do not match exactly those of erotica, both reflect a conflict between the realization, on the one hand, that images and sounds could convert the masses and reinforce dominant ideologies with their super-sensuous potential, and the need, on the other hand, to exert control over the sexual life, pleasures and bodies of their subjects. While Neoplatonic authors objected to erotic images and physical love because it detracted from reason, various writers on music relegated sounds that took aim at the body and not the mind to the realm of the irrational. Writers from the so-called Florentine Camerata through Giovanni Artusi denigrated polyphonic madrigals for their pictorialisms and contrapuntal errors, but couched their theoretical objections in terms that resonated with larger concerns over the proper balance of reason and pleasure. In railing against modern composers, Girolamo Mei writes that "It is a supreme hindrance in moving the soul to any affection to be chiefly preoccupied and almost bound by these straps of pleasure."[50] Likewise, Vincenzo Galilei faults those composers whose "sole aim is to delight the ear."[51] He criticizes the excessive dissonances and artifices that modern composers use to "allure our ears" and to bind the mind with "the snares of pleasure."[52] At the turn of the seventeenth century, Artusi repeats these accusations in his attacks against Monteverdi, insisting that "good music" appeal to reason and not just to the ear. He writes of lascivious composers that "They think only of satisfying the sense, caring little that reason should enter here to judge their composition."[53] He faults that which "corrupts the senses" by weakening the ear such that it "is so taken up with the other parts that it does not fully perceive the offence committed against it." [54] Certainly "Sì ch'io vorei morire" exhibits striking tonal tensions of the variety that infuriated Artusi and led him to accuse Monteverdi of appealing to the ear and not reason.

The writings of Mei, Galilei, and Artusi represent a strain of musical commentary that endeavored to regulate sonic pleasure and to protect the soul from the whims of the body with its appetite for irrational song. Music that appealed only to the body and led the mind away from reason could, in theory, like physical love, lead listeners to an intolerable state of disorder. At the same time musical gestures that aimed for pleasure rather than pure affects paralleled sexual acts that provided physical pleasure but did nothing for the soul.

Indeed, the collective anxiety about music and other sensuous experiences was not unfounded. Lyric and epic poetry, including many texts

---

[50] Mei, letter to Vincenzo Galilei in Palisca, *The Florentine Camerata*, 62.

[51] Strunk, *Source Readings*, 127.   [52] Ibid., 124.

[53] Artusi, "L'Artusi overo delle imperfettioni della moderna musica" (1600), translated in Strunk, *Source Readings*, 398–399.

[54] Ibid., 39.

Figure 3.4, Titian, *Three Ages of Man*. Duke of Sutherland Collection
on loan to the National Gallery of Scotland

set by madrigal composers, often implicated the act of singing itself as
essentially sensuous and libidinous. A quick survey of madrigal texts
reveals the predominance of singing sirens, from Tasso's musical sorceress Armida, who seduced innocent Christian soldiers with her voice,
to the object of Guarini's "Io mi son giovinetta," who ensnares her lover
with song.

Like composers and poets, visual artists had long recognized the inextricable intertwining of song and sensuality. In *Three Ages of Man*, which
features a woman playing a flute while looking into her lover's eyes,
Titian conflates making music with making love, and sound with sight
and touch (Figure 3.4). And famously, his *Venus and the Musician* series
depicts men and women locked in meaningful glances and connected
by sound (Figure 3.5). These paintings present musical situations in
which the male figure, either an organist or lutenist, plays in what looks
like an attempt to woo Venus while she sits languorously indifferent
(Figure 3.6).[55] In the paintings featuring an organist, she reclines, turns
her head away, and does nothing to conceal her body. Emphasizing the
tactile, she strokes the velvet cloth while gingerly touching the musician's waist with her foot. Meanwhile, he focuses not on his instrument
but on her genitals, wooing her with sound. In the paintings with a
lute, the musician plays to Venus, meeting her eyes and thus turning
his back to the viewer. She holds a flute in her left hand, and the music

---

[55] This interpretation is based largely on that of Goffen in *Titian's Women*.

Figure 3.5, Titian, *Venus and the Musician*. Reproduced by permission of the Bridgeman Art Gallery

lies strewn across the window suggesting that at some point they made music together – an activity that may substitute for making love. Rustic figures dancing to bagpipes in the background at once contrast with and encroach upon the courtly sounds of the lute, as if making music engendered a sensuousness that disengages hierarchies of the senses.

Not safe sex

The juxtaposition of the Renaissance understanding of song as an entity capable of altering the body, soul, and spirit with the imagined potential of erotic art to propel the sensations of pleasure now makes it possible to see how singing could be dangerously sexual. Madrigal performances produced for outside consumption the inner experiences of love and desire. They did so through musical conventions conceived as sonorous analogues to bodily motions. Through the medium of the human voice, musical gestures captured the flux of humors inherent in the sensations depicted by the words. Musical motion enacted bodily motion, so that rapid movement might present a state of excitement; harsh dissonances might suggest physical or emotional pain. Such musical devices for embodying sensual effect pervaded music of the sixteenth and seventeenth centuries.

110

Figure 3.6, Titian, *Venus and the Lutenist*. Reproduced by permission of the Metropolitan Museum of Art, New York

Madrigal performances presented complicated intersections of seemingly opposed ideologies, and their layered meanings rendered them liminal sites of discursive merges. The potential to configure in sound the humoral effects of both physical and spiritual desire precariously positioned them between the licit world of the *trattati d'amore* and the illicit world of Aretino's erotica. Performances of madrigals created a space in which high-minded and rhetorically conditioned spiritual yearnings for divine beauty rubbed up against lowly cravings for carnal pleasure. By using the powers of music and poetry to excite and stimulate the passions, madrigals could impel the listener either upwards to spiritual transcendence or downwards toward moral perdition.

To begin historicizing and anatomizing the musical manifestation of desire, musicologists have taken up Stephen Greenblatt's notion of erotic friction.[56] Greenblatt himself follows *Making Sex*, Thomas Lacqueur's influential study of Renaissance constructions of gender difference, and

[56] See, for example, McClary, "Constructions of Gender in Monteverdi's Dramatic Music," 37; Linda Phyllis Austern, "Nature, Culture, Myth, and Musician in Early Modern England," and Suzanne Cusick, "On Musical Performances of Gender and Sex," lecture presented at University of Pennsylvania, February 24, 1995.

reads *Twelfth Night* against legal and medical texts that elucidate early modern understandings of conception. [57] For conception to occur, erotic heat generated by chafing had to arouse both man and woman until they reached their boiling point – the ejaculation of orgasm. Since female bodies naturally maintained a lower temperature than their male counterparts, orgasm and ejaculation required a hotter furnace for women than they did for men. Reading this model of sexual chafing in conjunction with Shakespearean drama, Greenblatt argues that

> Shakespeare realized that if sexual chafing could not be presented literally on stage, it could be represented figuratively; friction could be fictionalized, chafing chastened and made fit for the stage by transforming it into witty erotically-charged sparrings. [58]

The concept of erotic friction recently has been very useful to musicologists dealing with issues of the early modern body. [59] Laura Macy translates Greenblatt's erotic friction into musical terms in order to advance an argument that madrigals functioned as controlled and constrained musical enactments of sex. She suggests that the erotics of late sixteenth-century madrigals emerged from the intimate physical nature of part-book singing, in which gestures like suspensions brought the

---

[57] Thomas Lacqueur, *Making Sex: Body and Gender from the Greeks to Freud* (Cambridge, MA: Harvard University Press, 1990).

[58] Stephen Greenblatt, *Shakespearean Negotiations: The Circulation of Social Energy in Renaissance England* (Berkeley: University of California Press, 1988), 89.

[59] Against Lacqueur and Greenblatt, I would argue that such erotic friction reflects neither an early modern utopian emphasis on female pleasure nor a mechanism for contained sexuality. That is historical fantasy. Female pleasure caused no social unrest when its furnace effect led to appropriate procreation. Indeed, not all medical theories upheld the necessity of female orgasm. Despite Galen's emphasis on female seed, Aristotelian ideas of conception rendered that seed extraneous, making women little more than human incubators. But when female pleasure extended outside matrimony, trouble ensued. Women who generated erotic heat for a purpose other than conception – courtesans, singers, and other lascivious ladies – were often violently disciplined. French and Spanish lesbians of the sixteenth century who used dildos to take on "male" roles in sexual situations, thereby rendering men irrelevant, received death sentences. They were killed for exercising pleasure without men. See Katharine Park, "The Rediscovery of the Clitoris," in *The Body in Parts*, ed. David Hillman and Carla Mazzio (New York: Routledge, 1997), 171–195. And Franco, for all her sexual agency, eventually stood trial before the Inquisition for the crime of magical incantations. See Margaret F. Rosenthal, *The Honest Courtesan: Veronica Franco, Citizen and Writer in Seventeenth-Century Venice* (Chicago: University of Chicago Press), 153–204. In arguing against the utopianism of Lacqueur's one-sex model, I follow a now well-worn critical path. For a concise discussion of the complexity of early modern approaches to the matter of gender difference and a critique of Lacqueur, see Katharine Park and Robert A. Nye, "Review of *Making Sex*: Body and Gender from the Greeks to Freud," *New Republic* 204/7 (1991): 53–55.

singers to articulate their lines in direct response to the other voices. For Macy, the physical sensations of this kind of performance mimicked sex, but the erotic energy it generated was ultimately contained by conventional poetic texts and courtly decorum. As an example, she argues that the central conceit of "Il bianco e dolce cigno," the joyful orgasm that makes the lover want to die a thousand deaths a day was both displayed and contained by its performative context.

It is not difficult to see how madrigals like "Il bianco e dolce cigno" might fulfill medical prescriptions for sexual arousal. The singers, in their small, physically proximate circle, recite wanton words in a context of musical friction . . . The madrigal's lightweight punch line, emphasized by the musical joke that sets it, now becomes an element of social control. When a suggestive text is combined with the physical pleasure of singing, sexual tension results.[60]

Macy historicizes her interpretation of madrigal singing by reading conduct books written by Castiglione and Doni, which describe strict boundaries of propriety and taste. Musical madrigals, like the poetic idioms of their texts, pushed but never broke the limits of decorum, providing a kind of safe sex. The singing of the madrigal constituted flirtation, but not foreplay; therefore the singers could enjoy this sexual tension without pursuing it to its conclusion.[61] Even the discipline and adherence to a strict set of rules, mandated by the activity of singing, Macy suggests, contained the erotic potential of music making.[62]

Susan McClary also uses "Il bianco e il dolce cigno" to explore the complicated relationship between musical expression and the body. She reads the piece as an early example of madrigalian codes for the representation of erotic experiences. The affective setting of words like "piangendo," with harmonies that slip momentarily out of the mode but never threaten its guiding musical dominance, allows for a controlled expression of lust. The subject's lust is coded and thus restrained within convention and decorum. She finds sexual excess at the piece's end when

---

[60] Laura Macy, "Speaking of Sex: Metaphor and Performance in the Italian Madrigal," *Journal of Musicology* 14/1 (1996): 15. Also, Susan McClary uses the concept of erotic friction in reference to trio sonata textures in "Constructions of Gender in Monteverdi's Dramatic Music."

[61] Macy, "Speaking of Sex," 15.

[62] In my dissertation, "Singing the Female Body: Monteverdi, Subjectivity, Sensuality," I argue that the discipline required of female singers is precisely what makes their voices subversive and challenging to convention. By learning to control their bodies physically and the music intellectually, they contest social tendencies to mark them as unruly and inferior.

Each line seeks desperately the sweetness of the cadence, yet their phrased superimposition causes them to cancel each other out. Every moment of would-be conclusion is swept along in the delicious flood of release, until gradually they all subside.[63]

Nevertheless, McClary understands that Arcadelt's "imagery is highly stylized – it does not, in other words, represent an unmediated experience of sixteenth-century sexuality."[64]

I want to build on McClary's and Macy's important work by further extending their consideration of song and sex as historically constructed and permeable. The sonority of madrigals – their dynamic motion – is crucial to understanding their functions. Certainly, at some level, madrigal composers did use discernible codes to represent sex. But these codes, however conventional, could not represent an entirely safe sex because they delivered a double blow to singers and listeners. They released at least two dangerous forces – love and sex. Rather than iconically or mimetically reflecting sex, they propelled the flux of humors similarly induced by erotic experience. Their performance projected the materials of the body out into the world and projected the psychology of emotions through experiences of the body. Considering the bodies of the performers makes it difficult to imagine, as Macy points out, that the intimate nature of part-book singing did not involve singers listening intently to each others' bodies and voices.

Excursus: the woman problem

The presence of women in madrigal performances greatly intensified their lascivious potential.[65] Women, like song and love, were considered unruly and enigmatic forces liable to slip into threatening excess. They, like the madrigals themselves, violated the natural order and were at once dangerous and enticing. Ficino warned that a woman could "bewitch a man like a sorceress," eroding his rational faculties.[66] Though singing could be unseemly business for both men and women, the transgression was far greater for female performers. Singing women threatened to dissolve at least some of the crucial biological distinctions that differentiated them from men. Like love and sex, gender distinctions

---

[63] McClary, "Music, the Pythagoreans, and the Body," 94.   [64] Ibid.

[65] Circumstantial evidence suggests that women probably did and certainly could have sung madrigals. We know that the madrigals to which Artusi responded involved female singers. In addition, a number of madrigals from *Il quarto libro de madrigali* are written in the style heavily influenced by the *Concerto delle donne* of Ferrara. We also know that Adriana Basile and other female singers participated in the Mantuan Friday afternoon "hall of mirrors" concerts for which Monteverdi provided music. Stevens, *The Letters of Monteverdi*, 75.

[66] Ficino, *Commentary on Plato's Symposium*, 98.

functioned as a set of analogous relationships that depended on the maintenance of both similarity and difference. The categories of male and female were connected in a dense web of correspondences. According to Galenic doctrines, women were inversions of men, while for Aristotelians they were colder versions of their superior, warmer male counterparts; both philosophers understood women to be anatomically similar to men. At the same time, medical philosophers understood gender difference metaphysically in terms of the following oppositions: perfect versus imperfect, formal versus material, active versus passive. By singing, and as I argued in chapter 1, raising their temperatures, women diminished physical differences and threatened fragile metaphysical dualisms.

Perhaps in response to this threat, poets and commentators on female singers connected their subjects to sex and often inflected their voices with seductive magic. Viewing pictorial representations of musical women and reading the sexual tropes involved in their description suggests that the liminality of song, like the liminality of love and of sex, opened up an erogenous zone in which women could claim an agency denied them in other areas of Renaissance life.

Taken together, the sexual connotations of the female singing voice and representations like Titian's musician paintings discussed above suggest that Renaissance society did have some spaces wherein women could claim an agency denied them by most segments of society. Like the activity of singing, Titian's paintings work against the tendency of Neoplatonic love to position women, like statues and pictures, as silent and absent objects of desire. In these paintings it is Venus who engenders the musician's existence. In the manner of Venetian courtesans, Titian's Venus and even Aretino's bawdy heroines can move bodies and minds. Moreover, the picture to which Dolce reacted, Titian's *Venus and Adonis*, reverses traditional gender roles: Venus desires and aggressively pursues the hunter.[67] Titian's fascination with the assertively sexual female body might relate to the power women wielded in the erotic underworld.

The raw sensuality – not sexuality – of Titian's figures reflects an acknowledgment, even within a patriarchal culture, that women could participate in love and sex, that they had access to the arresting power of sensuality, and that they could use that power to captivate men. Courtesans like the famed Venetian Veronica Franco wrote about their own desires and pleasures.[68] Though she participated in "involuntary"

---

[67] My interpretation of this picture is based largely on Goffen's discussion in *Titian's Women*. I am especially indebted to her understanding of pictorial codes.

[68] Other scholars have argued that courtesans by virtue of their social liminality were granted an intellectual and artistic agency denied to their more noble counterparts.

sexual performance, she also created a poetic universe in which the mind and soul of a courtesan talked back to male critics and patrons.[69] In an especially stunning poem, first published in 1565 by the author as part of a larger collection, Franco responds to a Petrarchan literary suitor by promising her erotic skill as a reward for proof of her seducer Marco Venier's wisdom and virtues.

> And in this way I'll give you so much pleasure
> That you may call yourself fully content
> And close to falling even more in love.
> I can become so lovely and delicious
> Whenever I'm in bed with any person
> To whom I feel myself pleasing and loved
> That then my sweetness will surpass all others
> So that the knot of love which seemed already
> so firmly tied will tighten all the time.[70]

Though playing on male fantasies of female eroticism made Veronica Franco a very rich woman, she also used that play to gain sexual agency. She claims a literary space for women, a voice in both high and low cultural debates about love and pleasure, and – perhaps more strikingly – a discursive space for female sexuality. And she, like other courtesans, also used music as an instrument of power and of pleasure.

Like Franco, Tullia d'Aragona advocated a love that includes women's intellectual and sensual capacities and inserts them into a discourse that would otherwise erase them. By equating the highest form of love with intellectual experience while denying women access to the life of the mind, Neoplatonists excluded real women's bodies from the experience of spiritual love. In contrast, Aragona makes room for real flesh-and-blood women. Her women come to life as more than just bland, silent vehicles for divine inspiration whose beauty emerges only when a man sees in it divine light. By acknowledging female intellect, she releases women from their containment in the physical side of human nature, and consequently challenges their perpetual associations with the body and the lower senses of touch, smell, and taste.

For the courtesan, her singing voice often comprised a key part of her self-performance and thus also became a metonymic symbol of her sensual power and sometimes her disrepute. Aragona herself was a poet,

Veronica Franco, Tullia d'Aragona, and Gaspara Stampa were all respected writers well skilled in contemporary Petrarchan and Neoplatonic conventions. See Rosenthal, *The Honest Courtesan*, and Anne Rosalind Jones, *The Currency of Eros: Women's Love Lyric in Europe, 1540–1620* (Bloomington: Indiana University Press, 1990).

[69] For more on Franco see Anne Rosalind Jones and Margaret Rosenthal, *Veronica Franco: Poems and Selected Letters* (Chicago: University of Chicago Press, 1998) and Rosenthal, *The Honest Courtesan*.

[70] Jones and Rosenthal, *Poems*, 69.

lutenist, and singer and owned an impressive collection of music prints and manuscripts in addition to her Latin and Italian books. Veronica Franco, though perhaps not a consummate musician herself, sponsored musical events in her home.

Monteverdian sensuality

The broad discursive picture painted in this chapter sets the ground for an exploration of madrigals as performances of sensuous experiences. Rather than functioning as iconic representations of sex, and hence as a static phenomenon, madrigals recover a performative dynamism that was, at its root, profoundly sensuous and sensual. As I stated earlier, the distinctions that poets and philosophers made between spiritual and erotic love were distinctions of language and rhetoric, not sensation. Song embodied sensation and thus made no such distinctions.[71]

The delightfully carnal potential of madrigals is abundantly evident in "Sì ch'io vorei morire." Unconcerned with Neoplatonic innuendo, this piece sings instead of foreplay and sex. Far exceeding the proprieties of Castiglione's conversation, it recalls Aretino's eroticism, emphasizing the licentious by slithering out of control and into the realm of sexual delight. It captures the anguished cries of a lover experiencing the pleasure of sex and, in so doing, introduces the listener to a musical and textual vocabulary for erotic experience which seems overzealous in comparison to the more restrained expression of most other pieces in the collection.

> Sì ch'io vorei morire
> ora ch'io bacio, Amore,
> la bella bocca del mio amato core.
> Ahi, cara e dolce lingua,
> datemi tant'umore,
> che di dolcezz'in questo sen m'estingua!
> Ahi, vita mia, a questo bianco seno
> deh, stringetemi fin ch'io venga meno!
> Ahi bocca, ahi baci, ahi lingua, torn'a dire:
> "Sì ch'io vorei morire"
>
> Now, let me die,
> love, now that I kiss
> the beautiful mouth of my beloved.

---

[71] My readings of these much-analyzed madrigals have been influenced by Nino Pirrotta, "Monteverdi's Poetic Choices," in *Music and Culture in Italy from the Middle Ages to the Baroque* (Cambridge, MA: Harvard University Press, 1984), 80–113; Tomlinson, *Monteverdi and the End of the Renaissance*; Alfred Einstein, *The Italian Madrigal* (Princeton: Princeton University Press, 1949); and Eric T. Chafe, *Monteverdi's Tonal Language* (New York: Schirmer Books, 1992).

> Ah, dear sweet tongue,
> give me such humors
> that from sweetness I expire on this breast!
> Ah, my life, to this white bosom,
> oh, press me until I swoon!
> Ah mouth, ah kisses, ah tongue, I say again:
> "Now, let me die."

Depicting the rising pleasure of a sexual encounter that begins with a kiss, this poem leaves little to the imagination. The speaker kisses first "la bella bocca del mio amato core" (the beautiful mouth of my beloved). Then he touches her "cara e dolce lingua" (dear sweet tongue) and finally expires on her "bianco seno" (white bosom). He begs her to "stringetemi fin ch'io venga meno" (press me until I swoon). Such frank eroticism almost suggests an Aretino-like satire, deliberately appropriating tools and conventions from courtly culture in order to reveal its hypocrisy. [72]

Monteverdi's music captures the erotic essence of the poetry by translating the feelings it portrays into musical utterances that detail the wanton words. This is not to say that sex is somehow in the notes or that Monteverdi thought consciously about most of what I will claim for the music. Instead, the sympathies between the words, the experiences, and the sounds were conventional and natural enough for composers, performers, and audiences that homologies between body and sound needed no articulation. As with all of the interpretations offered in this book, I do not presume to give definitive readings of already well-studied madrigals. Instead I hope to place them in a matrix that historicizes not only song but sensuality – bodies, desire, and pleasure.

In a way that text alone cannot, the performance of this piece foregrounds the body, especially the parts used for singing and for sex. Its text names body parts and its performance depends on them, which makes it impossible to ignore the corporeal elements so vehemently banished from Neoplatonic discourse. Enumerating the pleasures of the tongue articulated by the phrase "Ahi, cara e dolce lingua," each voice sings the affective exclamation, "ahi," on a long held second, followed by a quick declamatory statement (Example 3.1). The fast-repeated notes of "cara e dolce lingua" force the singer to use tongue and teeth – parts crucial for both kissing and singing. According to reigning Aristotelian doctrines, the voice or breath forces air from the chest up through the throat into the mouth, where the tongue, lips, and teeth give it articulation. At the same time, the repeated notes require throat articulation

---

[72] It also recalls the poems and songs with which Aretino peppers his work, including one written in praise of a singer/courtesan, Angela Zaffetti, and another that was supposedly set to music.

Example 3.1, "Sì ch'io vorei morire"

that taxed the body part medical practitioners connected to the uterus. Later in the piece Monteverdi brings out the textual anatomy by setting the line "Ahi bocca, ahi baci, ahi lingua" twice: first as a descending quarter-note bass sequence underlying an upper-voice sequence and then as a rising quarter note sequence in all five voices. Again the activity of singing highlights the body parts mentioned as performers open their mouths to articulate the vowels. At the same time, isolating and slowing down the music marks them indelibly in the listener's mind.

Saturated with expirations of all sorts, the piece is framed by a musico-poetic statement of desire for death of the orgasmic variety. The performance marks death through the effect of a sigh generated in the first, third and fifth measures on the word "morire," with a falling third. The gesture contains within it the dynamic of desire that runs through the piece. Melodically the figure resembles countless other sighs composed in the sixteenth and seventeenth centuries. But its repetition and structure gives it a rather different feel. It is constructed by failed leading tones which instead of ascending drop a third, giving the effect of something that is never quite realized – and the words clearly identify that something as desire (Example 3.2).

Example 3.2, "Si ch'io vorei morire"

Between the beginning and concluding gestures, "Sì ch'io vorei morire" embodies the escalation of desire, especially in its numerous sequences and suspensions. Rich in repeated harmonic progressions, it includes almost all of the sequence techniques found in his other works. Their rhythmic motion, pitch ascent and descent, and harmonic motion – dissonance/resolution – all sonically enact a play between arousal and fulfillment. More specifically, these sequences exchange motives between voices. If the voice comprises the same materials as blood, sweat, and seed, then an exchange of voice resembles an exchange of bodily fluids. At the same time, the repeated gestures seem to echo the Neoplatonic theory that physical pleasure breeds the desire for more pleasure – thus creating a hunger that can never be satisfied.

The sequences in "Sì ch'io vorei morire" enact rising pleasure through quickened rhythm, heightened pitch, and increasingly concentrated dissonances. For example, in the setting of "Ahi, cara e dolce lingua," the raised rhythmic intensity of the repeated notes suggests the rapid pulse rate of desire. The rhythmic pace slows and speeds up multiple times as the recitative-like declamation sets apart and highlights the exclamatory nature of the dissonant "Ahi." The gasp of air recalls Ferrand's statement that lovers' sighs result from their intense focus on the love object, which in turn causes them to forget to breathe. They must then "draw in the quantity of air in a single gasp that is taken in normally in two or three breaths."[73] The sequence reaches its peak at the words "datemi tant'umore," where humors are exchanged in a five-voiced texture; resolution finally arrives, bringing with it the point of maximum pitch and dissonance. The sonority, in other words, progresses with the humors to a climax.

The piece embodies resolution and fulfillment, the slowed pulse of desire's realization, through control of dissonance and rhythm. After the clash of humors on "datemi tant'umore," the musical motion abruptly slows to half notes. Harmonies move from dissonance to consonance on "di dolce" with a full-measure resolution as the subject expires on his lover's breast. The rhythmic motion stops altogether here, indicating a heart that has stopped beating. Immediately, however, the piece comes back to life with the exclamations of "Ahi vita mia." This phrase is exchanged between upper and lower voices – sound moves between participants in the manner of seed, saliva, and souls.

To be sure, all of these technologies were conventional symbols of pain in the early seventeenth century, and especially the pain of unrequited desire. But owing in large part to the continued dominance of humoral understandings of the body and the senses, they functioned at a very literal level. First, expressive dissonances represent erotic friction through their harmonic imbalance. But there is more to it than that.[74] Pushing this point somewhat further suggests that the erotic effect of such dissonances had to do with the way sound worked. If sound was imagined to be a physical entity that coursed from the throat of the singer to the ear of the listener, then each time a singer sang a note a humoral substance entered the air and ultimately the ear of the listener. When the pitches clashed they ran smack into each other, embodying the erotic friction mentioned earlier and causing a clash in the listeners' ears and souls.

The relation of sequences and dissonances in this piece to desire and arousal can be heard most dramatically in the long section that begins on the words "deh, stringetemi . . ." and continues until the return of the first line at the piece's end. Immediately after the expiration and at the rebirth of "Ahi vita mia" the rise and fall of desire begin again. Rising pleasure is embodied and drawn out by repeating the words "deh, stringetemi fin ch'io venga meno" (press me until I swoon) three times

---

[73] Ferrand, 280.

[74] Suzanne Cusick, "Gendering Modern Music: Thoughts on the Artusi–Monteverdi Controversy," *Journal of the American Musicological Society* 46 (1993): 10–26.

and setting them to descending and ascending fourth- and fifth-related sequences of dissonant suspensions (Example 3.3). Singers breathe as lovers breathe. The addition of bass notes on the third repetition of this sequence adds the bass–soprano polarity that Artusi found so "unnatural." Next, the sequence is reversed. The "deh, stringetemi" text drops out as all five voices, in a rising fourth pattern, denote the tactile elements of a kiss, "Ahi bocca, ahi baci, ahi lingua." These long dissonant chains that make first female and then male performers gasp for air capture the sensation of desire and the escalation of sexual energy, as sonorous instability mimics the bodily instability incited by sex. The exchange between upper and lower voices suggests an exchange between male and female partners.

On the surface, this piece seems utterly different from, and far more excessive than, "Cor mio, mentre vi miro," whose text by Guarini, as I mentioned at the beginning of this chapter, epitomizes disembodied and spiritualized Neoplatonic love. Guarini projects the restraint of his poetic content with controlled syntax. Eschewing textual indulgences, the poem avoids wordy constructions in favor of simple grammatical structures. In general, Monteverdi's setting avoids the emphatic gestural language of "Sì ch'io vorei morire" and uses musical devices that connect to the syntactic and semantic aspects of the text. Where the first piece basks in never-ending sequences and suspensions, this one uses subtler versions of the same gestures. "Sì ch'io vorei morire" traffics in the easily audible rise and fall of physical desire, privileging the body. In contrast, "Cor mio, mentre vi miro" reflects the connection between "gazing and being transformed," expressed in the first two lines of the poem, with staggered homophony. Each singer takes on the notes of the other, taking over the motions with tongues, mouths, and teeth. Like "Sì ch'io vorei morire," "Cor mio" makes listeners aware of the bodies singing, belying the textual evasion of the body. The transformation is further enacted in the second line of text where the music changes dramatically. Tonally, the piece moves from D dorian to A major, a tonal transformation and upward motion that is highlighted by the full-voiced setting that comes in at m. 6. The contrary motion of the soprano and bass parts that finally end on an A major chord might further represent the transformation (Example 3.4). Though the word "visibilmente" emphasizes visual pleasure, its repeated-note declamation makes use of the same tongue and teeth as the "cara e dolce lingua" passage of the racier madrigal and thus foregrounds the singing body, exceeding the spiritually disembodied realm of the text. The two passages in fact look and sound very much the same, despite their radically different meanings.

Like "Sì ch'io vorei morire," this piece centers on expiring humors. Monteverdi set the soul exchange narrated in the first part of the

Example 3.3, "Sì ch'io vorei morire"

Example 3.4, "Cor mio, mentre vi miro"

madrigal with a series of dramatic starts and stops. Most obviously, the judicious use of sighs on "In un solo sospir l'anima spiro" highlights the death encompassed in each sigh by stopping the action altogether. Each utterance of "sospir" is set apart by rests and expressed in a halting ascending melody that fails to cadence; the A to Bb motion of the first one, for instance, sounds particularly dramatic. The moment culminates with "L'anima spiro" set with a textural reduction that leads to a unison D and a full stop in the music – what Anthony Newcomb has called an evaporated cadence (Example 3.5). The unison is barely audible at this point. The dying away of the music mimics the expiring of the soul: the music completely stops moving as the subject breathes his final breath; sound stops as humors stop flowing. Though not the explicitly sexual death of "Sì ch'io vorei morire," this performance still enacts a transformative experience characterized by a disarming loss of self. Just as in "Sì ch'io vorei morire" the lover repeatedly expires and comes immediately back to life, in "Cor mio" the expirations lead first to repeated deaths until finally the silence of spiritual expiration erupts suddenly

Example 3.5, "Cor mio, mentre vi miro"

and exuberantly into a celebration of life on the words "O bellezza . . ."
The breath that the singers must take in order to soar both musically
and spiritually into the next measure all but covers up the cadence. The
singers' breaths engender the breath of life. The rebirth is emphasized
by an abrupt shift to a new tonal area, a leap of an octave in the soprano
voice, and a fuller texture filled in with almost all-triadic chords.

"Cor mio" marks the acceleration of desire, or the play between
arousal and fulfillment, through a succession of rising cadential
sequences whose building of harmonic tension propels the piece forward. The sequential harmonic rush capitalizes on the same sonorous
force and sensations that run through the more erotic madrigal.
Monteverdi set the affective exclamations "O bellezza mortale / O
bellezza vitale" to a rising melodic sequence that consists of a downward leap of a sixth followed by a mild suspended dissonance. Melodically, the falling sixth embodies a sigh of spiritual expiration, while
the following dissonance affects, in a much tamer version of the ever-
present dissonances in "Sì ch'io vorei morire," the humoral discord at

the moment of spiritual death and rebirth, when the soul leaves the body. The melodic and verbal exclamations are then heard in the tenor voice, underneath the upper voices' statement of the last two lines. The next line and a half, "poi chè sì tosto un core, per te rinasce," shoots out in a rapid rising melodic and cadential sequence, while the tenor continues the "O bellezza" sequence in the background. The increased rhythmic pace marks the increased heartbeat of rising desire. The seventeen measures of quick sequential homophonic declamation build harmonically and melodically until the third repetition, when four of the five voices join in for a passage that rises a seventh. This culminates in a slowed-down, stepwise ascending statement of the final words, "e per te nato, more," when the lover dies again. The rapid-fire declamation of the first line and a half embodies the increased energy and heartbeat of spiritual escalation, while the melodic fall leading to a rhythmic slow-down suggests the expiration and death that follows. The falling seventh between "nato" and "more" indicates the sigh of the lover (Example 3.6). For this final expiration Monteverdi brings back the full five-voiced texture that he has used only once before in the madrigal.

Notwithstanding the restraint of "Cor mio" and the excess of "Sì ch'io vorei morire," distinctions between Neoplatonic spiritualized love and sex apparent in their texts cannot help but disintegrate in the music. To be sure, the pieces differ in many important ways. The first exemplifies the kind of love enumerated by Ficino and his followers and the second suggests an experience closer to Aretino's world. The first articulates spiritual, disembodied love while the second remains grounded in the body. The first plays out, musically and poetically, the tension between love and death, whereas the second collapses them into one another. But these differences do not tell the whole story. Both pieces move and imitate the motions of the humors. The performative presence of these pieces involves similar gestures and tensions and embodies similar sensations. Both pieces capture a disharmony between body and soul, an increased pulse rate leading to a physical collapse. And the dissonances in both pieces cause voices to rub up against one another – forces clashing, like lovers, in the air. Marking the escalation of pleasure, sequences rise until the moment of their resolution, delaying harmonic consummation at the very last instant. The similar sensuality of the two pieces reveals that while the semantics of poetry and philosophy allowed distinctions between spiritual love and sex, the activity of singing tore through these dualisms. Writers could describe a difference between virtuous and vulgar experiences; sound simply conflated the two. The humoral effects incited by the extreme cases of "Cor mio" and "Sì ch'io vorei morire" did not oppose one another, but rather pushed up against one another.

Example 3.6, "Cor mio, mentre vi miro"

In most of Monteverdi's early madrigals lovers suffer inside as they gaze into each other's eyes. Only occasionally in a seemingly out-of-place piece like "Sì ch'io vorei morire" do they ever touch. This would all change by the second decade of the seventeenth century. By way of conclusion, I want briefly to allude to two madrigals from the 1619 *Concerto: Settimo libro de madrigali a 1.2.3.4. et sei voci, con altri generi de canti*, pieces that privilege musical logic and discrete sections over sensual expression. The control, musical and otherwise, of these pieces points out the dangerous sensuality of the madrigals already discussed in this chapter.

"Eccomi pronta ai baci," which I will discuss in much more detail in the final chapter, sings a different tune than anything from *Il quarto libro de madrigali*. The actions in this piece occur outside the body. The lady allows a kiss and the man bites her, leaving a scar; it is a *bacio* gone bad. Monteverdi captured this all with caustic accuracy as the angry lady vents her fury in an animated quick text declamation that does not slow down until the final cadence. Like other madrigals of the mid-seventeenth century, this piece displays a playful eroticism only hinted at in the fourth book of madrigals. Monteverdi's four *baci* madrigals from the seventh book of madrigals followed contemporary trends – forty-one of Marino's *baci* madrigals were set by other composers between 1603 and 1643.[75] The kiss served as a physical metaphor for intercourse rather than a sign of inner turmoil; the body stands as its own physical entity.

To be sure such coy eroticism bespeaks a shift from Petrarchan to Marinist ideals.[76] The lovers of Petrarch, Ficino, Bembo, and Castiglione were plagued by inner turmoil, clashing sensations, and humoral paradoxes. Neoplatonic and Petrarchan discourses built on ancient, medieval, and earlier Renaissance traditions conventionally explored the inner psychology and physiology of love. In contrast, Marino expressed the outward and tactile manifestations of erotic encounters. In this poetry, sound and sight met touch and smell, and lovers spent more time kissing and less time locked in meaningful glances. No longer a macrocosm of the human soul, nature became a tool for physical description and a panoply of objects awaiting exploration. The sensuality that in Petrarchan lyrics remained veiled by language of innuendo and hidden inside the body now resided on the body's edges, describing the surface experiences of touching, kissing and everything else.

"Eccomi pronta ai baci," like the other Marinist madrigals of Monteverdi's later madrigal books, bespeaks a widespread occlusion of conventional discourses and practices. These had previously worked to separate love from sex, relegating the former to the soul and the latter to the body. The shift from a poetry of innuendo that rarely mentioned the body or tactile experiences toward the tactile and playful erotics of Marino's lyrics might seem to indicate a more erotic sensibility. It is, after all, difficult to imagine Clorinda or most of the ladies serenaded in the fourth book allowing a kiss. Even Ariadne's ill-fated sexual encounter with Theseus remained invisible to the audience. This comparably sexy stuff notwithstanding, I would argue that the surface details of the new erotic play bespeak a taming of the powers of song, and, in this case, of madrigal singing – a taming which in turn effects a distancing marked by independent musical logic and fragmentation. In other words, though Marinist madrigals seem more exaggerated and erotic because they privilege the corporeal, their focus on bodily surfaces and not the forces that

---

[75] For discussions of poetic shifts and the *baci* madrigals as a whole, see Tomlinson, *Monteverdi and the End of the Renaissance*, and Lorenzo Bianconi, *Music in the Seventeenth Century*, trans. David Bryant (Cambridge: Cambridge University Press, 1987).

[76] Gary Tomlinson makes this argument in *Monteverdi and the End of the Renaissance*. For opposing viewpoints see Chafe, *Monteverdi's Tonal Language*, and Tim Carter, "Resemblance and Representation: Towards a New Aesthetic in the Music of Monteverdi," in *Con che soavità: Studies in Italian Opera, Song and Dance, 1580–1740*, ed. Iain Fenlon and Tim Carter (Oxford: Clarendon Press, 1995), 118–135.

course within the body's interiors effectively detach song from the spirit, muting its sensuality.

These are sexual as opposed to sensual. They relate explicitly to sex and to the erotic but not necessarily to the inward experience of something physical and carnal. In these songs, the texts address the body more directly, but the music itself is more disembodied. When composers made use of musical structures that privilege their own logic, they participated in a move away from the embodied sensuality that empowered Renaissance song, and toward the creation of a musical discourse that existed apart from language and the world. Instead of revealing invisible realms of the human body, the performance of these pieces constructs arbitrary connections between music and what it represents. By representing and not enacting sensuality, such performances might "rein in" the sensual power of song, possibly enacting the control that Macy and McClary find in "Il bianco e dolce cigno." As I will elaborate later in this book, the control here stems not from the musical gestures themselves but from the way they work within the music and how they work upon the listeners. Thus, for instance, the romanesca "Ohimè dov'è il mio ben," Monteverdi's setting of the tortured and introspective Petrarchan poem by Bernardo Tasso, begins with an intoxicatingly dissonant entrance of the second voice. The held second might seem to recall the "Ohimè's," "ahi's," and "O's" of the Book 4 madrigals. Dissonance, after all, had long served as conventional markings of the pangs of unrequited love. But here that dissonance derives its potency from the tension between the vocal lines and the relatively static harmonies of the basso continuo, from its musical construction and its location within a harmonic system that is not homologous to erotomania.

In all of this I do not mean to suggest that differences between "Eccomi pronta ai baci" and the polyphonic madrigals reside in the generic move to duet textures and the addition of a basso continuo part. That would be too easy. I want instead to think about the larger changes those changes effect. The presence of the continuo part may, for instance, relocate the control of musical logic in performance from the collective singers and listeners to one creative person, the instrumentalist who plays the accompaniment's framing logic or the composer himself. But more importantly, changes in Monteverdi's style resonate with shifting conceptions of the sonorous embodiment of human passions. The independent musical structures and vocal artifices that prevail in his later music would eventually sever song from the body and from speech. By the second half of Monteverdi's career, composers increasingly used musical devices that held together individual pieces instead of creating music whose meanings were perceived through larger cosmological relations. In philosophical terms, ontological truths about the body presented by natural philosophers were tempering the humoral experience of the body. Even more concretely, musical structures are always brought to sonic reality by singing bodies, but in Monteverdi's pieces these no longer direct the body's spirit in particular and logical ways; sensations are no longer channeled through the singing body. The gradually changing experience of song can be heard in the prevalence of gestures like sequences and repeated bass patterns that do not in any way reflect the humoral motions of the sensations and things they represent. This gradual shift relates to the waning of the *trattati d'amore* and the ideals that undermined them. The body is no longer so penetrable either by love or by sound; it is not a porous vessel that can be altered by the vicissitudes of love or the musical enactment of its ill humors. Of course the more controlled eroticism of the late madrigals does not mean that sensuality never exceeds rational control. Love's irrational pull still mystifies, still hurts, and still escapes control.

4

Emblazoning Angioletta: musical fantasies and dissection

Guarini's 1582 poem "Gorga di cantatrice" lyrically describes an erotic encounter between a seductive female singer and her admirer. In Monteverdi's striking setting of the poem "Mentre vaga Angioletta," published in the 1638 *Madrigali guerrieri e amorosi*, a male composer, a poet, and two singers offer a dissected and fragmented version of an ideal female voice by presenting it as a series of effects on the male listener. The text contains a stunning middle descriptive segment that lists twenty-two vocal effects; it works something like the Petrarchan blazon, a poetic tradition that reduced real women to linguistic fragments. The poem's speaker traces the experience of listening through individual elements that in the end add up to a transformative realization of desire. Monteverdi's setting demonstrates a similar process; his long descriptive segment matches Guarini's choppy lyric with musical fragments that propel male singers through a dizzying course of passaggi, gorgia, diminutions, and other flourishes popular during the late sixteenth and early seventeenth centuries. These descriptive musical passages represent the progression of the speaker's autoerotic stimulation, which culminates in the bursting forth of an aria-like conclusion that breaks the analyzing process, unifies aural fragments and easily assimilates love and song.

This piece about women's voices uses no actual women, marking a distinction between singing women and singing about women. In a sense, it reverses "O come sei gentile." Instead of two sopranos ventriloquizing a lover's sung amalgamation with a bird, two tenors ventriloquize the sexualized vocal virtuosity of a female singer. To discuss a piece without women might seem like an odd turn in a book specifically about women's voice, but I am interested in the responses that female voices elicited and in the myriad expressions of those responses. Rather than dealing with the female throat, or a piece that serves as a release for the female voice, this chapter explores its effects on male listeners and the manifestation of those effects. Like the last chapter, it confronts the connections between female virtuosity and male erotic fantasy. Along the way, it touches on some of the reasons why male voices were so much less eroticized than their female counterparts.

I read Monteverdi's musical gestures and Guarini's poetic rhetoric alongside the descriptive technologies employed by poets and anatomists in the late Renaissance, and relate the representational Angioletta to the real women whose voices she echoes. I also consider the concluding aria-like section in the context of a larger discourse that used images of birds, love, sex, and sirens to represent the female voice. This chapter mimics the structure of the piece itself, as it moves first through its descriptive – and dismembering – portion, then segues into an analysis of the women behind the description, and finally ends with a discussion of the transformative potential of song embodied in the madrigal's aria-like conclusion.[1]

That "Mentre vaga Angioletta" represents the female voice as an object of erotic fascination does not make it unique. Its text closely resembles many Renaissance tributes to female singers. To cite a few literary examples, three books of poetry celebrated the voice of Laura Peverara, the most famous member of the *concerto delle donne*. During his courtship of her between 1563 and 1567, Guarini wrote seventy-five poems in her honor.[2] A number of poets composed lyrics describing the Neapolitan virtuosa Adriana Basile, who was brought to Mantua at the turn of the seventeenth century. Called a "bella e vaga sirena" by Marino, she was described, in accounts perhaps closer to fantasy and thus similar to the subject of "Mentre vaga Angioletta," as a beautiful woman whose celestial harmonies and angelic sounds enchanted all who heard her. Into the next century, Giulio Strozzi published a volume in honor of the Venetian diva Anna Renzi with the Incognito Press, which contained poems that narrated her opera career and glorified the marvels of her voice.[3] On the musical side, composers such as Luzzaschi and Monteverdi composed countless pieces that serenaded the female voice and detailed its skills. But what does make "Mentre vaga Angioletta" unique is the complete absence of women as performers. In the manner of Petrarch's descriptions of Laura, it presents the lady's voice as a

---

[1] For an interesting and very detailed reading of this piece see Massimo Ossi, "A Sample Problem in Seventeenth-Century Imitatio: Claudio Monteverdi, Francesco Turini, and Battista Guarini's 'Mentre vaga angioletta,'" in *Music in Renaissance Cities and Courts: Studies in Honor of Lewis Lockwood*, ed. Jessie Ann Owens and Anthony Cummings (Warren, MI: Harmonie Park Press, 1997), 255.

[2] For details about Laura Peverara and her colorful life, see Anthony Newcomb, *The Madrigal at Ferrara* (Princeton: Princeton University Press, 1980), 187–190.

[3] Ellen Rosand, "The First Opera Diva: Anna Renzi," *Historical Performance* 3/1 (1990): 3–7.

series of effects and actions that render her less a real person than a male fantasy.

Many scholars working on this piece have focused primarily on trying to decipher the identity of Angioletta. Denis Stevens argues that the poem celebrates the virtuoso Adriana Basile, whose reign in Mantua during the first decades of the seventeenth century earned her the adoration of Monteverdi, Tasso, and other noted artists.[4] However, in an archival tour de force Stuart Reiner has refuted that claim, positing Anna Guarini, Angela Zanibelli, and other singers as possibilities. Reiner suggests that though Guarini's poem, originally written in 1592, may have served as a model for many other poems written in praise of Adriana, this particular one did not actually refer to her.[5] Despite the musicological ink spilled trying to discover whom the poem addresses, Angioletta's identity matters less than what her voice supposedly did to listeners, less than the desire her sounds enticed. Monteverdi and Guarini's *vaga ragazza* exists here as a vehicle for male expression and desire.

I am thus more interested in the "vaga" (charming) part of the title. Of all the words Guarini could have chosen from the colorful linguistic palette of sixteenth-century poetic idiom, *vaga* seems particularly apt. According to Angelo Firenzuola's 1541 treatise *On the Beauty of Women*, *vaga* relates to *vagabonda*, which connotes movement. Citing canonical authors such as Boccaccio and Petrarch, he says that moving objects entice more desire than those that stand still because they defy the viewer's gaze:

In this special sense, however, by which charm indicates that special beauty that has within it all those elements whereby anyone who looks upon it is obliged to become charmed (*vaga*), that is, desirous; and having become desirous, his heart is always wandering to pursue it and enjoy it, his thoughts travel to her, and he becomes a vagabond in his mind.[6]

Untouchable, virtuous, beautiful, and arresting, the charming woman inspires obsessive description by poets, painters, and other innocent bystanders. *Vaga* thus captures the effects of the female voice. An uncontainable force, it remains invisible and elusive. Emerging from a sensual body and sometimes a virtuous soul, its arresting power ensnares listeners. And like Firenzuola's charming woman, the female voice invites

---

[4] Denis Stevens, "Madrigali Guerrieri et Amorosi," in *The Monteverdi Companion*, ed. Denis Arnold and Nigel Fortune (New York: W. W. Norton and Company, 1968), 252–253.

[5] For a detailed discussion of who Angioletta might have been see Stuart Reiner, "La vag'Angioletta (and Others)," *Studien zur Italienisch-Deutschen Musikgeschichte* IX. (1974): 26–89. See especially 31–33.

[6] Angelo Firenzuola, *On the Beauty of Women*, trans. Konrad Eisenbichler and Jacqueline Murray (Philadelphia: University of Pennsylvania Press, 1990), 36.

men to pursue it, to enjoy it, to describe it, and to wander always to it in their minds.

Vocal effects

"Mentre vaga Angioletta" takes apart the female voice with music and language. A piece that attempts to convey the attraction of the poet to a singer and one dedicated to the erotic pleasure of the female voice, it uses descriptive rhetorics to colonize that pleasure. Both a printed text and a performance, it maps the effects of the female voice in which male composers and singers appropriate virtuosic female song. Guarini describes the actions of the woman's voice: its flexible sounds, twists, turns, and texture, along the way telling of the magic that it works on the poet, causing his heart to race, making it into a musical spirit, and ultimately transforming him into a singing nightingale.

Mentre vaga Angioletta	While charming Angioletta
ogni anima gentil cantando alletta,	attracts each gentle heart with her singing,
corre il mio core, e pende	my heart races and hangs
Tutto dal suon del suo soave canto,	completely on the sound of her sweet song,
e non so come intanto	and meanwhile mysteriously
Musico spirto prende,	takes on a musical spirit,
Fauci canore, e seco forma e finge	songful lips, and together with her forms and molds
per non usata via	in a strange way
garula e maestrevol armonia.	garrulous and masterful harmony.
Tempra d'arguto suon pieghevol voce	It tempers the flexible voice with ringing sound
e la volve e la spinge	flexing it and pushing it
con rotti accenti e con ritorti giri,	with irregular accents and twisted runs,
qui tarda e là veloce,	here slowly and there quickly,
e tal'hor mormorando	and at times murmuring
in basso e mobil suono ed alternando	with a low and liquid sound and alternating
fughe e riposi e placidi respiri,	turns and rests and calm breaths,
hor la sospende e libra,	now it suspends and liberates it,
hor la preme, hor la rompe, hor la raffrena	now hurries, now breaks, now restrains it,
hor la saette e vibra,	now shoots it and vibrates it,
hor in giro la mena,	now leads it in turns,
quando con modi tremoli e vaganti,	sometimes in tremulous wandering ways,
quando fermi e sonati.	sometimes firm and sonorous.

134

Così cantando e ricantando il core,	Thus singing again and again my heart,
o miracol d'amore!	oh miracle of love!
è fatto un usignolo	becomes a nightingale
e spiega già per non star mesto il volo.	and already, in order not to remain sad, takes its wings and flies.

The poet details the parts of the lady's voice, scrutinizing and reproducing it until it all but vanishes into the language of the male observers; his focus on the particulars leads the reader away from the larger whole. The poem's introduction situates the listener in the slow process of entering a state of rapture. The first word "Mentre" (while) immediately establishes the singing girl as the necessary precondition for the poet's experience – but not the main event. Guarini then introduces the poem's real subject, the poet's heart. He takes twelve lines to describe the effects of the singer, and the musical spirit's mysterious ways. The peculiar grammar of this section features a number of dependent clauses that take the reader's attention almost permanently away from the poem's subject and bring to the fore descriptive phrases. Finally the poet's heart returns to primacy at the climactic moment, rising in song and ultimately escaping his body as it "becomes a nightingale" and flies away.

The striking twelve-line middle section in which Guarini explicitly details the vocal effects gives the piece a profoundly fragmented feel. Rather than describing a song or a voice, he depicts the actions of the throat as it pushes, moves here and there, breathes, suspends, shoots, shakes, and so on. Guarini lists twenty ways in which the singer "tempers with clever sounds its flexible voice, " so that the reader focuses on individual vocal gestures and not on the larger structure of the poem. In the musical setting each descriptive phrase of the middle section gets its own musical gesture. The voices explode into melismas on the word "garula," an explosion that is highlighted by the first entrance of the second tenor. Monteverdi thus demonstrates the lady's vocal prowess by propelling the tenors' voices through the most daring vocal tricks of the day: wild scalar passiaggato for the "veloce" voice, slower parallel thirds and circular runs at the word "giro," sighing rests at "placidi respiri," alternated rests and short notes at "rotti accenti," and chromatically descending lines at "pieghevol voce." Each descriptive phrase involves excessive ornamentation of a melodic fragment. Her miraculous voice trembles, sings fugues, hurls, murmurs, and vibrates. Following Guarini's pace, Monteverdi wrote a disjointed piece that focuses on details and purposefully severs them from any sense of wholeness. Instead of explicitly cadencing, the gestures simply stop and start, divided only by a rest. Note especially the settings of "hor la raffrena" (restrains it) and "hor la saetta" (shoots it), in which

135

individual ornamental gestures are separated by rests over repeated chords. Harmony, melody, and rhythm are all going nowhere – nothing here moves except for the voice.

These ornaments and vocal flourishes in male voices imitate a kind of vocal writing usually associated with high voices, as in the case of "O come sei gentile." That Monteverdi wrote out a series of ornaments at a time when such maneuvers were often still left to the improvisatory whims of singers highlights his self-conscious imitative agenda. Also, the piece gestures towards the flashy high parts of madrigals written by Luzzaschi, Marenzio, and Monteverdi for the *concerto delle donne* – pieces that featured complicated diminutions, with some of Luzzaschi's madrigals demanding ranges of over two octaves.

The pages that follow situate the listener's pleasure within a larger discourse of gender and description – a discourse that suggests a slightly more disingenuous form of imitation.[7] My reading of the fragmentation in the piece differs then from Massimo Ossi's recent convincing interpretation of it as a mechanism for expressing the very individual and personal experience of the aesthetic rapture engendered by the Duke of Ferrara's *musica segreta*, and as part of Monteverdi's dedication to imitating the passion of listening.

Dissecting the female voice

In a letter dated August 20, 1581, Guarini presented "Gorga di cantatrice" to his patron, Alfonso d'Este:

Here is the canzonetta Your Highness ordered, in which I have endeavored to describe the sgorgheggiare and the tirate and the gruppi that are in music. This is a new and quite difficult undertaking, and as far as I can tell, one that has not been attempted by any other poet modern or Greek. Among the Latins, only the most divine Ariosto in one of his odes, and Pliny, the ancient scholar, have attempted it. I believe that the musician will find in it much invention by which to honor his skill.[8]

---

[7] For Ossi, both the music and the text are constructed to distinguish between "real" music and the fictional image that it occasions within the listener's soul. He describes the stream of vocal effects as a process of forcing the listener and/or reader to experience the disorientation of the listener's reverie. "Gorgia di cantatrice" mirrors the duke's private enjoyment of the concerto, physically and aesthetically removed from "the view of those he did not want to see him," as well as his concentration in following the texts being sung, and presumably also his anticipation of the details of their settings, which he must have known through repeated hearings. Finally it mirrors his intimate knowledge of the technical side of music, which would have made him aware of each musical figure as it occurred in the madrigals. Ossi, "A Sample Problem in Seventeenth-Century Imitatio."

[8] Newcomb, Document 24 in Appendix 5, p. 265. "Mando la Canzonetta, che mi fu da V. A. ordinata, nella quale mi sono ingengnato di descrivere lo sgorgheggiare et le tirate

The poet makes it clear that he intended the poem to be set to music and felt hard-pressed to describe the voice of a singer. His words suggest something more intense than the countless other poems written by him and his contemporaries that serenaded the marvelous female voice. Guarini's desire to describe the pleasure of listening to the female voice and to recreate that pleasure for his readers is in keeping with descriptive impulses usually associated during this period with writers, artists, and natural philosophers who were exploring the powers of excitation as a means for describing novel territories. In these discourses the ideal reader reconstitutes, rather than just imagines, the described experience and the text produces the physiological illusion of reality. "Mentre vaga Angioletta" takes these descriptive impulses to a performative level. In it, music, language, and male voices serve as tools for the description and discovery of the enigmatic female voice. Like the medical dissector, the explorer, or the author of the anatomical blazon, music and verbal gestures mapped the effects of the female voice, taking it apart in a musical and poetic rhetoric of violent dismemberment, partitioning something that once possessed an organic unity. The end product is a printed text and a performance that relies on the virtuosity of male composers and singers in order to appropriate the prowess of the female voice.

This impulse toward a linguistic and, in this case, musical description of a mysterious phenomenon relates to the concurrent attempts of natural philosophers to explain the inner workings of things, to make occult forces manifest. These new structures of knowledge, which I discuss more fully in the final chapter of this book, attempted to control nature through description and display. They represented a commitment to discovering the secrets of nature – in the case of this madrigal, the secrets of the female voice. And in particular, they participated in a new dedication that began at the end of the sixteenth century to making the secrets of nature public knowledge.[9] Such descriptions of female singers made public the private musical events – the *musica segreta* – that only a select few ever had the opportunity to hear. Not only were the performances ostensibly private, but also in many cases the singer's handlers kept pieces composed for them out of the public eye. Duke Vincenzo Gonzaga, for example, did not let his ladies sing in public until the 1608 festivities. And some of Luzzaschi's pieces composed for the Ferrarese *concerto delle donne* were not published until after Duke

et i gruppi, che si fan nella musica, cosa nuova et difficile assai et, per quell ch'i habbia fin qui veduto, da nium rimatore, nè tampoco da poeta Greco, et tra' latini dal diviniss(mo) Ariosto in una sua ode et da Plinio, prossatore antico, solamente tentata. Nella qual credo che'l Musico troverà molta invenzione di farsi honore . . ."

9 For more on this descriptive impulse see William Eaton, *Books of Secrets in Medieval and Early Modern Culture* (Princeton: Princeton University Press, 1994).

Alfonso's death. The term *musica segreta* itself highlights the intimate and esoteric nature of the performance and may well relate to the fascination with secrets which was manifested in books and other representations that demonstrated the secrets of nature, the secrets of women, and the secrets of just about everything else.

As a catalogue and poetic dismemberment of the female voice, "Mentre vaga Angioletta" musically performs the mapping of the body and body parts that so preoccupied sixteenth-century artistic and medical practitioners. Dissection and the linguistic tropes that went with it worked to put the body under surveillance. The process of anatomizing the body was one of violent and destructive dismemberment – an attempt on the part of doctors, artists, and writers to render powerless the body's inner workings by dividing the whole into parts.[10] Anatomists carved the body into a series of small, detached parts, thereby removing the wholeness that defines it as human. Such endeavors followed late Renaissance efforts to control one's own and others' bodies. And the noted potential violence of description also has echoes in ancient and Renaissance traditions – recall that it was Lucretia's husband's excellent description of her that led ultimately to her rape.

Reflecting the divide-and-conquer ideology that lay beneath scientific explorations of the body's mysterious interior, Monteverdi and Guarini's musical and poetic descriptions of the effects of the singer's throat reach beneath the singer's skin to reveal the secrets of her voice. Put perhaps too crassly, just as doctors opened up women's bodies in an attempt to understand and contain the womb – the mysterious organ that expelled menstrual blood and births of the monstrous and normal varieties – Monteverdi and Guarini anatomized in detail the effects that a devilishly talented singer had upon male listeners in an effort to explain, and thus control, her voice. Because doctors and artists no longer trusted ancient texts to prove what lay within the body's shell, they set about discovering, recording, and most importantly disseminating the "truth" themselves. While Michelangelo and Leonardo took apart cadavers to better depict muscular structures, doctors opened up human bodies in order to decipher their insides. The so-called anatomical Renaissance of the sixteenth and seventeenth centuries witnessed the development of a new language for describing the body. Beginning with Vesalius's publication of *De humani corporis fabrica* in 1543, anatomists mapped in detail body parts and their workings that had previously remained veiled: Eustachio mapped the ear; Falloppius the female reproductive organs;

---

[10] Both Katharine Park and Jonathan Sawday have made this argument, Jonathan Sawday in *The Body Emblazoned: Dissection and the Human Body in Renaissance Culture* (New York: Routledge, 1996) and Katharine Park in "The Criminal and the Saintly Body: Autopsy and Dissection in Renaissance Italy," *Renaissance Studies* 47/1 (1994): 1–33.

Columbus and Fabricius the venous system; and Michael Servitus the pulmonary passages.[11]

What relates most significantly to the madrigal in question is not, however, the discoveries themselves, but rather the intense desire to make visible the interior of the human body and to do so in a performative and aesthetically pleasing manner meant to entice the viewer. More important than his correction of Galen's errors was Vesalius's novel desire to expose the details of human anatomy to the human eye. The most remarkable feature of his publication was the presence of countless illustrations that aimed to reveal for a wide viewing public the secrets that lay beneath the human skin. Vesalius understood the power of a picture and of visual description.

The dissections that led to his famous illustrations did not come to pass in the sterile and quarantined spaces of modern medical labs, but instead occurred most famously in anatomy theatres which staged a public confrontation between the anatomist and the dead body, a theatrical ritual of discovery and domination. These productions aimed to seduce the reader and the spectator with the pleasure of the image. Vesalius's now famous cover illustration features the presentation of the entrails of the exposed female body to male observers.[12] In that illustration, Vesalius peels back the dead women's abdomen, revealing her naked womb to the dissector and the raucous spectators.

Scientists, like artists and writers, endeavored to excite the passions with descriptions of their discoveries that made their experience palpable. The careful production of beauty and wonder in countless scientific texts of the period suggests that scientific knowledge carried with it a compulsion to turn information into an aesthetically pleasing possession.[13] Similarly the literature of travel and exploration overflowed with descriptions that were as much about pleasure as about exposing the truth.[14]

The blazon

Roland Barthes's *S/Z*, a book American critics have found particularly productive for discussing the power of the singing voice, follows a

---

[11] For a more detailed discussion of these anatomical developments, see Sawday, *The Body Emblazoned* and Nancy G. Siraisi, *Medieval and Early Renaissance Medicine: An Introduction to Knowledge and Practice* (Chicago: University of Chicago Press, 1990).

[12] For a detailed argument about this cover page, see Park, "The Criminal and the Saintly Body."

[13] For a more detailed argument about the aesthetic of printed texts see ibid., especially page 67.

[14] See Mary Baine Campbell, *Wonder and Science: Imagining Worlds in Early Modern Europe* (Ithaca: Cornell University Press, 1999).

description of the power of the castrato's voice with a vignette on the blazon. Barthes's ruminations on the artist Sarissime include a discussion of his attraction to the castrato La Zambinella. He knows La Zambinella only as a series of disconnected parts: "Fragmented woman is the object offered to Sarissime's love . . . she is merely a kind of dictionary of fetishized objects."[15] The castrato does not represent a whole or unified body, but instead leaps from the page as the dissemination of partial objects, a dissected body reassembled by the artist into a Pygmalion-like fictive unity.

> The spitefulness of language, once resembled in order to utter itself, the total body must revert to the dust of words, to the listing of details, to a monotonous inventory of parts, to crumbling: language undoes the body, returns it to the fetish. This return is coded under the term Blazon. The blazon consists of predicating a single subject, beauty, upon a certain number of anatomical attributes.[16]

Barthes writes about a nineteenth-century literary process of dissection, in which a list of parts attempts to reproduce the whole. But the tradition he captures stretches as far back as the ancient world and of course, to Petrarch's obsessive descriptions of Laura.

Such literary fascination with dismembering the human body can be traced to the Petrarchan blazon – a code of beauty based on dividing the whole woman into a collection of luscious fragments and fetishized parts.[17] To be sure, Petrarch provided a model for expressing a complex inner psychology of love. But his insistent particularization of Laura's body also provided a model for a descriptive practice that privileged the parts over the whole and thus distorted them. In literary fragmentation, like medical dissection, a new textual body replaces the material body: just as dissection takes apart corporeal unity in order to make public a discovery, so too does poetry linguistically dismember the body, replacing the whole with the poetic production of a part.[18] Both anatomist and poet virtuosically display their artistic prowess in the production of printed texts that made a body part public. In Nancy Vickers's words, "it is in the masterful publishing of the secrets of the body by means of a masterful wielding of an instrument that the medical dissector's art meets that of the poet-rhetorician."[19]

In the manner of the blazon, Monteverdi's madrigal takes as its subject female song and the erotic ecstasy it produces. His piece reduces

---

[15] Roland Barthes, *S/Z*, trans. Richard Miller (New York: Hill and Wang, 1974), 108.

[16] Ibid., 109.

[17] For the definitive study of the Petrarchan blazon see Nancy Vickers, "Diana Described: Scattered Women and Scattered Rhyme," *Critical Inquiry* 8/2 (Winter 1981): 265–279.

[18] The argument here is derived from Nancy Vickers's essay "Members Only," in *The Body in Parts*, ed. David Hillman and Carla Mazzio (New York: Routledge, 1997), 3–23.

[19] Ibid., 7.

140

Angioletta to an erotically charged voice. But the madrigal performs this substitution of voice for singer more viscerally than a literary text. The act of singing intensifies what Barthes called the spitefulness of language, giving it a physical presence. The throat of the male singer is a much more potent instrument than the pen. Monteverdi and Guarini both turn the throat into a metonymic representation of the female singer herself. The poet depicts a flexible voice, and all of the actions done by the voice – pushing, suspending, freeing – are things that act on the throat. The composer sets these words to actions that highlight the work of the female singer by reproducing it with the parallel male body part. In performance, the represented female voice leaps from the page through a male voice.

The descriptive rhetoric of "Mentre vaga Angioletta," and particularly its focus on the throat, also relates to the more bawdy anatomical blazon – a genre that celebrates a specific body part through a catalogue of "evocative units." The poems appeared in multi-authored anthologies that consisted of musings on particular body parts. Most fashionable in France during the second half of the sixteenth century, these satirical poems written by poets like Clement Marot involved satirical pontifications on every part: nose, breast, finger, etc. The blazon of the nose, for instance, was addressed to "O noble nose, odorous organ."[20] With their catalogues, comparisons, metaphors, and figures of repetition, these poets did not aim to make wholes from collections of parts; rather they aimed for parts. Like the anatomical blazon, "Mentre vaga Angioletta" is one big metaphor, using a series of conventional poetic and musical gestures to put on display for public consumption the particularized female body.[21]

Such descriptive tactics permeated Renaissance culture where dialogues, treatises, and other pastimes like poetry and art reveled in ideal beauties but trafficked little in live women. For instance, taking Petrarch's lyrics as a starting point, a popular parlor game of the sixteenth century involved memorizing groups of Petrarchan lines that described a particular body part – eyes, mouth, breasts.[22] In addition, artists and philosophers published numerous tracts detailing the beauty of women by culling parts and features from the texts of famous authors and the bodies of notable ladies. Luigini da Udine's *Libro della bella donna*, printed in the 1540s, depicts a hunting trip in which four men

---

[20] J. N. Darles, "Blason du Nez," in *Les Blasons anatomiques du corps féminin* (Paris: Charles Langelier, 1543).

[21] Vickers, "Members Only," 7.

[22] For a description of these games see Naomi Yavneh, "The Ambiguity of Beauty in Tasso and Petrarch," in *Sexuality and Gender in Early Modern Europe*, ed. James Turner (Cambridge: Cambridge University Press, 1992), 137.

141

describe their beautiful ladies.[23] The signori create the perfect figure by citing a wide range of sources, from Italian vernacular poets to ancient mythology.

Firenzuola's *On the Beauty of Women*, the work to which I referred at the beginning of this chapter, makes a perfect woman from the parts of six different ladies, a process which renders her possible only in the creative imagination. In the course of the dialogue, the leading gentleman verbally takes apart his companions, dismembering them in order to assemble an ideal, but impossible, whole. During this process, he anatomizes the parts of a woman in general and focuses his descriptive energies on the parts of individual ladies. His end product then is made beautiful by its parts. Within the dialogue, Selvaggia possesses the ideal throat, and of her throat the character Celso says that, "We will then take hers, perhaps the most beautiful throat that I have ever seen, and we add it to our drawing and it will supplement with its presence what I have not been able to draw with the rough paintbrush of my words."[24] Her throat is fair and thin enough to show veins and muscles. "When it bends down it should make certain circular wrinkles around in the shape of a necklace. When it bends up it should stretch completely as if to imitate the sensuous little stock-dove with its neck tinged in gold and purple. One likes a throat with very delicate skin, slender, long rather than short. At its border with the bosom it should reveal a little declivity, all filled with snow."[25] This is precisely the part whose insides Monteverdi and Guarini describe in luscious detail. Celso here describes one body with enough detail that the body to which it is attached matters hardly at all.

Visual artists also tended toward fragmentation, finding little use for real female bodies. Rather than attempting to recreate an actual thing, Renaissance artists revealed an image filtered through ideal concepts of beauty, harmony, and divine proportions. Understood as a search for divine perfection, artistic productions of beautiful women did not reproduce living female subjects but rather invented perfect, but impossible, objects of visual fascination. Thus artists like Alberti and Raphael revered as a paragon the ancient painter Xeuxis, whose failure to find any single woman beautiful enough to serve as a model for a portrait of Helen led him to work from the composite parts of many models.[26] In his mid-fifteenth-century treatise *On Painting*, Alberti wrote of the ancient painter that "He chose, therefore, the five most beautiful young girls from the youth of that land in order to draw from them whatever

---

[23] Federico Luigini, *Il libro della bella donna* (Venice, 1554).

[24] Firenzuola, *On the Beauty of Women*, 60.   [25] Ibid.

[26] For more on the artistic ramifications of these idealized figures see Paolo Tinagli, *Women in Italian Renaissance Art* (Manchester: Manchester University Press, 1997), 2.

beauty is praised in a woman. He was a wise painter."[27] Later, in the sixteenth century, Raphael made reference to the same story, saying that in order to paint a beautiful woman he had to see many, then basing his painting on a "certain idea."[28] He too created an ideal female form that did not represent an individual woman.

"Mentre vaga Angioletta" presents the lady, in particular her sounds, as a series of effects and actions that make her less a real person than an idealized version of the female voice. She might be almost any early modern singer. A product of Guarini's poetic wit and Monteverdi's musical craft, her parts could come from any of the best singers from the turn of the seventeenth century. Both the poet and composer fabricate a lady's voice that does not necessarily connect to an individual body. Thus Angioletta's identity hardly matters at all.

Real singers

"Mentre vaga Angioletta" does of course contain traces of real singers, culled from the rich palate of singing virtuose. We know that both Monteverdi and Guarini were intimately involved with a number of singers and had plenty of experience working with and on singers. Monteverdi's wife and daughter sang, and he trained and maintained chapel singers at Venice and Mantua, while Guarini's wife Taddea and daughter Anna were both noted virtuose in the late sixteenth century. It is not surprising that, in addition to reflecting scientific and literary modes of description, their madrigal parallels conventional depictions of leading women singers of the day. The rhetoric they used to display Angioletta's traits, attributes, and effects matches the music written for, as well as the poetry and commentaries dedicated to, women who sang in Renaissance courts and on the Venetian operatic stage. Perhaps the most striking description with respect to Guarini's poem is Vincenzo Giustiniani's nostalgic recollection of the various consorts of female singers in the 1580s, in which he recounts a duel between the ladies of Ferrara and Mantua fought with voices – with timbre, runs, trills, and talent. Even his pacing seems to match Guarini's.

The ladies of Mantua and Ferrara were highly competent and vied with each other not only in regard to the timbre and training of their voices but also within the design of exquisite passages delivered as opportune points, but not in excess. Furthermore they moderated or increased their voices, loud or soft, heavy or light, according to the demands of the piece they were singing; now slow, breaking off with sometimes a gentle sigh, now singing long passages

---

[27] Leon Battista Alberti, *On Painting*, trans. J. R. Spencer (New Haven: Yale University Press, 1966), 93.

[28] Ibid., 43.

legato or detached, now groups, now leaps, now with long trills, now with short, and again with sweet running passages sung softly to which sometimes one heard an echo answer unexpectedly.[29]

Like Guarini, Giustiniani anatomizes the female voice for a reader, attempting to capture the sounds and the experience of listening to them on paper. His narrative description employs the same lyrical pace as that of the poet; listing actions of the throat using similar rhetorical patterns and emphasizing the same flexibility and variety of effects. Also important in this description is Giustiniani's insistence that the ladies did all of this "without excess." Virtuosic display had to remain within the limits of virtue.

In addition to its striking resonances with Giustiniani's description of the *concerto delle donne*, Monteverdi and Guarini's *vaga ragazza* closely resembles countless others. On the tomb of Caterina Martinelli, the Roman prodigy whom Duke Vincenzo Gonzaga brought to Mantua and for whom Monteverdi imagined the role of Arianna, the Duke of Mantua inscribed the following words:

Caterina Martinelli of Rome, who by the tunefulness and flexibility of her voice easily excelled the songs of the Sirens and the melody of the heavenly spheres, dear above all to Vincenzo, Serene Duke of Mantua for that famous excellence, the sweetness of her manner, her beauty, her grace, and charm, snatched away, alas by bitter death.[30]

Like Angioletta, Caterina is charming, tuneful, and flexible. And like Angioletta, her siren-like voice moves even the heavens. Using similar language almost one hundred years later, Giulio Strozzi praised the "felicitous passages," "lively trill," and "most perfect voice" of Anna Renzi, the singer most known to musicologists for her performance as Ottavia in the 1643 production of *L'incoronazione di Poppea*.[31] Recall that, when these commentators talk about flexibility or about the ability to make a trill, they refer explicitly to how singers use materials of the throat, materials that had direct associations with reproductive body parts.

By imbuing their Angioletta with charm and beauty, Monteverdi and Guarini placed her in the excellent company of familiar virtu- ose like Angela Zanibelli and Adriana Basile. In addition to sporting good voices, singers needed to possess the charm, beauty, and grace required of all court ladies. Whoever she might have been, Angioletta

---

[29] Vincenzo Giustiniani, *Discorso sopra la musica* (1562), trans. C. MacClintock (New York: American Institute of Musicology), 68. Also published in Solerti's *Le origini del melo- dramma* (Turin, 1903).

[30] As cited in Edmond Strainchamps, "The Life and Death of Caterina Martinelli: New Light on Monteverdi's L'Arianna," *Early Music History* 5 (1985): 170.

[31] Rosand, "The First Opera Diva," 5.

was certainly not the only singer aptly described as *vaga*. Zanibelli's patroness wrote to the Duke of Mantua: "I am sending this pretty singer of ours. I hope she will conduct herself well . . ." After describing the young lady's vocal talents, she added, "May it please God that her voice give satisfaction – her face at all events will be no liability."[32] Descriptions of Adriana Basile penned by poets and noblemen highlighted her beauty and charm, describing her blond hair, black eyes, charming form, beautiful hands, and lovely countenance.[33] Upon hearing Basile in Rome, Cardinal Gonzaga wrote to his father Vincenzo that "she is more beautiful than anything else."[34] The priest Gregory di Palio praised her "most exquisite diligence and honesty."[35] The Estean prince Giulio Felice described La Basile as possessing "charm, countenance, and voice."[36] Concluding a brief comparison of La Basile with her rivals Settima Cacti and Hippolita Marotta, Monteverdi applauded Adriana's vocal and other qualities. "At Mantua, I heard Signora Adriana sing, play, and speak extremely well. Even when she is silent and tunes up, she has qualities to be admired and worthily praised."[37] Monteverdi here seems to say that Adriana's appeal stretches beyond her musical ability.

And Adriana was by no means alone. By the end of the sixteenth century, trends in Italian court life made the female voice a hot commodity – both as a status symbol for reigning nobles and as currency for the advancement of the singer. Singing and singing women had long been a part of nearly every court activity. Actresses of the commedia dell'arte had regularly sung on the stage in the sixteenth century. In addition to the well-known Isabella and Virginia Andreini, almost all of the women of the Gelosi troupe were lauded for their fine voices. These women, defined as actresses, helped pave the way for the female court musicians in northern Italy.[38] The *concerti delle donne* of the 1580s

---

[32] Reiner, "La vag'Angioletta (and Others)," 37.

[33] Ademollo cites many such poems capturing her appearance: see A. Ademollo, *La bell'Adriana ed altre virtuose del suo tempo alla corte di Mantova* (Città di Castello: S. Lapi Tipografo, 1888), 122.

[34] Ibid.,122. "è più bella che altro."

[35] Ibid., 126. "Per quanto ho possuto raccorre con esquisitissime diligenze, onestà di vita . . ."

[36] Ibid., 128.   [37] Stevens, *Letters of Monteverdi*, 72.

[38] Ann MacNeil highlights the career of the exceptional sixteenth-century actress/singer Virginia Andreini and demonstrates previously unknown ways in which women participated in musical and theatrical life in the sixteenth century. *Music and Women of the Commedia dell'Arte in the Late Sixteenth Century* (NewYork: Oxford University Press, 2003). Nina Treadwell's dissertation provides a wonderfully complete look at singing women in sixteenth-century court cultures. Nina Treadwell, "Restaging the Sirens: Musical Women in the Performance of Sixteenth Century Italian Theater" (Ph.D. dissertation, University of Southern California, 2003).

differed from their predecessors in that they were hired – and imported often from other courts – as ladies in waiting for their beautiful voices.[39] Their voices were then further developed through extensive training and rehearsals. Installed in a court position, singers provided endless hours of amusement for the nobility, serving as one of many necessary ornaments for a court.[40] As Anthony Newcomb has discussed, the Florentine Ambassador Urbini's fascination with the Ferrara ladies suggests their intense novelty.[41]

As early as 1581, the Duke of Ferrara displayed his *concerto delle donne* for important visitors and took them on tour as a symbol of his court's greatness. His court composers wrote music that displayed his ladies' voices, and his coaches trained them in grueling rehearsals that pushed their voices past the technical pinnacles of the day and choreographed their movements, gestures, and even facial expressions. Apparently, the packaging worked well. In a letter written during the summer of 1583, Alessandro Lombardini described the visit of the Duc de Joyeuse to whom the three ladies "sang very nicely, alone, in duets, in trios all together; they sang Echo dialogues and many other beautiful and delicious madrigals."[42]

While women had sung in almost every facet of court life, the *musica segreta* marks the first institutionalized concerts that featured singing ladies, imbuing them with high cultural and leisure capital. Giustiniani writes of these Ferrarese events, "The Duke took the greatest delight in such music, especially in gathering many important gentlewomen and gentlemen to play and sing excellently. So great was their delight that they lingered sometimes for whole days in some little chambers they had ornately outfitted with pictures and tapestries for this sole purpose."[43] These were moments of double exposure, exposing the singers themselves and the duke's musical wealth. By the end of the sixteenth century, such concerts had spread beyond Ferrara, taking place regularly in Mantua and other courts. Monteverdi described Friday afternoon

---

[39] Men too served other functions: Giulio Cesare Brancaccio, the star bass singer at Ferrara in the 1580s and famous among musicologists for complaining about the attention given the ladies, was an impoverished noble whose protests at having to follow the Duke's orders bespeak a consciousness about his own servile position, but who also worked to show off his skill as a courtier and a soldier. Giulio Caccini, in addition to composing and singing, possessed gardening and penmanship talents. See Newcomb, *The Madrigal at Ferrara*, 185–186.

[40] See Anthony Newcomb, "Courtesans, Muses or Musicians? Professional Women Musicians in Sixteenth-Century Italy," in *Women Making Music: The Western Art Tradition 1150–1950*, ed. Jane Bowers and Judith Tick (Urbana and Chicago: University of Illinois Press, 1985), 90–115.

[41] Newcomb, *The Madrigal at Ferrara*, 22.   [42] As quoted in ibid., 25.

[43] Vincenzo Giustiniani, "Discorso sopra la musica de' suoi tempi." In *Le origini del melodramma*, ed. Angelo Solerti (Turin: Bocca, 1903) 105.

concerts in the hall of mirrors, giving equal attention to Adriana Basile's talents and to the impressive list of nobles in the audience.

> Every Friday evening music is performed in the Hall of Mirrors. Signora Adriana comes to sing in concert, and lends the music such power and so special a grace, bringing such delight to the senses, that the place becomes almost like a new theatre. And I think that the carnival of concerts will not end without His Highness the Duke (Vincenzo) having to post guards at the entrance for I swear to Your Eminence that in the audience this last Friday there were not only their Highnesses the Duke and Duchess, the Lady Isabella of San Martino, the Marquis and Marchioness of Solferino, ladies and knights from the entire court, but also more than a hundred other gentlemen from the city too.[44]

Monteverdi's comment suggests that the event displayed not only the singers, but also the watching nobility.

These concerts and other musical functions made singing a valuable enough commodity that a woman in possession of a good voice could do well at court largely because courts trafficked in singers, trading them with neighboring courts and farming them out to singing teachers in still other courts.[45] Singers could be placed in service if their families could not afford dowries. Annibale Guasco, for example, writes of sending his daughter to work for a princess out of necessity, because he could not afford a dowry, given the expense of placing two other daughters and some brothers.[46] The most successful singers were quite conscious of their need to keep the dukes pleased. Giustiniani writes that the ladies "made every effort to win fame and favor of the Princes, their patrons, who were their principal support."[47] In addition we know that courts paid their lady singers well. In 1620, when Monteverdi was negotiating with the Mantuans about possibly returning there from his position in Venice, he complained about earning less than singers and claimed that he asked "for even less than Adriana used to get, and perhaps Settima, but he asks only for what he gets now."[48] He also cited as one of his reasons for not returning to Mantua the problems of making music for

---

[44] Stevens, *The Letters of Monteverdi*, 75.

[45] For detailed discussions of the careers of Catarina Martinelli and Adriana Basile, see A. Ademollo, *La bell'Adriana ed altre virtuose*.

[46] Thanks to Suzanne Cusick for making me aware of this amazing document. Annibale Guasco, "Ragionamento a D. Lavinia sua figliuola della maniera del governarsi ella in corte; andando per Dama." Turin, 1586. Guasco wrote this letter to his daughter just before she left to serve as lady-in-waiting at the court of Catherine of Austria, who was newly married to Carl Emmanuele of Savoy. The is discussed at length in Stefano Lorenzetti, "'Quel celeste cantar che mi disface.' Immagini della donna ed educazione alla musica nell'ideale pedagogico del rinascimento italiano," *Studi musicali* 23 (1994): 241–261. It also figures prominently in Lorenzetti, *Musica e identità nobilare nell'Italia del Rinascimento: Educazione, mentalità, immaginario* (Florence: Leo S. Olschki, 2003).

[47] Giustiniani, "Discorso," 70.   [48] Stevens, *The Letters of Monteverdi*, 192.

a corrupt and fickle court in which the Duke valued all kinds of people, including lady singers, more than him and in which the treasure could "dry up on the death of a Duke or at his slightest ill humor."[49]

Many female singers rose fairly quickly up the court ladder. All three of the original singing ladies of Ferrara – daughters of minor nobility – advanced themselves by marrying courtiers.[50] This was due largely to the Duke's careful control over the marital status of his female singers. Laura Peverara married Count Annibale Turco, whom Duke Alfonso d'Este accepted as a gentleman of the court and to whom he gave the palace apartments of his late sister.[51] Of course not all the marriages ended happily. On a macabre note, Anna Guarini (daughter of the poet) ended up murdered by her jealous husband, with the assistance of her own brother. Such drama was not unusual in sixteenth-century court culture; under an elaborate system of patronage, ruling nobles could both protect and threaten their subjects.

Yet singing was often not the only skill that brought these women to court. Many were also employed in other aspects of court life. Thus, for instance, Angela Zafreti, brought to Mantua in 1607, also served as a weaver and embroideress. Adriana Basile was known for her quick wit in conversation and Laura Peverara of the *concerto delle donne* was also known for her beautiful body. The Florentine ambassador to Ferrara, Urbini, wrote, "He (Duke Alfonso) saw a young lady who was rather beautiful and, in addition, had the virtue of singing and playing excellently. He thereupon conceived the desire to have her in Ferrara and, upon his return here, he had the Duchess send to obtain her as one of her ladies in waiting."[52]

Guasco makes it clear that making music was only a very small part of what his daughter could do. Lavinia was expected to fulfill every wish of her padrona. Perhaps the most important part of her job involved maintaining proper comportment, of which singing of course must have gotten in the way. She was to stand perfectly still without fidgeting – an activity which would reveal an "unstable personality." And especially when in the presence of the Duke or other men, she was to keep "her head and eyes on her needlework." And of course the most important thing she had to do was guard her virginity, "There is nothing more worth saving than your soul, unless it be your reputation for chastity, for there is nothing more precious to a woman."[53]

---

[49] Ibid., 190.

[50] For a discussion of the possible social agency of these women see Suzanne Cusick, "Thinking from Women's Lives: Francesca Caccini after 1627," in *Rediscovering the Muses*, ed. Kimberly Marshall (Boston: Northeastern University Press, 1993), 206–227.

[51] Newcomb, *The Madrigal at Ferrara*, 188.   [52] See ibid., 11.

[53] Guasco, "Ragionamento," 10.

Ironically, the training necessary to perform as a musician often worked against the demure indifference required of court ladies.[54] Singers and their handlers had a variety of pragmatic and discursive means for confronting the impact of vocal activity on a woman's reputation. Giulio Caccini's daughters' performances were mostly restricted to music written by their father. During negotiations for her delivery to Mantua in 1610 Adriana Basile worried about the effects the move would have on her reputation. Once there, she carefully preserved her honor by refusing to sing on the public stage.

Given the negative connotations of overly cultivated skills in general, the erotic potential of singing in particular, and the precarious nature of any woman's chastity, it is not surprising that descriptions of singers, from the *concerto delle donne* through the earliest divas of the Venetian operatic stage, display an almost unseemly interest in the chastity of their subjects. In his aforementioned exuberant assessment of the court singers, Giustiniani makes it clear that the singers he described used only appropriate gestures and eschewed "awkward movements of the mouth or hands or body which might not express the feeling of the song."[55] His need to assert that the singers did not flaunt their bodies emerged from the focus on their bodies engendered by his discussions of their vocal attributes.[56]

Duke Vincenzo seems to have had a rather ecstatic enjoyment of the ladies even as he attempted to contain their bodies. By the middle of 1581 performances of the *concerto delle donne* occurred almost daily and were a source of intense pleasure. Urbini, the Florentine ambassador to Ferrara, reports with some bafflement that "The Duke is so inclined to and absorbed in this thing that he appears to have placed there not only all his delight but also the sum total of his attention. One can give him no greater pleasure than by appreciating and praising his ladies, who are constantly studying new inventions."[57] Perhaps in response to his own obsession with the ladies, Duke Vincenzo exercised his own control and protection most obviously in the aforementioned arranged marriage. By providing his singing ladies with carefully chosen, nobly born husbands, a dowry, and a place to live within the palace, he effectively contained their sexuality. At the same time their fringe benefits rendered their salaries almost irrelevant, thus assuaging the implications of singing for money. Moreover, the carefully prescribed or "secret" performance

---

[54] For a discussion of the problematic nature of female performers in England, see Linda Phyllis Austern, "Alluring the Auditorie to Effeminacie: Music and the Idea of the Feminine in Early Modern England," *Music and Letters* 74 (1993): 343–354.

[55] Giustiniani, "Discorso," 68.

[56] Anthony Newcomb also makes it clear that the members of the concerti were most likely ladies-in-waiting and not courtesans. See Newcomb, *The Madrigal at Ferrara*, 54.

[57] Ibid., 24.

situations mentioned earlier deliberately kept the ladies from the potentially lascivious act of performing in public. Guests usually included only members of the inner courts and visiting dignitaries, and performances were often held in the private chambers of the duchess.

Ideologies die hard. Thus the emergence in mid-seventeenth-century Venice of an institutionalized genre created a space for women to sing from the public stage, but they still had to contend with unwanted assaults on their chaste reputations. Thus, as with the *concerto delle donne*, commentators and advocates went to great lengths to verify the women's virtue, insisting that whatever unseemly behavior they enacted on the stage necessarily served verisimilitude. For instance, Giulio Strozzi describes Anna Renzi as "a sweet siren who gently ravishes the souls and pleases the eyes and ears of the listener."[58] But he carefully reminds readers of Renzi's taciturn nature and her skill at imitation – reminding them that she would not naturally have expressed herself so excessively and insisting that she always remained within the limits of decorum. Describing her natural verbal restraint he writes that she "is a woman of few words, but those are appropriate, sensible, and worthy for her beautiful sayings of the reward of praise."[59] Of her verisimilitude he writes, "Our signora Anna is endowed with such lifelike expression that her responses and speeches seem not memorized but born at the very moment. In sum, she transforms herself completely into the person she represents."[60] She can so accurately represent because she quietly observes what is around her: "helped by her sanguine temperament and bile, which fires her (without which men cannot undertake great things) [, she] shows the spirit and valor learned by studying and observing."[61]

Love songs

"Mentre vaga Angioletta" is just the kind of not-so-innocent description that got singing ladies in trouble. In addition to its focus on corporeal matters, accentuated by the title of Guarini's version, "Gorga di cantatrice," the piece addresses the transformative potential of song. When the lover's heart is transformed into a nightingale and then flees his body, he has reached a Neoplatonic consummation in which love leads to the annihilation of the self.[62] As I argued earlier, such a transformation did not lie far from erotic experience. The whole song turns singing into a sensual and sexual activity by making it into a commodity exchanged

[58] As quoted in Rosand, "The First Opera Diva,"4.
[59] Ibid., 5.   [60] Ibid., 5.   [61] Ibid.
[62] One might also argue that he has been subtly feminized given Ovid's story of Procne and Philomela in which the latter turns into a nightingale.

by lovers. Renaissance thinkers imagined love as an exchange of spirit or seed. In this madrigal the poet makes voice the commodity: the lovers merge through singing a virtuosic duet. The intercourse of the voices captures the sexualized interaction between the lover and his love object. The speaker here has become the bird of "O come sei gentile," the very thing he covets. The piece begins with a soft slow reciting tone on A that moves to D when the words discuss the poet's heart. The music speeds up as the speaker's heart races, the vocal escalation reflecting erotic excitement. Monteverdi chose not to embellish the word "canore," which would have been conventional, but instead composed the only melismatic passage on the word "core" in the opening section, immediately making a connection between song and self. When the heart assumes a musical spirit on the words "musico spirto," the instrumental accompaniment finally comes in and fills up the sonorous space of the madrigal. This change in mood is accentuated by a move to a G minor tonality (Example 4.1).

The recitative texture ends abruptly at the word "garula," with an ornamental flourish that is emphasized by the entrance of the second tenor in parallel thirds. The second tenor enters as the poet's voice takes on the musical spirit and moves with the throat of the singer, mingling both throats and singing. As music increasingly overwhelms language in the work of description, the shared vocal range of the singers presses lover and love object together, which makes distinguishing them increasingly difficult. The admirer has literally turned into the singer by putting his voice in her mouth. The fragmentation of the midsection culminates in a lyrical climax that musically enacts the transformation of lover and love object into one another – of lover into nightingale and of body into soul. At the same time, the focus on individual physical attributes leade up to an eruptive event recalling "Sì ch'io vorei morire," which, as discussed in the last chapter, portrays the details of an erotic encounter leading up to a final consummation.

The shared transformative power of love and song appears most potent when the music shifts to a triple-meter aria, an easy emblematic representation of song, beginning with the poet's "così cantando e ricantando il core" (singing again and again my heart). This is the first real melody we have heard. At this moment, the madrigal – which has sounded almost like a catalogue of ornamentation until this point – loses its virtuosic edge. The striking absence of the fragmented virtuosic music emphasizes its previous prevalence. Within this concluding aria, during which the fragmented sounds of the piece's vocal catalogue become part of a whole, the parts are no longer the point. Meaning takes precedence over the disjointed passaggi that have preoccupied the piece. One might argue that this push toward coherence is mirrored in tonal movements as the piece moves to A in the first "così cantando" and

Example 4.1, "Mentre vaga Angioletta"

D in the second, finally ending on a plagal cadence that seems to highlight the mystery insinuated in the piece's slow introduction. Monteverdi emphasizes the "miracol d'amore" with a rising melodic sequence that leads to the highest pitch in the piece (Example 4.2). Thus while resolving the fragmentation of voice the music still insists on its status as a miracle and a wonder of nature.[63]

Virtuosity does not disappear in this section, but it is absorbed into a larger structure. Monteverdi reserves virtuosic gestures for the last line of the poem, when by the experience of listening the poet is transformed into a nightingale and then takes flight, leaving the body – at least temporarily – in the manner of Neoplatonic consummation. Virtuosic gestures now emphasize the words "spiega" and "volo" as fast

---

[63] Monteverdi creates a similar juxtaposition between description and unifying devices in "Zefiro torna," though in this case singing seems to liberate the poet from his torment.

Example 4.2, "Mentre vaga Angioletta"

triplet rhythms erupt out of the melodic passages. Singing becomes the vehicle of transformation, the erotic materials of exchange.

Throughout "Mentre vaga Angioletta" the charming girl's song courses through the singer's throat, mingling with the spirit as it "forms and molds" her lover's spirit into a matching song. This reflects the Renaissance understanding of the sensuality of song, in which both love and singing move the soul and alter the body's precarious humoral balance. Such concepts also permeate lyrical and prose writings, implicating the act of singing as essentially sensuous. For instance, in a letter to Monteverdi praising the composer's virtues, Grillo innocently, or not so innocently, describes Adriana Basile as moving the hearts and souls of her listeners. He writes: "She wins our hearts with her sweet enchantment; we are carried to Heaven although our bodies remain on earth."[64] In effect, the listeners undergo a transformation like that of love or sex, through which they reach some kind of divine fulfillment. Grillo goes on to say that, "While the beautiful Angioletta delights all sensitive spirits with her singing, my heart hastens to listen, and remains there

---

[64] A. Grillo, *Delle lettere*, vol. II (1616), 137–138, quoted in part in Neri, "Gabriello Chiabrera e la corte di Mantova," *Giornale storico della letteratura italiana* 7 (1886), 337. It is translated in Einstein, "Abbot Angelo Grillo's Letters as Source Material for Music History," in *Essays on Music* (New York: Norton, 1956) 176–177, though my translation is a bit different.

magically entranced by the sound of her sweet song."[65] In contrast, when depictions of male singers drew on Neoplatonic rhetorics they tended to highlight harmonies of the spheres, as in the description of Francesco Rasi, who played Orpheus in the first production of *L'Orfeo*, "who to the harp made the woods echo with celestial harmony."[66]

These descriptions could also imply something very libidinous. For instance, Ercole Bottrigari's description of what one hears when a group of nuns sing together touches on the many, and sometimes conflicting, tropes for representing the female voice in late Renaissance Italy and echoes Monteverdi and Guarini's portrayal of their "vaga ragazza."

How you would melt away when you see them convene and play together with as much beauty and grace and such quietness. You would certainly think you were either dreaming or seeing one of those imagined incantations of the Sorceress Alcina or perhaps one of these German dolls which by means of tempered steel springs move along the table playing instruments which have been made by their ingenious fabrication.[67]

The singer is a sorceress; she is a trained machine; she brings the listener to another state of consciousness; she entices the listener and herself to submit completely to the ecstasy of the moment. And of course this is what makes her so very threatening. Her image then meshes with the conventions established within lyric poetry and letters to mobilize a rhetoric of sorcery, magic, and seduction (and their angelic analogues) against female singers.

Descriptions of singers associated them with muses and other liminal figures who straddled the borders of the natural, uncivilized world, blurring the lines between art and nature, between the real and the imaginary. Tipping his hat to Tasso's Armida who seduced innocent Christian soldiers with her voice, the Abbot Angelo Grillo described Adriana Basile as "a siren alluring and enticing but in a marvelous way a Neapolitan Armida."[68] And dozens of poems referred to her as a "beautiful and charming siren."[69] Grillo's language of magic and love resonates with writings in praise of singers that infuse the female voice with a sexual and magical power.

Armida, Adriana, and other singing enchantresses – both real and fictional – recall the mythological sirens; half bird and half woman,

---

[65] As cited in Denis Stevens, "Madrigali Guerrieri et Amorosi," 253.

[66] Warren Kirkendale, *The Court Musicians in Florence During the Principate of the Medici* (Florence: Leo S. Olschki Editore, 1993,) 573.

[67] Ercole Bottrigari, *Il Desiderio* (Venice: Amadino, 1594). Translation based on Ercole Bottrigari, *Il Desiderio*, trans. C. MacClintock (New York: American Institute of Musicology, 1962), 58.

[68] Ademollo, *La bell'Adriana*, 126. "ma peraltro una sirena allettatrice e lusinghiera, a meraviglia, un'Armida napoletana."

[69] See for example ibid., 108.

their irresistible chants offering erotic pleasure that bewitched mortal men and forever detached them from reason.[70] Sirens could kill with their voices, devouring the hearts of all those who came in contact with them. In *Gerusalemme Liberata*, Tasso insistently associates Armida with erotic pleasures and dangers. Armida embodies the dangers of song as she employs magic, charms, and spells. Moreover, her sirens lull Rinaldo to sleep.[71] Like this fictional siren, it was believed that female singers could ensnare men with their voices, inspiring the Neoplatonic love–death connection.

The poem's concluding image of a singing nightingale alludes to the very popular image of tame nightingales, at once constrained and empowered by song, and follows a tradition that linked female song to bird song. Detailing the process of bringing Adriana Basile to Mantua in the early seventeenth century, one of the counts wrote of trying to obtain "uno de questi uccelletti" (one of these little birds) and finding in Adriana a "cardellino" (gold finch). In a vituperative critique of overly-ornamented singing, Zacconi wrote of the female singers in question: "These render such pleasure and delight that we seem to hear just so many trained birds, who with their singing steal our hearts and leave us well contented with their song."[72] This association was not just an Italian phenomenon – in the French chanson, early modern understandings of birds as essentially libidinous and unrestrained by courtly love positioned the songbird as a metaphor for sexual discourse itself and for carnal pleasure.[73] The idea of virtuosity as the art of imitating sounds from nature continues through the Baroque period and as far as the nineteenth century. For instance, despite Paganini's amazing feats of "pure virtuosity," in some ways he was most acclaimed for his uncanny imitations of farmyard animals, chickens and donkeys.

The conflation of the ravishing female voice and equally ravishing bird song situated both forces in the natural untamed world, a space ripe for colonization by some rational force. Early modern cosmologies imagined that birds, like sirens and muses, wielded a natural song that always already existed in the world – a richly sensuous, primordial, and enchanting sound that if left uncontrolled could ravish the spirits of those who heard it. The pervasiveness of aviary and magical language

---

[70] For more on sirens, see Meri Lao, *Sirens: Symbols of Seduction* (Rochester: Park Street Press, 1998). See also Austern, "Nature, Culture, Myth and Musician in Early Modern England."

[71] Melinda J. Gough, "Tasso's Enchantress, Tasso's Captive Women," *Renaissance Quarterly* 54 (2): 523–552.

[72] Carol MacClintock, *Readings in the History of Performance* (Bloomington: Indiana University Press, 1979), 69.

[73] Kate van Ordern, "Sexual Discourse in the Parisian Chanson: A Libidinous Aviary," *Journal of the American Musicological Society* 48, no. 1 (1995): 1–42.

circumscribed the female voice in the primal, uncontrolled world of nature in which birds, sirens, shamans, muses, and nymphs by virtue of their voices exist somewhere between the real and the unreal, savagery and civilization.[74] Many compositions used melismatic luxury – the most labor-intensive brand of singing – to equate bird songs with the voices of women. This convention carries a disconcerting disjuncture between a poetic fascination with the natural passion of the female voice and a technical mastery that, as I argued earlier, was anything but natural.

Both Monteverdi and Guarini used these metaphors of birds, sorcery, transformation, and love in works other than "Mentre vaga Angioletta." But again, most of these works featured female singers and thus embodied rather than described their effects. For instance, in the fourth book of madrigals Monteverdi set two of Guarini's texts on singing: "Io mi son giovinetta" and "Quel augellin che canta." Both pieces resemble the canzone style associated with the Ferrarese *concerto delle donne* and Monteverdi's second book of madrigals, as well as with the kind of woman to whom Monteverdi and Guarini paid homage in "Mentre vaga Angioletta." "Io mi son giovinetta" laughs and sings in the spring season.

"Io mi son giovinetta E rido e canto alla stagion novella"	"I am a young woman And I laugh and sing in the new season"

Cantava la mia dolce pastorella
  quando subitamente
a quel canto il cor mio
cantò, quasi augellin vago e ridente
	Thus sang my sweet shepherdess
	  when suddenly
	in response to that song
	my heart sang like a charming and happy bird:

All participants here sing with the florid gestures that were hallmarks of the *concerto delle donne*. Love for the lady and ravishment by her voice transforms the speaker into a singing bird, filling him with birdlike utterances as he too begins to sing of the coming of spring. Like Angioletta's admirer, his heart takes on the sounds of his lover. Both pieces conflate singing with burning desire and the transformation of song with that of love. In the first madrigal, the lady "rido e canto alla stagion novella" (laughs and sings in the new season). In the second madrigal, the little bird sings sweetly and merrily in tones that, were they human, would say "Ardo d'amore, ardo d'amore" (I burn with love, I burn with love). Bird song stands in for human song, which in turn marks a site of burning and, of course, frustrated desire. As in most polyphonic madrigals, the distinction between the narrative and

---

[74] Austern, "Nature, Culture, Myth and Musician in Early Modern England."

diagetic voice remains fuzzy, enhancing the sung embodiment of lovers transformed into one another and in turn into singing birds.

Reflecting similar connections between song and love, "O come sei gentile," which I discussed in detail in chapter 1, features the virtuosic soprano voices that "Mentre vaga Angioletta" attempts to capture. The poem compares singing to the inescapable prison of love where the singing lover is captured like the singing bird: "io prigion, tu prigion." Both the lover and the bird sing for the love object who bound them, but, as the poet tells the bird, "vivi cantando, ed io cantando moro" (singing you live, but I, singing, die). For these words, Monteverdi composed one of his most luxurious soprano duets ever. As love transforms lover and beloved into the same sonorous fabric, the two sopranos increasingly sound almost indistinguishable.

Conclusion: echoing Orfeo

Most vocal works that display a virtuosity like that of "Mentre vaga Angioletta" were written for soprano voices. But its flashy male voices certainly do not stand as entirely unique. The continuo madrigal, which Monteverdi published well into the Venetian phase of his career, gestures back toward the Mantuan *L'Orfeo*; its vocal style and the position of virtuosity parallel Orpheus's most famous aria, "Possente spirto," and the duet between Orpheus and Apollo with which the drama concludes. Orpheus's songs, like "Mentre vaga Angioletta," describe the effects of the female body – this time not just the voice, but the whole silent female body. They also use virtuosity as a means of expressing desire, confirming once again the inextricable intertwining of song, carnal, and spiritual love. And once again song serves as a vehicle for expounding on the effects of, and responses to, the female body.

"Possente spirto," Orfeo's famous attempt to convince Charon to let him enter Hades, foregrounds virtuosity.[75] In this striking aria, Orpheus musters up all of his musico-rhetorical prowess in order to woo all who hear his powerful plaints. Monteverdi puts in Orpheus's mouth the tricks of a well-trained seventeenth-century virtuoso, the same he used to create his Angioletta. Euridice is the vehicle for his expression. Like "Mentre vaga Angioletta," "Possente spirto" involves an escalation of virtuosity as Orpheus's pleas get more and more ornamented up until the fourth strophe.[76] Even the instrumental accompaniment in this piece

---

[75] "Possente spirto" has been widely analyzed in the Monteverdi literature. The two accounts most influential for me are Gary Tomlinson, *Monteverdi and the End of the Renaissance* (Berkeley: University of California Press, 1987) and Eric T. Chafe, *Monteverdi's Tonal Language* (New York: Schirmer Books, 1992).

[76] Monteverdi wrote two versions of this piece – one ornamented and one not.

157

calls attention to the virtuosic potential of music as the instruments – a pair of violins, followed by a pair of cornetti, and finally a double harp – match the voice passaggio for passaggio. But then, as in "Mentre vaga Angioletta," virtuosity climaxes in an arioso-like segment. As Orpheus's thoughts turn to Euridice, and indeed toward a perfect Neoplatonic consummation through meaningful glances – "o de le luci mie, luci serene..." (O clear eyes, the light of my own eyes...) – the music recedes to an only slightly ornamented line. As in "Mentre vaga Angioletta," one might argue that the arioso style serves as an emblem of love. Virtuosity cannot adequately render love.[77] Charon refuses to let Orpheus pass and the singer abandoning virtuosity and song hurls his final plea in an emotional recitative.

Like "Mentre vaga Angioletta," this moment contains no real women – Euridice hardly sings at all throughout the drama. She is his silent muse, his absent "Angioletta." Monteverdi and Striggio's final version left out the Ovidian ending to the drama with its aggressive women, the dancing bacchantes drowning out Orpheus's sounds as they tear him to shreds. Instead Apollo, the sun god and father of Orpheus, leads his son to the heavens where he forever imagines Euridice's likeness in the sun, clouds, and stars. The dearth of women reflects the drama's general lack of female presence. Even Euridice, La Messaggera, and La Musica were likely played by castrati – not exactly real women.[78]

But female absence inspires Orpheus's expression, even if it fails to do its job of persuasion. His miraculous music moves everyone who hears it – just not quite in the right way. Charon falls asleep, Proserpina feels such empathetic "pietà" that she pleads on his behalf, and Pluto's thoughts wander to his own beautiful wife. Perhaps here Monteverdi means to say that not even Orpheus can really control the force of song. As the chorus tells us, "Pietade oggi e amore / trionfa ne l'inferno" (Compassion and love have triumphed in the infernal realms today). Music's victory does not end here. Instead, it once again triumphs and replaces love as Orpheus and Apollo join in a virtuosic duet almost as ornamented as "Possente spirto," rising with song toward the sky. If, as La Musica's prologue would lead us to believe, the primary message of *L'Orfeo* is the power of music and that Euridice exists merely as a vehicle for the expression of that message, then one might make the same case for "Mentre vaga Angioletta." For song, and not virtuosity, captures the

[77] The 1589 *intermedi* to *La Pellegrina* contain a strophic variation aria that very closely resembles "Possente spirto" and also seems to argue for the miraculous power of music.
[78] Susan McClary also makes a gendered analysis of "Possente spirto" though her interpretation is different. She reads the piece as an out of control, and thus feminizing, expression. See Susan McClary, "Constructions of Gender in Monteverdi's Dramatic Music," in *Feminine Endings: Music, Gender, and Sexuality* (Minneapolis: University of Minnesota Press, 1991), 35–53.

poet's love for his lady, at once unifying the fragments that came before and foregrounding just how fragmented they once were.

Orpheus and his virtuosic escapade reveal some important differences between male and female singers and the imagined effects of their songs. Put another way, Orpheus wields as much power as the women I have discussed in these pages but his power carries different strengths. While Monteverdi and Guarini's Angioletta sings for singing's sake, Orpheus does so with the specific persuasive intention of convincing Charon to ferry him across the Styx. His ornamentation thus escapes the realm of the feminized overzealous. Monteverdi and Striggio embraced the idea of Orphic power captured in Giuseppe Orologgi's annotations of Giovanni Andrea dell'Anguillara's Italian edition of *Metamorphoses*. His description of Orpheus's rhetoric matches the language used by the Florentine humanists to describe music written in the recitative style.

The Story of Orpheus shows us how much strength and vigour eloquence can have, like her who is the daughter of Apollo who is none other than Wisdom. The lyre given to Orpheus by Mercury is the art of speaking properly which like the lyre moves the affections with sounds, now high now low, of the voice of the delivery so that the woods and the forests are moved by the pleasure that they derive from hearing the well-ordered and clear speech of a wise man.[79]

Orologgi infuses Orpheus's song with a masculine energy that opposes the potential dangers of female song as described by the commentators, poets, and observers quoted in this chapter. He exudes strength, speaks properly, and moves the affections. The pleasures of his voice come from the "well ordered and clear speech of a wise man." He is neither a bird nor an Armida-like siren whose ornamentation threatens at any moment to exceed decorum. And he is certainly not lascivious.

Guarini's treatment of male virtuosity in his poem "Il basso del Brancaccio" dedicated to Giulio Cesare Brancaccio, an off-and-on male member of the Ferrarese *musica segreta* between 1577 and 1583, further highlights differences between the reception of male and female voices. Eschewing the rhetorics of magic, sorcery, and love that he used to emblazon his Angioletta, Guarini instead focuses on the singer's physical power.

Quando i più gravi accenti	When the deepest sounds
da le vitali sue canore tombe	from the living somber depths of his voice
con dilettoso orror Cesare scioglie,	Cesare loosens with pleasant horror
par che intorno rimbombe	it appears that everywhere

[79] F. W. Sternfeld, "The Orpheus Myth and the Libretto of Orfeo in Claudio Monteverdi's *Orfeo*," in John Whenham, *Claudio Monteverdi, Orfeo* (Cambridge: Cambridge University Press, 1986), 22.

l'aria e la terra. E chi n'udisse	the air and earth thunder,
il tuono	and those who hear their rumble
senza veder chi'l move e chi l'accoglie,	without knowing who causes and harbors it
diria: "Forse il gran mondo	might say "Perhaps it is the great world
è che mugge con arte? e dal profondo	that bellows with such art? and does such a musical sound
spira musico suono?"	breathe from deep within it?"
O crederia che l'ampio ciel cantasse,	Or perhaps they might think that it is the endless heavens that sing
se l'ampio ciel con melodia tonasse.	were the endless heavens to thunder with such a melody.[80]

Brancaccio makes the earth rumble. Rather than leading listeners to a celestial love-induced transformation, the heavens vibrate with his melody.

The power of song became ambivalent when wielded by women. The erotic inflection, technical mastery, and ability of the female voice to move the human spirit made women who sang far more arresting than the average Renaissance love object. That they wielded such a powerful force also inspired patriarchal discomfort and control. Such control took the form of virginity tests, idealized descriptions, and behavioral mandates. But it also worked at the level of discourse as we have seen in the analyzing and dismembering rhetoric of "Mentre vaga Angioletta." Put another way, this piece's musical and poetic analysis was both a celebration of its subject and an attempt to gain rhetorical control over an enigmatic and potentially unruly force. By using male voices to capture the effects of the female voice, Monteverdi and Guarini can be said to reassert control over women who learned to manipulate their own voices and, by extension, their bodies. This musical and poetic dissection represents discursively the domination of the female throat inherent in the intense vocal training endured by singers. Thus, the untamed sounds of the female voice reached the state of articulate language only when controlled by a masculine rational function. The most powerful protection against the musical and erotic threat of the female voice in "Mentre vaga Angioletta" was to exclude actual women from the space of description and celebration.

[80] Battista Guarini, *Opera*, ed. Marziano Guglielminetti, 2nd edn. (Turin: Unione tipografico-editrice torinese, 1971), 301.

5

Angry ladies: changing experiences of sensations

In the spring of 2000, I asked a group of undergraduate music majors to write about Monteverdi's *L'Arianna* as if they had attended the 1608 wedding festivities. They chronicled dissonances crashing through their ears and boiling blood rushing through their bodies. Thanks to Suzanne Cusick's article, "'There was not one lady who failed to shed a tear,'" the students all described a flood of tears at Ariadne's memorable sighs.[1] Though their pseudo-seventeenth-century accounts sounded authentic, not one of them actually cried or took ill. Bred in a world of punk sounds, the Walkman, telephones, and car alarms, these students listened with millennial ears conditioned by sounds that did not exist in the seventeenth century. Rather than implying some callousness on the part of my students, this Collingwood-esque fantasy reminds us to think about sound and sensation as culturally contingent experiences.[2]

This chapter considers four of Monteverdi's angry ladies – Ariadne, Armida, Clorinda, and the unnamed subject of "Eccomi pronta ai baci" – as momentary embodiments of the seventeenth century's slowly shifting soundscapes. They provide points of access to what I will call Monteverdi's experimental efforts and have important implications for the experience of sensation and the meanings attached to women's voices and women's singing at the end of the Renaissance. Within larger questions of musical sensibility, the representation of female rage makes a particularly effective investigative space because it elicited from Monteverdi distinct musical vocabularies and theoretical justifications.

The primary musical comparison in this chapter distinguishes the technologies of anger in the laments of Ariadne and "Eccomi pronta ai baci." Virginia Ramponi's 1608 performance of Ariadne's ire at

---

[1] Suzanne Cusick, "'There was not one lady who failed to shed a tear': Arianna's Lament and the Construction of Modern Womanhood," *Early Music* 22(1994): 21–45.

[2] I refer here to R. G. Collingwood's idea of history as a matter of getting into the head of historical subjects. R. G. Collingwood, *An Essay on Philosophical Method* (Oxford: Clarendon Press, 1933).

Theseus for abandoning her on an island after a night of honor-stealing lovemaking was a corporeal event defined by the *physical movement* of air. Her embodiment of anger enacted a particular kind of disturbance in the air between one person's mouth and another person's ear. Performed only five years after the publication of the fourth book of madrigals, it emerges from the same expressive world as the madrigals discussed in chapter 3, "Sì ch'io vorei morire" and "Cor mio, mentre vi miro." In contrast, the anger of Ergasto's lady portrayed in "Eccomi pronta ai baci" exists as an explicitly musical gesture. In this piece, published in 1619, two tenors and a bass envoice Ergasto's lady as she reacts to an unwelcome love bite by singing harmonic and rhythmic patterns that *represent* anger. Ariadne reflects a world where passions act on the body like winds and rains on the world, while Ergasto's lady lives in a space more like ours in which emotions comprise physiological events that arise from some external or internal stimulus. To make more lucid the distinction between these two pieces, I will also discuss angry ladies that Monteverdi drew from Torquato Tasso's *Gerusalemme Liberata*. Armida's polyphonic lament from the 1592 third book of madrigals, "Vattene, pur crudel," features a middle section in which five voices project rage with an emotional intensity that parallels Ariadne's lament.[3] Monteverdi returned to Tasso's epic for the text of *Combattimento di Tancredi e Clorinda*, a piece that was first performed during the 1624 Venetian Carnival season and published in the 1638 *Madrigali guerrieri e amorosi* (Book 8).

The treatment of Monteverdi's music in this chapter necessarily engages the work of scholars who have already used the composer's prolific musical compositions and theoretical writings to place him at the intersection of distinct moments in early modern music making – one Renaissance and one decidedly more modern. Musicologists have rightly situated Monteverdi's involvement with nascent solo-voiced genres, public opera, and basso continuo at the forefront of change in musical fashion and in the development of new techniques. Interpreting these novelties in a broader light, some scholars more recently have drawn on the work of Michel Foucault to explain the composer's conflicting styles as a shift from a musical lexicon based on a ubiquitous sequence of resemblances to one grounded in autonomous musical gestures that construct a sonic world of arbitrary connections.[4] Adding gender and body to this discussion suggests a movement toward music

---

[3] These pieces appeared just a decade before the Monteverdi/Artusi debate that ultimately spawned a statement of purpose for the *seconda pratica*.

[4] See especially Gary Tomlinson, "Music and the Claims of Text: Monteverdi, Rinuccini and Marino," *Critical Inquiry* 8 (1981–82), 565–589; *Music in Renaissance Magic: Toward a Historiography of Others* (Chicago: University of Chicago Press, 1993); and *Monteverdi and the End of the Renaissance* (Berkeley: University of California Press, 1987). Tim Carter

making that was severed from the body and thus a less threatening force more acceptable for women.

To broaden even further the context for turn-of-the-seventeenth-century shifts in musical practice, the musical gestures discussed in the early descriptive portion of this chapter can be read as a series of experiments with sound. Such a reading suggests an intimate connection between this new style, which has been described as objective or mimetic, and attempts by natural philosophers to study, control, and contain nature.[5] The development of codified musical styles that depended on instrumental mediation reflects efforts to manipulate nature through instruments, experiments, and collections – efforts alluded to in my earlier discussion of dissection. The taking of natural objects out of their contexts by museums and experimentalists had musical analogues in conventions such as the *stile concitato*, which severed sound from what it represented.

By calling attention to the conceptual similarities between musical thought and natural philosophy, I follow a long line of scholars who have been fascinated by their concordances. In 1964, Stillman Drake responded to Claude Palisca's claim that scientific discovery had nudged along aesthetic tastes by positing music as the original impetus for experimental physics.[6] As both men noted, the astronomical discovery that the universe lacked any essential harmony rendered implausible the notion of music as a microcosm of the universe. At the same time, studies of the dynamics of vibration and sound displaced the theory of number symbolism as the root cause of music's effect on the senses and the mind. I would add that the decay of conceptions of the body as a vessel dedicated to maintaining the appropriate balance of humors and temperament – systems equally affected by events outside and inside the body – undermined notions of song as a material force that kept the body in motion.

To build on, and complicate, the work of Palisca and Drake, I draw on more recent work of historians of science who have embraced the convergences and non-convergences between practice and theory and

worked with Tomlinson's ideas in "Resemblance and Representation: Towards a New Aesthetic in the Music of Monteverdi," in *Con che soavità: Studies in Italian Opera, Song and Dance, 1580–1740*, ed. Iain Fenlon and Tim Carter (Oxford: Clarendon Press, 1995), 118–135. See also Eric T. Chafe, *Monteverdi's Tonal Language* (New York: Schirmer Books, 1992).

[5] For an elaboration on the objective and mimetic style see Tomlinson, *Monteverdi and the End of the Renaissance*.

[6] Claude Palisca, *Studies in the History of Italian Music and Music Theory* (Oxford: Clarendon Press, 1994), and Stillman Drake, "Music and Philosophy in Early Modern Science," in *Music and Science in the Age of Galileo*, ed. Victor Coelho (Dordrecht: Kluwer Academic, 1992).

who highlight the blurring of boundaries between emergent practices and their residual contexts. This provides the groundwork for a reading of Monteverdi's various stylistic innovations as experiments with sound. These changed the soundscape and in turn helped to propel new theories of the mechanisms by which human beings absorb sensation and by which song does its work on listening and singing bodies.

Such soundscapes, combined with other expansions of sensory experiences, also led to new theories of sensation that would eventually be most famously articulated by René Descartes. My suggestion here upends traditional causal arguments about the relationship between shifts in music and epistemology at the turn of the seventeenth century. Such arguments have tended to interpret writings like Mattheson's on the musical representation of affections as reactions to Descartes's enumeration of the passions. In contrast, my contentions suggest that practice preceded theory, and that Descartes's ideas synthesized reactions by the broader community of natural philosophers to changes in sensory experience that emerged from new mechanisms for looking, listening, feeling, and understanding. This does not mean that Monteverdi reacted to Descartes or necessarily had any awareness of Descartes's ideas. Nor does it imply a chronological process in which Monteverdi's later music reflected new scientific ideas. Instead, the sounds of Armida, Ariadne, Clorinda, and Ergasto's lady – and of course countless other represented women – changed the soundscape in ways that led to a reconfiguration of the world, which would eventually be characterized by Descartes as mechanized.

Excursus: the gender problem

This chapter may seem to take a strangely ungendered turn. Rather than eschewing the question of women, it explores the crucial supplementary realm of the sensual in order to provide a larger context for the work done in earlier chapters. Situating the expressive modes discussed in previous chapters on a continuum between emergent and residual understandings of sound and the sonic transmission of passions gestures toward the metaphysics that worked in tandem with the physicality emphasized in this project. It purposefully implies that a book about gender must also be a book about the subject and that a book about the body cannot ignore the metaphysical realms that surround it. The chapter unpacks the suggestion made earlier that Monteverdi worked at a moment of profound shifts and that his music thus reflects the unsettled atmosphere of transition. The discussions that follow broaden my suggestion in chapter 1 that the instrumental writing of "Chiome d'oro" reflected a mechanization of the voice by detailing the emergence of a mechanical understanding of the human body. The descriptive violence of "Mentre vaga Angioletta" that I related to dissection and the blazon in chapter 4 also reflects the desire on the part of natural philosophers to codify and thus colonize nature. And finally "Eccomi pronta ai baci, "discussed in chapter 3 as a playfully erotic contrast to the threatening sexuality of polyphonic enumerations of physical pleasure, is here reconceived as a distinction between enacted intercourse and observed erotic theatre. Such theatre was produced by a new emphasis on the creation of fictional spaces that remained safely isolated from observing audiences. These new spaces help explain why madrigals now trafficked in a playful eroticism that exceeded the spiritual disembodied love of Neoplatonic fame. This does not mean that epistemological shifts resulted in new strategies for representing women and understanding their voices. Rather, it suggests that, like the conceptions of sensation that are the main focus of this chapter, deployments of women's voices moved in tandem and sometimes even preceded important changes in structures of knowledge.

This chapter locates the philosophical divide in the emergence of ideas that would eventually be capstoned by Descartes. Descartes himself was curiously and coolly silent on the issue of gender and women. He is most famous for driving a wedge between mind and body and for suggesting that all "mankind" had access to reason. At the same time, his anatomical discussions simply ignored the concept of temperament, locating sexual difference entirely in sexual organs. Rather than being cosmological opposites, men and women were different kinds of machines. This idea might seem liberating to women because it released their minds from their bodies, the primary locus of sexual difference and hierarchy. If there is mediation between mind and body then the problems with the female body no longer imply moral problems with her soul. But as Genevieve Lloyd has argued, given the existing associations of women with matter and men with reason, Descartes's separation of mental and physical efforts and effects reified existing gender hierarchies by making the unmarked male the guardians of rational thought and relegating the body to the province of women.[7] Despite the appearance of gender neutrality, when "man" separated himself from nature he also divorced himself from woman.

The distancing of song from the body that I will argue moved concurrently with these epistemological shifts might have allowed women to escape the open secret of the court for the public venue of the operatic stage. To be sure, women who performed in public still faced unpleasant scrutiny but they were probably spared the virginity tests that Catarina Martinelli had to endure. The location of women's power in their performance, virtuosity, and acting ability implied, and perhaps

---

[7] Genevieve Lloyd, *The Man of Reason: "Male" and "Female" in Western Philosophy* (Minneapolis: University of Minnesota Press, 1994) 38–50.

even helped, to prompt a loss of the inextricable connection between song and spirit. And when temperament lost currency, singing women stopped threatening gender hierarchies by heating themselves up to the range of male bodies. They no longer wielded inherently threatening and excessive bodies or existed within temperately precarious gender hierarchies. The taking on of roles removed the problems generated for female performers by taking on the physical experience of the sensations depicted in the music. Characters and representations were emblems of women's voices, not stagings of their bodies and souls. And the stage was a contained and fictional space which might not invade the very pores of the audiences who now clapped at the end of a performance but did not cry or feel their blood boil. They watched stories but did not experience them in the manner of the ladies at the 1608 festivities.

At the same time the tendency toward mechanization created a new kind of male control. If the body was a machine and if women were still associated with the body then they were in effect machines or wind-up toys operated by the invisible hand of the male composer. The invisible hand here is Descartes's unmarked male, a rational being who colonizes nature; women's voices and bodies. Perhaps musically this is enacted and instigated most clearly in the harmonic patterns underpinned by the continuo. In them instruments and constructed musical gestures that contain the solo female voice by inserting a musical space between her and her listeners, making women's voices of the real and imagined varieties subject to the descriptive power of men. This effect is highlighted in "Eccomi pronta ai baci,'" which has no women. Male voices present a fictional woman. Similarly the playful eroticism of this piece suggests the replacement of naturalized motions by mechanical interactions. Pieces could talk directly about physical touching and body parts because those parts remained radically distinct from what happened on the inside.

Bitten and abandoned ladies

The laments of the abandoned Ariadne and Armida capture in sound the pathos of women stung by love and hurled into tempests of passions. Embodiments of the female excess I discussed earlier in the book, their rage provides musical access to what the experience of those passions might have been at the turn of the seventeenth century. It is not by coincidence that the earliest examples are laments; laments as a genre exist within a long tradition that did, and does, provide a space for extreme musical passion. The trope of the angry abandoned woman permeates musical literature, from ancient Greek tragedy through opera and more recently, the blues, torch songs, and countless popular ballads.

166

In the laments of Ariadne and Armida, passions exceeded in importance the characters themselves. In the manner that Nietzsche attributed to all lyric poetry, the expression of a pathos exists independently of a single speaking I.[8] Both pieces are emblematic of *stile rappresentativo*, an expressive ideal that endeavored to embody through singing the vibrancy of a character's inner passions and affective reactions. Composers working in monody and polyphony set texts in ways that conveyed vibrant emotions from desperation to joy.[9] As I have argued in previous chapters, in terms of the body and sensation, sung performance at the end of the Italian Renaissance could mimic and incite humoral activity, propelling in listeners and performers interior sensations that induced a series of physiological and psychological processes. Thus, the laments of Ariadne and Armida could move the audience to tears because collisions between the physical properties of air from the singer's voice and the listener's ear caused palpable reactions. This collision when instigated by women was particularly dangerous.

Since its first performance *L'Arianna* has attracted all kinds of accolades. As early as 1633, Monteverdi himself identified Ariadne as his most perfect realization of the affective powers of music. In the twentieth century, countless scholars pored over the extant lament, most rightly calling attention to the famous repetition of the "Lasciatemi morire" motive and to its derivative motive attached to Ariadne's frequent cries of "O Teseo." My interest lies in assessing the means by which the gestures most famous for communicating the lady's passions would have worked within a late Renaissance horizon of experience. If my question in earlier discussions of this piece was what do all of the tears shed at the first performance tell us about woman's bodies, here my interest lies in what those tears tell us about the experience of sensation. I thus revisit the lament with a focus on the climax of the abandoned heroine's anger, which occurs in the fourth section. At this point, Ariadne already has dramatically expressed love, grief, and hopelessness, crying out for Theseus to turn back and rescue her from languishing with the wild beasts. She has accused him of giving her misery instead of the gold and jewels he once promised. She has just cried out, "O Teseo, o Teseo mio, Lascierai tu morire" (Ah Theseus, my Theseus, will you leave me here to die?). In the fourth stanza she seems finally to realize that her lover will never return.

---

[8] Friedrich Nietzsche, *The Birth of Tragedy*, trans. Shaun Whiteside (New York: Penguin Books, 1993), 29.

[9] Nino Pirrotta has discussed this style at length. See "Monteverdi's Poetic Choices," in *Music and Culture in Italy from the Middle Ages to the Baroque* (Cambridge, MA: Harvard University Press, 1984), 280.

Ahi che non pur rispondi!	Alas, he still answers me not!
Ahi che più d'aspe è sordo a' miei lamenti!	Ah, he is more deaf than a serpent to my lament!
O nembi, o turbi, o venti,	O thunder clouds, O whirlwinds, O tempests
Sommergetelo voi dentr'a quell'onde!	Drown him beneath those waves!
Correte, orche e balene,	Hurry, sea-monsters and whales,
E de le membra immonde	And fill your bottomless depths
Empiete le voragini profonde,	With his foul limbs.
Che parlo, ahi!, che vaneggio?	What am I saying? Ah, what is this raving?
Misera, ohimè! che chieggio?	Alas! O miserable me, what am I asking?
O Teseo, O Teseo mio,	O Theseus, my Theseus,
Non son, non son quell'io	It was not I, no not I,
Non son quell'io che i feri detti sciolse:	Not I who spoke such savage words;
Parlò l'affanno mio, parlò il dolore;	my woes spoke, my anguish spoke;
Parlò la lingua sì, ma non già 'l core.	My tongue spoke, yes, but not indeed my heart.

Monteverdi captures the anger and remorse of Rinuccini's rhetoric with a gut-wrenching fluency that powerfully employs rhythm and pitch to project outward Ariadne's inner turmoil. The rhythm of her speech becomes highly irregular and her musical syntax moves seamlessly from an agitated expression of anger to large leaps and struck dissonances as she temporarily harnesses the power of her wrath. The section begins with rhythmic uncertainty as Ariadne realizes that Theseus does not hear her sobs. Her cries of "Ahi" in lines 1 and 2 stop the flow of musical speech as the singer gasps for breath (Example 5.1, mm. 76–77). Ariadne's speech stops, her heart stops, her body stops moving in anguish. Meanwhile a focus on harmony would point out the jarring tritone leap from A to D♯ in the bass and the abrupt shift to a G major area as in anger, she calls upon clouds, winds, and gales to destroy her former lover, sending him to the realm of the sea monsters. More interesting from my perspective is the increased speed of her pulse. Monteverdi composed for Ariadne a series of falling thirds reminiscent of the Theseus motive that she now uses to implore nature to destroy her former lover.

In this passage of rage, rhythm and pitch matter most because they are most capable of mimicking the body's motions. The fast repeated-note declamation resembles the *stile concitato*, which will be discussed later. The rhythmic speed reflects the heightened pulse of anger. Meanwhile the pitches themselves rise and fall with each curse, from B, to D, to C, and back to E. The shift to a G sonority harmonically enhances the

Example 5.1, *Lamento d' Arianna*, mm. 76–88

shift in mood to a higher pitch of anger. The increasingly high-pitched notes move toward a range that at once constrains the singer's throat and powerfully assaults the ear of the listener – her voice is literally rising in the manner of a temper tantrum. (Example 5.1) At the end of her curse Ariadne orders the heavens to send Theseus to the "voragini profonde," the bottomless depths. Monteverdi emphasizes her growing anger by setting these words with the highest pitch in the phrase and highlighting that sound by halting the quick rhythmic declension. This goes against the madrigalian word-painting convention that would have set the bottom of the sea with the lowest pitch possible; emotional peaks trump stylized conventions.

Immediately after this outburst Ariadne checks herself and reins in her anger on the words "che parlo." Again the falling third harkens back towards Theseus. Harmonically, Monteverdi marks this self-doubt with a pause and an abrupt shift to a Bb harmony that contrasts with the B cadence of the first phrase and sets up an opposition between durus and mollis. But more importantly for my purposes, the rhythm slows, reflecting her slowing pulse. Again she sighs. The rest, followed by a sigh figure on a falling major sixth, emphasizes first the cessation of her passion and again the utter despair of her body as its inner motion stops and as her now sluggish humors droop (Example 5.1, mm. 82–85). Exhausted from rage, her speech returns to the halting pace of the section's beginning, rising to an E and then falling back to the D of "Teseo." The pitch falls into a spoken range as she brings her body back under control. And then finally she remembers Theseus with the familiar "O Teseo" motive. The section ends with a rather stunning, if not somewhat depressing, moment in which Ariadne declares that she did not speak these words; her tongue and her anguish spoke but not her heart. Her body and not her soul did the damage. But even in this passage Ariadne cannot totally banish her anger: the *stile concitato*-like passages return for the articulation of the words "tongue" and "words," still escaping from her body even as she apologizes for them.[10] In this passage harmonic and motivic devices exist but only to enhance the musical passions not as the primary mode of conveying Ariadne's anger.

Armida speaks the same language as Ariadne, but she does so polyphonically, which reasserts the point that the shifts in the sensory experience of music I am talking about did not result from a change in fashion from polyphonic to monodic music. For his polyphonic settings of Tasso, Monteverdi chose emotional vignettes that stop the drama in its tracks. At the point where Monteverdi's three-part setting of her lament from the third book of madrigals picks up Tasso's story, Armida has seduced and been abandoned by Rinaldo. Throughout the epic Armida is presented as a lascivious, demonic, and aggressive sorceress who ensnares Christian warriors with her magic. Like Theseus, Rinaldo chose honor and duty over love and, like Ariadne, the sorceress laments her fate in a dizzying emotional trajectory of fury, vengeance, and resolve.

In this piece, music, speech, and passion become one so that the experience they embody supersedes even the subject herself. Envoiced through multiple bodies, this piece seems more about expressing an affective trajectory than about representing a character.[11] The opening "Vattene pur crudel" (Go, you cruel man) marks her wrath, projecting and inciting movements of the spirit, channeling its invisible psychological and physical motions. It begins with a repeated-note declamation that moves to a large leap of a minor sixth on "Crudel"(Example 5.2).

---

[10] I will leave alone the interesting motivic relationships between this passage and the "Lasciatemi morire" motive. Eric Chafe and Suzanne Cusick have discussed them extensively. See Chafe, *Monteverdi's Tonal Language* and Cusick, "There was not one lady."

[11] This discussion is influenced by Gary Tomlinson's discussions of Monteverdi in *Music and Renaissance Magic*. See especially pp. 239–245.

Example 5.2, "Vattene pur crudel"

Prima parte

This leap, an enraged cry, is an angry version of Ariadne's famous cry. Instead of using an affective dissonance Monteverdi relies on a melodic leap that emphasizes the physical qualities of the word, as if anger has literally heightened her speech. The leap also releases the agitation of the repeated notes. Utterly caught up in rage, Armida has forgotten to breathe, and the singers, embodying this in their performance, must then release their breath. The solo soprano voice stands out in the polyphonic madrigal and the repetition in the soprano and then quinto part give the cry an incessant quality – she will not give up. An analysis focusing on harmony would suggest that Armida's initial cry is excessive and irrational in its utter lack of defining mode or key. Harmonically we could be anywhere. Next, Armida threatens the furies:

Me tosto ignudo spirt' ombra seguace Indivisibilmente a tergo havarai.	Soon my naked ghost will stalk threatening your every step
Nova furia, co' serpi e con la face.	Like a new fury, with snakes and burning torches.
Tanto t'agiterò quanto t'amai.	I shall torment you as much as I once loved you.

Monteverdi highlights Armida's tenacity by setting in all four voices the repeated-note exclamation of "Indivisibilmente" and "nova furia." Setting her words of fury in all four voices intensifies her rage. She expresses a painful combination of love and hate on the line "Tanto t'agiterò quanto t'amai" (Example 5.3, mm. 30–40). The rhythmically agitated, repeated-note enunciation of "Tanto t'agiterò" captures the quickened pulse of her anger followed by the collapse and exhaustion it incurs. This leads into the slowed and drawn out melodic descent of "quanto t'amai." The radical difference between the two halves of this poetic line reflects the inner dissonances of her hate and love, the

171

Example 5.3, "Vattene pur crudel"

tenderness that lies beneath her rage. The rhythms capture the rhythm of her soul in what sounds like a stylized version of the music of the pulse described in chapter 1 in which song could work directly with the body's rhythm. Here, musical pacing mimics Armida's emotional motions.

Like Ariadne, Armida cannot sustain her anger; it ultimately leads to defeat and physical collapse, which the narrator describes and embodies in a slow chromatic descent that begins at the second half of the *ottava* (Example 5.4, mm. 25–37).

Example 5.4, "Vattene pur crudel"

Hor qui mancò lo spirto a la dolente,

né quest'ultimo suono espresse intero;

e cadde tramortita e si diffuse
di gelato sudore, e i lumi chiuse.

At this point breath failed the grieving maiden

and she did not utter completely these last sounds

and fell in a faint and, covered with cold sweat, closed her eyes.

Armida cannot utter her last words, and the bottom three voices drop
out as the upper two parts begin a long-drawn-out, twenty-one-bar
chromatic descent. Gone are the repeated exclamations that have sustained her speech; unable to produce words, she communicates only in
a dramatic collapse. The reduced air being moved by the singers mimics
the reduced air of her failing breath. The chromatic descent marks the
descent of her spirits. Slowed musical pacing captures the slowing of
her pulse, which accompanies the movement from anger to exhaustion.

"Eccomi pronta ai baci" comes from a different expressive world.
It traffics in a more mediated expression of anger beginning from the
very mechanism of its presentation. In contrast to projecting the fluid
emotions of Ariadne and Armida, this piece shows a specific response
to a particular action by staging a scene in which the lady allows Ergasto
a kiss, if he promises not to bite. Predictably, he bites. The bite leaves
a scar. She yells. Rather then embodying inner physical processes, the
piece demonstrates one emotional response – anger – to one action – the
bite.

Eccomi pronta ai baci;	Here I am, ready for kissing;
baciami, Ergasto mio, ma bacia in guisa	kiss me, my Ergasto, but kiss so that
che coi denti mordaci	your biting teeth
nota no resti nel mio volto incisa,	leave no sign etched upon my face
perch'altri non m'additi, in essa poi	whence others might point at me and in these
legga le mie vergogne e i baci tuoi.	read my shame and your kisses.
Ahi! tu mordi e non baci!	Ah! You're biting, not kissing!
Tu mi segnasti ahi!	You've scarred me, alas, alas!
Possa io morir, se più ti bacio mai!	I'll die before I'll kiss you more!

The two tenors and bass accentuate the main dramatic action – the
bite – with a pause followed by a shift in texture from a solo tenor
line to excited imitative polyphony that pits the upper voice against the
lower two (Example 5.5). Monteverdi set the lady's cry with an imitative
passage that moves by fifths and that does so very quickly in comparison to the slow tonal motion of the rest of the piece. In this passage,
the music's organizational features trump the natural expressiveness
of the gesture. Without the irregular speech-like inflections of Ariadne's
lament, the quickened angry speech that collapses into sighs in the sonic
shape of an actual woman's passion, this moment lacks both the naturalness of her anger and the verisimilitude of opera. And the emotions
themselves never spin into the realm of excess that characterizes the
lamenting women. Even the final dogmatic "ahi" seems more invested
in a cadence than an inner sigh. A long-drawn-out cadence, it concludes
on A the sequence that seemed to be leading toward D. This is followed immediately by another long sequence based on circle-of-fifth

Example 5.5, "Eccomi pronta ai baci"

progressions. Monteverdi fashioned the emotion of Ergasto's date in harmonic and rhythmic patterns that represent anger. The particular disturbances of air that enacted Ariadne's distress produced unheard clashes of air, in addition to the heard ones. Her anger was a *physical* event while the anger of Ergasto's lady was a *musical* event.

Perhaps the most striking difference between Ariadne, Armida, and the lady of "Eccomi pronta ai baci" lies in the motion of their emotions. The earlier ladies moved irregularly between fluid states of feeling. This bitten woman responds with a single contained emotion – anger – that masks the complex sensations of a "real" person. Her emotional responses lack the excessive and explosive emotional shifts of Ariadne and Armida. Musically, the discrete sections of "Eccomi pronta ai baci," marked by emphatic cadences at the end of each poetic line, give it a fragmented feel. The first line of text is set with one line of music

that ends on an emphatic V-to-I D major cadence. Meanwhile, dissonances, sequences, and tonal shifts mark textual changes. The independent musical logic of these gestures supersedes their incumbent sensual
effects. This tendency toward representing discrete and acted-out emotional states and actions pervades Monteverdi's music and his letters
from the 1620s, especially the correspondence with Alessandro Striggio around the composition of *La finta pazza Licori*. To explain Licori's
feigned madness as a musical imitation of specific words and actions
rather than a complex psychological state, he writes "When she [Licori]
speaks of war, she will have to imitate war, and when of peace, peace,
when of death, death, and so forth."[12] Like Licori, the anger of the lady
in "Eccomi pronta ai baci" is acted out by singers who represent her
specific emotional state.

Monteverdi took this predilection for creating distinct and contrasting emotional states to new heights in the famous rapid-fire sixteenth
notes of the *stile concitato* and its showpiece, the *Combattimento di
Tancredi e Clorinda* – a piece which presents a series of contrasts and
quick changes in mood through shifts in instrumentation and style. This
musico-poetics of opposites plays out tonally in modal contrasts that pit
the combat between Tancredi and Clorinda and the *concitato* passages
in G major against the *cantus mollis* G minor of lyrical and passionate moments. During the narrator's description of the battles between
Clorinda and Tancredi, musical instruments sonically represent their
anger and vexation.[13] Each of the warriors grasps a sharp sword, and
poised for battle,

E vansi incontro a passi tardi e lenti   And they come towards each other
                                            with slow and lingering steps
quai due tori gelosi e d'ira ardenti.   like two bulls, jealous and inflamed
                                            by wrath.

As the narrator speaks about the "flaming" anger of Tancredi and
Clorinda, the string of passages of sixteenth-note crescendos represent
their emotional state. Unlike Ariadne's melodically escalating anger or
Armida's rhythmic rage, this does not resemble the sounds a real person would make. This representation stands disembodied from the passionate subjects, neither emanating from the voice nor marking bodily motions. While expressive devices in earlier madrigal settings were
held together as much by homology between sound and body as by
musical structure, these later musical gestures existed as autonomous

---

[12] Denis Stevens, *The Letters of Claudio Monteverdi* (Cambridge: Cambridge University
Press, 1980), 315.

[13] For more on Monteverdi's use of the warlike style see Robert R. Holzer, "'Ma invan la
tento et impossibili parmi,' or How 'guerrieri' are Monteverdi's madrigali guerrieri,"
in *The Sense of Marino*, ed. Francesco Guardiani (New York: Legas, 1994).

gestures, which helped to create a fictional, non-verisimiliar universe. At the same time the musical gestures that represented emotional responses served to contain those emotions, making them far less threatening than the unbridled passion of a lamenting woman. Within the fictional universe one woman's voice is thoroughly ventriloquized into gestures that become emblems of a woman's metaphoric voice. Real women are replaced by abstract representations of female forms which, as in "Mentre vaga Angioletta," completely erase the female voice.

A space of their own – or not

"Eccomi pronta ai baci" and the *Combattimento* create fictional arenas that contrast markedly to the live pulsating spaces inhabited by Ariadne and Armida. In both pieces, the mimetic gestures, scenic tableaux, and presence of a narrating voice bifurcate the world of the performance and the audience, placing the listener outside the action. A miniature dramatic scene, "Eccomi pronta ai baci" features a fictional character and the illusion of events that occurred in a specific time and location, which an autonomous subject can observe from a safe distance. To relate it back to the discussion of erotics and desire in earlier chapters, it is a scene of observed eroticism as opposed to an instance of enacted sex such as "Sì ch'io vorei morire." Listeners must accept the probability of the scene on its own theatrical terms as they hear three male singers play one woman in a depiction of an imagined unity, a fictional world marked as different from the world they inhabit.[14] In this non-verisimilar universe an individual woman's voice is ventriloquized into gestures that become components or emblems of a female voice. This representation of a discrete subject works differently than Armida's polyphonic lament in which five voices embody generalized passions. Here, song participates in the creation of a discrete fictional universe. Rather than moving between the mouth of the singer and the ear of the listener, altering the bodies and spirits of both, it imposes a space between the individual and the cosmos, between the material body and immaterial soul.[15]

[14] My thinking on this has been influenced by Catherine Belsey, *The Subject of Tragedy: Identity and Difference in Renaissance Drama* (New York: Routledge, 1993).

[15] By making so much of the scenery, I do not mean to suggest that scenic theatre was a new invention. Clearly, countless sixteenth-century productions made use of elaborate stage sets. Instead, in the *Combattimento* the effects of scenery that attempted to look "real," combined with a testifying narrator, creates an overall effect of distance that was likely not present in earlier productions. Early productions trafficked in a performative magic of marvelous stage sets, which was not much troubled by modern questions of verisimilitude. The willing suspension of disbelief separating audience and stage was not yet in place.

Framed by costumes, staging, and the commentaries of the narrator, the *Combattimento* creates an even more detached space in which characters possess individual monodic voices, wear military armor for costumes, and act. Tancredi even rides a live horse. In Monteverdi's words, "since this was intended to be performed with dramatic action," the characters should dress in armor, ride horses, and enact "passi et gesti" (paces and gestures) ordered by the text. He writes that together the instrumentalists and singers create "a unified representation."[16] In this complete and closed-off scene, gestures strengthen the impact of the words, confirming their reality within the illusory world of the theatre. "The paces and gestures are to be performed in the manner expressed in the text, neither more nor less, the actors carefully observing the tempi, strokes, and movements from place to place." By Monteverdi's account, at least, the staging worked well. The "polished production" performed at Carnival in 1624, he writes, was a novel success: "it was a genre of vocal music never before seen or heard."[17]

In addition, the *Combattimento* is dominated by a mediating and omniscient narrator, named *testo* in the score, who speaks far more than either of the protagonists, instructing the characters and the audience what to feel and do. Commanding and dictating a sequence of actions, this *testo* remains, except in rare moments of empathy, outside the drama, testifying about a series of events that occurred previously in some fictional universe. His monodic and declamatory voice remains largely severed from Tancredi and Clorinda, and the sonorous world they inhabit. Monteverdi made this point himself, instructing the narrator to "be some distance away from the instruments, so that the text may be better understood."[18] Not about generalized emotion or pathos, the comprehension of a specific scene demands a context. To provide background information on the characters, the narrator informs the listener that Tancredi believes Clorinda to be a man. Later, passing judgment on the actions, he berates Tancredi for the pride he takes in wounding his enemy. "Misero, di che godi! O quanto mesti/siano i trionfi ed infelice il vanto!" (Wretched man, what pleases you! Oh how sad will be your triumphs and unlucky your boast!). As part of an elaborate frame, the narrator's voice removes this story from the time and space of the viewing audience. By using the narrator as a mediating voice, Monteverdi eschews the speaking subject altogether and thus ensures that passions are produced by technologies of representation that remain apparent to the listener.

The audience of the *Combattimento* and the listener of "Eccomi pronta ai baci" respond to individuated characters. In terms of an incipient Cartesianism, impersonation renders Ergasto's lady and Clorinda

---

[16] Stevens, *The Letters of Claudio Monteverdi*, xvii.   [17] Ibid.   [18] Ibid.

reflections of seeing subjects who exist apart from an objectifiable world. For if, as Descartes would eventually say, bodies are discrete entities filled with animal spirits and individual souls, those bodies can also be filled with fictional souls. Impersonation might fill one body with one fictional voice, as the performer's body is temporarily inhabited by the soul and voice of a fictional character. In "Eccomi pronta ai baci," the lady comes to life through three male singing voices. The *Combattimento* presents a low voice singing the role of Tancredi and a high voice for Clorinda; Monteverdi's performance instructions for the *Combattimento* define the characters as entities entirely separate from one another. He writes that "Clorinda is to speak when it is her turn, the Narrator falling silent, likewise Tancredi."

In contrast to the separation of audience and character implied by the narrator of the *Combattimento*, Clorinda and the subject of "Eccomi pronta ai baci," both Ariadne and Armida speak directly to the audience and affect the audience's bodies. Ariadne obviously sings her own words. And even when Armida is spoken about her voice remains indistinguishable from the narrator. She speaks through the same performance forces as the voice that speaks about her, which precludes a distinction between dramatic and diagetic presentations. For instance, after Armida's collapse, the narrator describes her recovery: "Poi ch'ella in sè, tornò, deserto e muto/quanto mirar potè d'intorno scorse" (When she returned to herself, she found everything empty and silent), but the musical fabric does not change. In the text, the narrator continues to depict Armida until half-way through the *terza parte*, when she arises: "'Ito se n'è pur,' disse, 'e ha potuto/me qui lasciar de la mia vita in forse?'" Monteverdi uses texture to signal a shift in narrative mode. Just as Armida regains her voice, the musical phrase ends on a long C chord, over which the canto leaps an octave, declaiming a short phrase over the sustained C chord in the other four parts. The immediate imitation of the figure in the lower voices belies any temptation by modern listeners to ascribe a representational role to the canto.

To return to the later pieces, the aural creation of a fictional space and the segregation of spectator and stage created by dramatic madrigals relate to the project of monocular perspective, initiated by Alberti and Brunelleschi, in which attempts by painters to reproduce a faithful version of reality sever the viewer from a represented object and the objectified world. As Erwin Panofsky has argued, such perspective "creates distance between human beings and things, but then in turn it abolishes this distance by, in a sense, drawing this world of things, an autonomous world confronting the individual, into the eye."[19] The

---

[19] Erwin Panofsky, *Perspective as Symbolic Form*, ed. Christopher S. Wood (New York: Zone Books, 1997), 65.

distancing, even alienating, effects of these art forms participated in a process that Panofsky describes as the "objectification of the subjective" and the triumph of "the distancing and objectifying sense of the real."[20] Perspective depicts the world according to a rational and repeatable procedure that, for instance, does not depend on the uncontrollable pathos of one character. It also isolates the viewer from a re-presented world. Linear perspective allowed for the creation of a world that existed only in the imagination of the viewer and that implied a distance between viewer and object.

Like linear perspective, scenic theatre segregates the spectator and the stage. The increasing spatial, temporal, and ideological detachment of stage worlds from the real world opened up a rift that willing suspension of disbelief that filled the arts of representation were predicated on the audience accepting the probability of the production on its own theatrical terms. Perhaps this impulse led the anonymous author *of Il Corago* to postulate the principal task of the poet as inventing plots and characters whose believability, according to some system of probability, militates against the "unnaturalism" of the theatre.[21]

This reconfiguration of theoretical spaces had a material parallel in the intense proliferation of museums, laboratories, botanical gardens, and anatomy theatres. The desire to gaze at objects, to decontextualize them, fostered the building of structures designed specifically to impose this distance, which perforce promoted a demand to fill these spaces. Anatomical theatres put the once-living body on display and separated the anatomist from his students. And the museums that emerged in the late sixteenth century as a sacrosanct place for the examination and codification of nature inserted a space between object and observer – between humans and nature.[22] To extend this to the realm of gender if men were the unmarked subject and women were associated with nature then this reconfiguration also created a space for the emergence of a modern male subject who colonized the female object. Men could ventriloquize women because they were separate from them.

---

[20] Ibid., 67.

[21] *Il Corago* is an anonymous treatise written between 1628 and 1634 on how to be a *corago* (director). It depicts shifting theatrical tendencies in the early decades of the century. Paolo Fabbri and Angelo Pompilio, *Il Corago o vero alcune osservazioni per metter bene in scena la composizioni drammatiche* (Florence: Leo S. Olschki Editore, 1983). For a similar argument about *Il Corago*, see Lorenzo Bianconi, *Music in the Seventeenth Century*, trans. David Bryant (Cambridge: Cambridge University Press, 1987). Bianconi also provides a good introduction to the heated seventeenth-century debate about the necessity of a unity of time and space in opera libretti.

[22] Paula Findlen, *Possessing Nature: Museums, Collecting, and Scientific Culture in Early Modern Italy* (Berkeley: University of California Press, 1994).

Experiment

The wealth of new objects and knowledge garnered by new technologies like the telescope, new spaces for collection like the museum, and new places encountered by Europeans in their explorative voyages all slowly eroded conventions of natural philosophy that first emerged in the ancient world. The acquisition of things not described or understood by books, particularly in ancient sources, led to the gradual replacement of a culture of books with a culture of nature in which, as Francis Bacon asserted, truth lay in observation and nature and not in the authority of ancient texts. This quickly led to an emphasis on manipulating nature rather than observing it.

Though historians have tended to think of Baconian academies as the primary locus for the evolution of experiment as a formal structure, the Italian natural museums of the sixteenth and seventeenth centuries provided an arena for the acquisition of knowledge; they manipulated and codified nature through objectifying it as a phenomenon separate from the subjective observer.[23] This new emphasis on experience rendered sensory evidence crucial to obtaining knowledge. As Gabrielle Fallopius wrote to Alfonso d'Este of Ferrara in 1560, "One delights in practical natural philosophy, which one learns from ocular testimony."[24]

In 1603 the Roman Prince Federico Cesi founded the Accademia dei Lincei, named for the legend of the sharp-eyed lynx whom Pliny had described as "the most clear-sighted of the quadrupeds." This collective of naturalists, mathematicians, and virtuosi pitted themselves against text-bound scholars and set itself the task of redefining natural history. Though their origins lay in a firm dedication to scholastic forms of science that revealed the secrets of the universe, they soon became avid proponents of new empirical approaches practiced by their most infamous member, Galileo Galilei. They emphasized more and more the visual characteristics of the world. By finding truth in nature, and not in books, they contributed to the corrosion of textual authority. Fabbio Colonata, one of their founding members, wrote in 1618 that "therefore we hold that one ought to believe more in the observation of natural things than in imagined objects and suppositions derived from one sole observable principle without the means and end of the thing itself, from which one can construct a rule."[25] This impulse also stood behind the anatomical Renaissance discussed in the last chapter, with its emphasis on seeing the way the body worked instead of reading about it. Bodies were now atomized and made knowable by material specifics.

---

[23] For details about these institutions see ibid.
[24] As cited in ibid., 205.   [25] As cited in ibid., 207.

The new science carried with it a gendered language of discovery that implied a colonizing of interior spaces which, in the case of "Mentre vaga Angioletta," was the female voice.

Experiments were not yet understood in terms of the conventional scientific method that we know today, in which a specific outcome is generated by either doing or preventing an action. Instead, an *experimentum* in early seventeenth-century terms identified a loose set of practices deeply engaged with objects and directed towards an audience. Peter Dear explains such experiments as "a historical event in which an investigator experiences the behavior of a contrived setup, or apparatus, and uses or might use a report of that historical event as an element in constructing an argument intended to establish or promote a knowledge claim."[26] Various manipulations of nature used measurements and other technical methods to make sense of enigmas. To be sure, this was not entirely new. Even Aristotle had understood sensory experience as the primary mechanism for acquiring knowledge. But what experience meant changed dramatically in the early modern period. The scholastic notion of experience emphasized common knowledge while early modern philosophers defined it as the specific description and behavior of a natural phenomenon.

A number of musicians gave musical currency to the privileging of physical and sensory evidence – to seeing (or hearing) for oneself – perpetuated by Vesalius's anatomy project, natural museums, and scientific academies like the Cimenti in Florence and the Lincei in Rome. In music, as in natural philosophy, new spaces of production and new kinds of sounds led to practical and philosophical quandaries that would eventually erode existing structures of knowledge. Perhaps most crucially, sound, like natural objects, was understood as a force to be manipulated by instruments, observers, and thinkers. One might read musical practice from the turn of the seventeenth century as an experimental practice, an attempt to manipulate nature in the form of sound and the physiological effects of those sounds. The writings of Vincenzo Galilei in the 1580s and Monteverdi in the first and third decades of the seventeenth century position sound as an object for observation and manipulation and as a force separate from sonorous numbers and the cosmos those numbers embodied. Placing more value on evidence than textual truths, their writings suggest a conceptual shift that resonates with the movement in natural philosophy away from reliance upon ancient texts for truth and toward reliance upon experience.

---

[26] Peter Dear, "Narrative, Anecdotes, and Experiments: Turning Experience into Science in the Seventeenth Century," in *The Literary Structure of Scientific Argument: Historical Studies*, ed. P. Dear (Philadelphia, University of Pennsylvania Press), 138.

All four of the pieces discussed in this chapter emerged from that experimental process of creating new musical languages. Written between his vehement polemic with Artusi over the *seconda pratica* and the publication of the *Madrigali guerrieri et amorosi*, "Eccomi pronta ai baci" falls into a period during which Monteverdi worked with a variety of different ways of creating passions, musically codifying and representing nature, and, of course, for giving voice to female subjects. Beginning with his infamous dispute with the self-proclaimed guardian of tradition, Artusi, Monteverdi's musical practices and their accompanying theoretical justification posited music as the manipulation of sounds that the human ear could measure.

By the end of the sixteenth century, changes in musical practice had begun to erode reigning theories about music. The rise of instrumental music prompted debates on the proper tuning of pipes and strings, while vocal music that exceeded accepted diatonic, modal, and consonant sounds engendered discussions of the nature of consonance and dissonance. More specifically, vocal ornamentations, part-singing, and emphasis on text expression produced previously unorthodox dissonances, while the increased use of instruments rendered received notions of absolute tuning and acceptable sounds problematic. The gestures that irked Artusi in his dispute with Monteverdi and which later became conventions of the new musical language emerged in part from the improvised ornamentation of singers – accenti, rapid runs, appoggiaturas, and *rottare* (broken passages). At the same time, the advent of the basso continuo, in which a continuous harmonic bass freed the voice parts from having to provide continuity, made for quick contrasts that infringed on the musical consistency advocated by Zarlino and practiced by *prima pratica* composers like Palestrina. Now voice parts could isolate specific contrasts, allowing the musical mood to change suddenly without sacrificing flow. While progressive thinkers like Zacconi could endorse these new techniques because they promoted "cantar con grazia" (singing with grace), conservative writers like Artusi never forgave their transgression of Zarlino's rules.[27]

New vocal and instrumental styles challenged the Pythagorean predilection for acoustically pure intonation of octaves, fifths, and fourths derived from the sonorous numbers 1, 2, 3, and 4, which had allowed for only limited sounds and did not include the combinations found in polyphonic or multi-instrumental works. A mathematical theory of proportions, the Pythagorean approach defined consonance and dissonance according to numbers related as ratios. In its strictest usage, arithmetic theory was valorized above acoustic pleasure and

---

[27] Anthony Newcomb, *The Madrigal at Ferrara* (Princeton: Princeton University Press, 1980).

numbers determined acceptable sounds. This did not place undue limits on composition in ancient and medieval music, which was dominated by monodic and homophonic styles that remained confined to specific modes.

By the end of the Renaissance violations of the rules used for specific expressive purposes had become appealing. At the same time keyboard instruments, lutes, viols, and recorders rose in popularity. Unlike the human voice, their construction set limits on the notes they could produce. Enter more sophisticated temperaments, which violated Pythagorean rules; and thus ensued the tuning polemics that began in the late fifteenth century and were in full swing between the 1520s and 1640s. Zarlino, one of the more conservative participants, still believed that only numbers could justify sounds, and that since voices should govern instruments, any limitations this system placed on composition were fully justified. Zarlino modified the Pythagorean system in order to improve the intonation of the thirds and sixths that were so prevalent in the music of his days.

Zarlino's theories came under attack by many instrumentalists, including his student, the lute player Vincenzo Galilei, who advocated relying on the senses as opposed to abstract mathematical theories. Describing the primary rift between self-proclaimed conservative and progressive factions in music theory, Stillman Drake writes that, "In one corner stood the mathematical theory of antiquity, which took sonorous numbers as the cause of concord . . . In the other was the human ear, with that curious taste for pleasant sounds that goes along with – or at least once went along with – the composition and performance of music."[28] In his 1581 treatise proving correct the actions of practicing musicians, Galilei stated and explained the by then conventional departures from Zarlino's tuning system according to a theory that distinguished the corporeal (moving bodies) brand of sound from the incorporeal (innate numbers). "For what Zarlino says in chapter 15 of the first [book] of the *Istitutioni* maintaining that number is sonorous, cannot stand in any case, for not having in itself body – for sound is not produced without the percussion of some body capable of rendering a sound – a simple number consequently cannot be sonorous, just as time and a line which also lacks body are divisible."[29]

For Galileo Galilei, numbers do not possess sonorous properties in and of themselves, but rather exist in relation to some sonorous body. He explained sound as fundamentally a physical process that existed apart from any essential numerical qualities:

---

[28] Drake, "Music and Philosophy," 492.

[29] Claude V. Palisca, *The Florentine Camerata: Documentary Studies and Translations* (New Haven: Yale University Press, 1989), 83.

Sounds are created and are heard by us when – without any special "sonorous" or "transsonorous" property – a rapid tremor of the air, ruffled into very minute waves, moves certain cartilages of a truncation within our ear. External means capable of producing this ruffling of the air are very numerous, but for the most part they reduce to the trembling of some body which strikes upon the air and disturbs it; waves are thereby very rapidly propagated and from their frequency originates a high pitch, or from their rarity's deep sound.[30]

Sonority does not exist as a real quality that modifies the naturally silent essence of the bell; instead, it is the result of mechanical phenomena on the sense organs.[31]

Refusing to accept theories on faith, Vincenzo Galilei performed his own experiments to determine the true ratios of consonance. His experiments are important both because they proved that numbers did not cause sounds and because they suggested a use for numbers that related to the material world and related instruments of measurement. He proved that the standard Pythagorean numbers did not apply to suspended weights or the volumes of bells and organ pipes. More specifically, his experiments on the unison exemplify both his reliance on the senses and his commitment to properties other than those determined by sonorous numbers. He writes that "Therefore a unison is the sound of those strings between which the sense knows no difference of any kind either of quantity or quality." He goes on to demonstrate his use of the senses as a metric through an analogy to sight: "The same happens to the ear as happens to the sight when two lines are so close to being parallel that in the space of a hundred paces they depart only by a fourth of an arm's length. This difference divided by one hundred is so minimal that it would be undetectable to the sense nor would the sense discern it in the space of a single pace but in one hundred yards."[32] What matters is what the senses detect. Despite his nascent empiricism and lack of a traditional humanist education, Galilei still could not completely dispense with ancient authorities. He, like a number of thinkers interested in mechanics, grounded his studies in the ancient "engineer" Aristoxenus. Translated from the Greek in 1562, Aristoxenus had in his *Harmonika Stoicheia* insisted on the judgment of magnitudes of intervals by the ear and thinkers moving away from Platonic ideals of proportion found him invaluable.[33]

---

[30] Galileo Galilei, "The Assayer," in *The Controversy on the Comets of 1618* (Philadelphia: University of Pennsylvania Press, 1960), 311.

[31] Daniel Chua has also written about these issues in *Absolute Music and the Construction of Meaning* (Cambridge: Cambridge University Press, 1995), 17.

[32] Palisca, *The Florentine Camerata*, 205.

[33] Claude Palisca has shown that this treatise was well known by Vincenzo Galilei, Artusi, and Doni and that most late Renaissance theorists, with the exception of Zarlino, had

Like Vincenzo Galilei's tuning polemics, the Monteverdi/Artusi debate, which I discussed for its gendered implications in Chapter 2, can be read as a clash between a conservative reliance on ancient texts and a progressive devotion to sensory evidence. Performances during the late 1590s of Monteverdi's polyphonic madrigals "Cruda Amarilli, che col nome ancore" and "Anima mia, perdona" so inflamed the conservative Artusi that he wrote a treatise using these two pieces to lambast these "modern destroyers of the good established rules." Artusi saw these compositions as working against nature because they violated established rules passed down from the ancients. Published in 1600, Artusi's document beat the madrigals into print by five years and inaugurated a contentious exchange with Monteverdi and his brother Giulio Cesare. Artusi faulted the compositions for their use of unprepared dissonances between the bass and high voices, unorthodox modulations, accidentals, and irregular cadences – all of which ignored Zarlino's rules for dissonances. "I do not deny that discovering new things is not merely good but necessary. But pray tell me first why you wish to employ these dissonances as they employ them . . . why do you not use them in the ordinary way, conforming to reason?"[34] Artusi accepted new sounds, but only if they follow the rules. In this "ordinary way," dissonances had to move from one consonance to another without compromising the integrity of the mode. Under these strictures, accidentals and irregular cadences committed transgressions because they compromised modal structures.

In his second exchange with Monteverdi, Artusi took up the problem of temperament and of tuning, declaring that modern composers had gone from bad to worse. He took exception to Monteverdi's use of unorthodox intervals such as the diminished fourth, which resulted from a ratio totally outside Pythagorean doctrines, and faulted Monteverdi for producing so-called new intervals that were unsound: "They sometimes use intervals which they themselves do not know, and say that they are something new even though they are older than the cuckoo-bird, like the following, the first of which is not a sixth or a seventh but sounds good to their ears, which are purged."[35] The text

associated it with equal temperament. Claude Palisca, *Studies in the History of Italian Music and Music Theory* (Oxford: Clarendon Press, 1994), 188–199.

[34] Translations of Artusi taken from Paolo Fabbri, *Monteverdi*, trans. Tim Carter (Cambridge: Cambridge University Press, 1994), 35.

[35] "ci rapportano interualli tall'hora, che loro stessi non li conoscono, dicono però che sono cose noue, se ben sono più uechie, che il Cucco; come li seguenti, il primo de quali dicono che non è ne sesta, ne settima, ma che consona benissimo alle sue orecchie, che sono purgate." Giovanni Maria Artusi, "Considerationi musicali, del r.p.d. Gio Maria Artusi": in Seconda parte dell'Artusi overo Delle imperfettioni della moderna musica, nella quale si trattò de' molti abusi introdotti dai moderni scrittori, & compositori. Nuovamente stampata (Venice: Forni, 1968).

declares intervals improper based on their proportions that are "false for singing but good for playing on lutes." The voice, he argues, cannot negotiate unnatural intervals because it does not have "a preset stopping place like an artificial instrument."[36]

The Monteverdi brothers privileged practice over theory by putting empirical evidence and observation before myth and metaphysics. When they replaced Zarlino's rules with a new scheme, the "seconda pratica," founded on truths of reason and sensation, they implied a method but not a governing numerically based theory. Their thought process made room for the aural experience of listeners – practice, in other words, preceded theory.[37]

Despite never completing his promised *seconda pratica* treatise, Monteverdi did formalize a set of practices exhibited in the *Combattimento di Tancredi e Clorinda* and enumerated in the preface to the *Madrigali guerrieri et amorosi*. To be sure, this statement of purpose does not mark any new activity. It does, however, bespeak an important rhetorical shift that resonates with the modulation of experience into experiment effected by natural philosophers. An experiment at this time involved the use of experience and achieved currency through the status of its author. If, in the seventeenth century, as Peter Dear has argued, the account of an experiment comprised as important a part of its performance as the scientific activity itself, then Monteverdi's statements must be taken to heart for their form as much as their content.

Taking the reliance on sensory perception from the dispute with Artusi one step further, Monteverdi's preface to his *Madrigali guerrieri et amorosi* explicitly articulates a theory grounded in aural and experimental evidence."[38] The performative document most likely does not describe a process that actually occurred but can rather be read as a musician's attempt to use an empirical sensory method. Monteverdi's experimental document illustrates the relation of the new sciences to earlier Renaissance searches for the secrets of nature. In addition to promoting a specific method, his process involves a search for sounds in nature and for the codification of those sounds. This resonates with the attempts by natural philosophers like Girolamo Cardano, who, in his *De secretis* (On Secrets) first published in 1562, attempted to categorize and catalogue the various kinds of secrets. As a statement of a lexicon of musical

---

[36] Ibid.

[37] Palisca made a similar argument in *Studies in the History of Italian Music and Theory*.

[38] Nino Pirrotta described this document as "a theorization ex post facto for manners and movements that Monteverdi must have found spontaneously and madrigalistically." Nino Pirrotta, "Music and Cultural Tendencies in Fifteenth-Century Italy," in *Music and Culture in Italy from the Middle Ages to the Baroque* (Cambridge, MA: Harvard University Press, 1984), 312.

affect it follows the general trend towards cataloguing that I discussed in relation to "Mentre vaga Angioletta."

Rather than explaining isolated gestures or letting the music speak for itself in the manner of the Artusi controversy, Monteverdi's articulation of an intellectual process situates composition as an experimental activity in which he uses his own experience. He details his discovery of the musical representation of "contrary passions." The three primary affections, "anger, temperance, and humility," correspond to three vocal ranges – high, medium, and low – and three styles – *concitato* (agitated), *temperato* (temperate), and *molle* (languid). The *concitato* or *agitato* style supposedly demanded the most cognitive effort since ancient sources provided no examples of sounds that Plato described as "those that imitate the voice and accents of a man going bravely into battle."[39]

Appropriating the rhetoric of a natural philosopher, Monteverdi explains that "with no little research and effort, I set myself the task of discovering it." After "cogitating on the semibreve" and performing a series of experiments with faster and faster notes, he determined that after dividing the semibreve into sixteen semiquavers (sixteenth notes) and combining them with a text of vexation, he "heard in this small example the similitude of the emotion I was seeking."[40] His real epiphany came, however, during his encounter with Tasso's impassioned description of the conflict between Tancredi and Clorinda, which he pursued "in order to obtain a better proof." In addition to using sensory evidence to determine the veracity of this representation, he interpreted the applause of noblemen after the 1624 performance of the *Combattimento* as evidence that "the trial succeeded in imitating wrath." Monteverdi describes his experimental process as one of composition. After the "apparent success of my first attempt to depict anger, I proceeded with greater zeal to make a fuller investigation and composed other works in that kind, both ecclesiastical and for chamber performance." That investigation, presumably to make sure that the *Combattimento* had not been just a fluke or dependent on Tasso's language involved writing many compositions that employed *agitato* style. As another kind of evidence, he wrote that the praise and imitation by other composers of his style proved the success of these compositions and the gestures they included. The imitation by other composers of his musical gestures prompted Monteverdi to claim that "For this reason I have thought it best to make known that the investigation and first essay of this genus, so necessary to the art of music, came from me."[41] We know from the host of composers as far-reaching as Schütz who quickly wrote in this style that Monteverdi's new technique did have widespread ramifications.

---

[39] Stevens, *The Letters of Claudio Monteverdi*, xvii.   [40] Ibid., xiv.   [41] Ibid.

In claiming to divide up the semibreve, Monteverdi wrote of manipulating a natural phenomenon – sound. His process resembles Bacon's commitment to enhancing sound as part of the process of gaining control over nature. Equally important was his use of his own ear as a measuring device. Monteverdi's process was one of auralization, or the aural equivalent of observation. As such, whether or not he actually experimented with semibreves interests me less than the parallels between the rhetoric of his description and that of seventeenth-century natural philosophers who explained and presented their experiences as truths verified by observation and the senses. In this his work mirrors that of Galileo Galilei. The jury is still out on whether Galileo actually performed the physical manipulations he described in his "inclined plane experiments," in which he claimed to have rolled balls down a smooth ramp in order to prove the mathematically expressed laws of gravity. Though he professed to have done the experiments "as often as a hundred times," his proof lies in the memory of many instances. And the significance of the work does not depend on its having occurred. In these early writings, rather than reporting a singular historical event Galileo offers his experiences of nature as proof. For Monteverdi and Galileo the testimony matters as much as the activity.

Bacon's acoustical experiments went even further than Monteverdi's compositions, dedicated to understanding and expanding the soundscape. For instance, his sound houses, which he described in the *New Atlantis*, published twelve years after Monteverdi's eighth book of madrigals, represented utopian spaces in which all kinds of physical manipulations modified and extended the sounds that nature provided. He writes of "harmonies which you have not, of quarter sounds, and lesser slides of sounds," and "diverse and artificial echoes," created through trunks, pipes and other materials.[42] Bacon published his most detailed accounts of sound in the *Sylva sylvarum*, in which he performed experiments to discover the nature of sound. He professed intense interest in the "majoration" of sound, by which he meant the enhancement of sounds as a part of increasing human control over nature.

Instrumental excursus

Many musical experiments including Monteverdi's demanded instruments, and their new prominence ultimately extended the early modern soundscape. In the realm of natural philosophy Bacon identified musical instruments as the best sphere for investigating the effects of sounds and harmony. He derived this view at least in part from his realization that

---

[42] Francis Bacon, *The great instauration; and, New Atlantis*, ed. Jay Weinberger (Arlington Heights: Harlan Davidson, 1986).

instrument makers could use their own art to capture the natural properties of sound and extend them. In the realm of musical composition, instruments violated rules and thus demanded new ones. Even the most conservative thinkers tolerated certain kinds of novel intervals and harmonies in instruments. Zarlino and Artusi both faulted their opponents for allowing the unnatural, mechanically constructed instruments to dictate to the more natural human voice. Artusi writes that "It is known that the ear is deceived, and to this these composers, or new inventors apply themselves with enthusiasm. They seek only to satisfy the ear and with aim toil night and day at their instrument to hear the effect which passages so made produce. The poor fellows do not perceive that what the instruments tell them is false."[43] Artusi later insisted that intervals useful in lute music are useless for vocal music.

Vincenzo Galilei's theories emerged from his experience as a lute player but ultimately had consequences that related as much to the material construction of sound as to his own experience as a performer. In his discourse concerning the unison, he explained that unison pitches depend on the material characteristics of the instruments making the sounds. He first describes the unison in terms of two coins constructed of the exact same material:

It is similar to having two coins made of the same material, of the same thickness, size, height, and weight and of an impression so similar that the sense cannot detect any difference of any kind, and these can truly be said to be unisonant and uniform.[44]

His reference to materials begins his grounding of tone in physical properties, not numbers. Comparing the sounds made by copper, gut, and steel strings, various thickness, and diverse striking forces, he insists that unison sounds depend as much on the materials as on proportion. Differently constructed strings are only as unison as their material properties allow. "But they are unisonant only in so far as the diversity of material of which they are made will allow. They will disagree not only in the variety of sound because of the diversity of the material of which the sounding bodies are composed but with respect to shape as experience tells us."[45] Galileo goes on to explain this theory through an analogy between the sounds of different materials and the different boiling points of oil and water.

Monteverdi also relied on instruments for both the derivations of theories and musical composition. That instruments are valued over the natural voice reflects a new emphasis on the possibility of mechanical instruments to both represent and deconstruct nature. It

---

[43] As quoted in Fabbri, *Monteverdi*, 41.
[44] As cited in Palisca, *Studies in the History of Italian Music and Theory*, 201.   [45] Ibid.

also suggests interesting ways in which technological developments changed perception. In the preface to the *Madrigali guerrieri et amorosi*, he tells his reader that the *stile concitato* worked better with instruments than voices because "the voice did not attain the velocity of the instruments." Both "Eccomi pronta ai baci" and the *Combattimento* use instruments to indicate dramatic shifts and to express passions. Ergasto's lady expresses her anger in phrases whose harmonic movement in fifth- and fourth-related patterns is driven by the continuo. Moreover, the singers' voices, which sound like singing and not like heightened speech, are used as artificial instruments of representation. Instruments serve as one more way in which the expression of a fictional woman's voice is alienated from any real woman's body, enhancing the artificiality already implied by the three male voices.

The predilection for instruments sounds most explicitly in the *Combattimento* in which instrumental passages continuously comment on the text through autonomous musical gestures. The slow repetition of the D major chords at the beginning of the piece that accompany the narrator's description of Clorinda circling the mountain on foot while Tancredi slowly approaches on horseback sounds like the stomping hooves of the horse. Such iconic and instrumental gestures continue to underpin, or represent in music, the narrator's description of Tancredi and Clorinda's battles. As the narrator speaks of clashing swords and flailing arms, the music mimics the battle actions and the protagonists gesture in the manner of fighting soldiers. During the narrator's description of the warriors, "dansi coi pomi e infelloniti e crudi,/cozzan con gli elmi insieme e con gli scudi" (they hit each other with the pommels roughly and cruelly, they butt each other with their helmets and shields), instruments mimic the described effects by plucking their strings, making a percussive sound that imitates clanking metal.[46]

Though not much work has been done on changes in early modern soundscapes, historians of science are currently exploring the effects on vision of new scientific methods and instruments such as the telescope and microscope. Rather than focusing only on the discoveries facilitated by instruments, these scholars attend to the ways in which seeing the tiniest details and most distant planets implicated the experience of vision. Microscopes and telescopes proved that the outside of a substance could not explain its interior and that planetary motion held complexities beyond the discerning power of the naked eye. When the microscope revealed mechanical structures that existed beneath the level of ordinary perception, it made accessible sub-visible material causes of

---

[46] Monteverdi's instruction in the score, "Qui si lascia l'arco, e si strappano le corde con duoi ditti" (Here one puts aside the bow and the strings are struck with two fingers), stands as the first known appearance of this technique in Italy. Fabbri, *Monteverdi*, 191.

191

phenomena that contradicted explanations based on sympathies and correspondences.[47] This is not to say that instruments and experimental technologies eliminated mystical harmonies and correspondences between macrocosms and microcosms, but rather that the new accessibility of hidden regions of the heavens and the tiniest details of matter made those correspondences manifest.

During the sixteenth and seventeenth centuries instruments became increasingly important in the investigation and codification of nature. The discovery in 1575 that lenses could counter the effects of myopia made them invaluable. Galileo Galilei promoted the microscope as a means to gain knowledge beyond the capabilities of human perception. In the 1630s, Cartesian optics aimed to raise the eye from an instrument of self-preservation to one of scientific knowledge. In the *Dioptrics* published in 1637, Descartes suggested strongly that instruments allowed humans to transcend the limits of their eyes. Descartes preached the invention of innumerable devices and Bacon, the idea that science should overcome human limitations.

By revealing the inner substance of things, the microscope demonstrated that features invisible to the naked eye did not necessarily correspond to the surface. In other words, new technologies made people realize that what they saw on the surface was not everything there was to see. Translating this to the realm of hearing, instruments could make heard sounds that had previously been impossible. Just as the telescope expanded the visual universe, musical instruments expanded the sonic universe. What notes sounded like no longer necessarily revealed what existed below their surface or corresponded to anything else. Musical sound no longer necessarily revealed anything beyond itself. Composers presented new ways of using voices, harmonies, and instruments that would eventually sever the link tying musical sounds to the represented emotions and the inner forces of the human body. This opened up a space which they filled with new musical conventions and which philosophers explained by separating the object that is sensed from the sensation.

Metaphysics

As musical practice slowly eroded existing theories, so too did the new reliance on sensory experience change the assumptions of natural philosophy. The changes in soundscape wrought by novel gestures eventually led to new ways of understanding the sensory effects of sound and to new representations and implications of women's voices. By way of

---

[47] See Catherine Wilson, *The Invisible World: Early Modern Philosophy and the Invention of the Microscope* (Princeton: Princeton University Press, 1995.

giving a philosophical context to the technologies of anger represented by Monteverdi's four angry ladies and to the enactments of gender and desire discussed throughout this book, I will discuss the differences between the thought of Plato and Aristotle, who served as foundations for Renaissance understandings of sensation, and Descartes, who would eventually summarize the ideas and developments that had been percolating since the turn of the seventeenth century.

The writings of Descartes from the 1630s and 1640s, with their dedication to a process of abstraction, can be read as a culminating gesture to large changes in practice and theory that had occurred across Western Europe in the early seventeenth century. An ambivalent Platonist, Descartes, like his predecessors, understood sensation as a process of physiological movement. But where for Plato sensation existed as an entirely physical force in which material and immaterial things outside the body traveled through various orifices, causing internal physical and psychological reactions, Descartes imagined a process of translation between actions outside the body and their internal comprehension and effects. In other words, he inserted a space between the pure existence of matter – sound or image – and the sensation it incurred. Objects are "received by the external sense organs and transmitted by the nerves to the brain."[48] Mapping this idea onto music, the *stile concitato* translated the sensation of anger into instrumentally derived sounds that were then received by the sense organs – the ears – and understood by the listener as a representation of anger via a process of retranslation.

Early experiences of sensation and sound such as those embodied by Ariadne and Armida, or the sensual effects of the Book 4 madrigals, were solidly rooted in ancient ideas. When Virginia Ramponi performed the bodily and vocal gestures that her world understood as anger, she did so through embodied sounds that required no translation. Her vocal motions matched the physical motions of anger and moved directly from her body to the listeners. Though Plato and Aristotle disagreed on how objects entered the body, they shared an understanding of vision and hearing as modalities of touch, in which objects outside the body eventually struck the soul directly. Aristotle derived his assertion that sensation was similar to "the way that wax receives the impression of a signet ring" from Plato's materialist conception of sensory perception first articulated in *Timaeus*.[49] According to both men, perception occurred when an external thing – either immaterial or material – acted

---

[48] René Descartes, *The Philosophical Writings of Descartes*, trans. John Cottingham, Robert Stoothoff, and Dugald Murdoch, vol. I (Cambridge: Cambridge University Press, 1985), 165.

[49] One of the earliest Greek works translated into Latin, this dialogue remained influential through the Aristotelian world of the middle ages, the emergence of Neoplatonism in the early Renaissance, and the rise of scientific rationalism in the seventeenth century.

on a perceiving subject through a sense organ or through the body as a whole.

Such disturbances would occur when the body encountered and collided with external fire [i.e. fire, other than the body's own] or for that matter with a hard lump of earth or with the flow of gliding waters, or when it was caught by a surge of air-driven words. The motions produced by all these encounters would then be conducted through the body to the soul, and strike against it.[50]

Plato goes on to explain sensation as a chain reaction: parts affect other parts until they arrive at the "center of consciousness. In other words, motions moved directly from body to soul.[51]

Within Plato's scheme, song sounded when air from the singer's mouth met air from the listener's ear. "Sound is the percussions of air by way of the ears upon the brain, and blood which is transmitted to the soul, and hearing is the motion caused by the percussion that begins in the head and ends in the place where the liver is situated."[52] Like the singing teachers of the sixteenth century, Plato defined song as a material entity that worked with animating spirits. Pitch depended on the speed of percussion and volume, on the force of percussion. Sound was thought to acquire meaning through its physical properties. The physical motions of the singers envoicing Ariadne's and Armida's sonic enactments of anger, for example, propelled a particular disturbance of air between one person's mouth and another person's ear – a motion that paralleled the material disturbances of anger. As I argued earlier, the pace of their musical anger sped up in conjunction with the increasing pulse of their anger. Similarly, Aristotle imagined sound as a collision of air moving at different speeds: "The air in the ear, on the other hand, is built in deeply and tends to be motionless, so that the sense of hearing can sense accurately all the differences of the motions."[53]

As Neoplatonism morphed into scientific rationalism, sound modulated from a sensual entity to a mechanical force that acted on sense organs. Returning to "Eccomi pronta ai baci" and the *Combattimento*, instead of reflecting a phenomenological essence or the invasion of a physical force, the lady's rage and the narrator's descriptive passage cause a movement of nerves which the brain understands as a representation of anger. Such a conception of sensation as residing in the brain and as a representation of the soul's reaction to bodily occurrences implied a space between action and reaction, and between body and soul. The soul, not the body, is the province of sensation, which means that song no longer works directly on the bodily humors.

---

[50] Plato, *Timaeus*, trans. Donald J. Zeyl (Indianapolis: Hackett Publishing Company, 2000), 31.

[51] Hippocrates Apostle, *Aristotle's On the Soul* (Grinnell, Iowa: Peripatetic Press, 1981), 40.

[52] Plato, *Timaeus*, 43.   [53] Aristotle, *On the Soul*, 67.

At the same time the perception of sound was dematerialized, as can be seen in Descartes's critique of Plato. He writes that

Most philosophers maintain that sound is nothing but a certain vibration of air which strikes our ears. Thus, if the sense of hearing transmitted to our minds the true image of its objects then, instead of making us conceive the sound, it would have to make us conceive the motion of the parts of the air which is then vibrating against our ears. But not everyone will wish to believe what the philosophers say. [54]

Instead of sonic bodies directly causing sound movements, the nerves that approach the ear "make the soul hear sounds." Descartes goes on to radically decontextualize those materials of sound by arguing that ideas in the brain have little to do with the objects they reflect and that rather than grasping the pure existence of matter they effectively translate patterns, pressures, and motions to the brain. This is most apparent in his discussion of language, which no longer assumes that meaning has any relation to sound. For Descartes, words

bear no resemblance to the things they signify, and yet they make us think of these things, frequently even without our paying attention to the sound of the word or to their syllables. Now if words, which signify nothing except by human convention, suffice to make us think of things to which they bear no resemblance, then why could not nature also have established some sign which would make us have the sensation of light, even if the sign contained nothing in itself which is similar to this sensation?[55]

Here he at once asserts the conventional nature of language and the mediation inherent in all sensation. He reasserts the artificial nature of language in a discussion of how humans make words:

Suppose we hear only the sound of some words, without attending to their meaning. Do you think the idea of this sound, as it is formed in our mind, is anything like the object which is its cause? A man opens his mouth, moves his tongue and breathes out: I do not see anything in these actions which is not very different from the idea of the sound which they make us imagine.[56]

According to this logic, musical representations of passions did not need to contain the passions themselves. The cries of Ergasto's lady are projected through a sonic motion that stands apart from her anger and is understood as something other than the sounds that they make. These ideas have important implications for music. For instance, these dictums give a philosophical context to the actuality that the angry music of Ergasto's lady or of the narrator's description of Clorinda was no more a natural embodiment of anger than were angry words. Such gestures did not acquire meaning through sonorous properties but through a

---

[54] Descartes, *Philosophical Writings*, vol. I, 94.   [55] Ibid., 81.   [56] Ibid., 86.

man-made musical grammar. Musical gestures made listeners imagine the sensation of anger.

Both Plato and Descartes wrote more about vision than hearing, and a brief consideration of sight thus makes clearer the differences between the materiality that they ascribed to the process of sensation. The space that Descartes inserted between Plato's material spirits and the perception of those spirits stands out clearly in these discussions. For Plato, sensation physically alters self and depends on the flow of external fire through the eyes. "We describe the ray of sight as a body that comes into being with daylight as an extension of ourself."[57] When daylight surrounds the visual stream and its fire coalesces with that of sight, it makes

a single homologous body aligned with the direction of the eye ... And because this body of fire has become uniform throughout and thus uniformly affected, it transmits the motions of whatever it comes in contact with, as well as of whatever comes in contact with it, to and throughout the whole body until they reach the soul. This brings about the sensation we call seeing.[58]

If a particularly strong fire from the outside meets a fire that jumps out of the eyes like a "lightning bolt" then one perceives color. If something other than fire penetrates the eye then the eyeball's hidden passages expel a "glob of fire and water," otherwise known as a tear.[59] In contrast, after summarily squelching Plato's combustive flames, Descartes insists that nothing material passes from the object to the senses. This is something very different than the process I argued for in my discussion of "Sì ch'io vorei morire," and "Cor mio, mentre vi miro," in chapter 3, with respect to Renaissance embodiments of sensuality. In those polyphonic madrigals, song worked by the movement of materials – namely air – which carried all kinds of sensations and resonances with them.

The following illustrations of the process of sight should clarify the above mentioned differences. (See Figures 5.1 and 5.2) The first is a modern representation of Plato's ideas and the second is Descartes's own figure. For Plato, vision occurred in daylight when fire coming from the eyes met fire coming from the object and created a uniform column of fire. In the Cartesian diagram, sight still involved the movement of material spirits but it now depended on an added layer of complexity, whereby an object is first received and then transmitted, mediated by fibers in the brain. For Descartes, light is "formed in our imagination by the mediation of our eyes." Rays from objects strike the senses through the optic nerves that attach the back of the eye to the internal surface of the brain. So far this sounds very much like Plato. But then Descartes explains that

---

[57] Plato, *Timaeus*, 58.   [58] Ibid., 33.   [59] Descartes, *Philosophical Writings*, vol. I, 165.

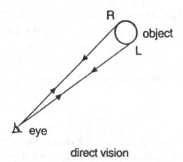

direct vision

Figure 5.1, A modern representation of Plato's conception of vision described in *Timaeus*. Reproduced from Plato. *Timaeus*, trans. and ed. Donald J. Zeyl. Hackett Publishing Company, Indianapolis, 2000

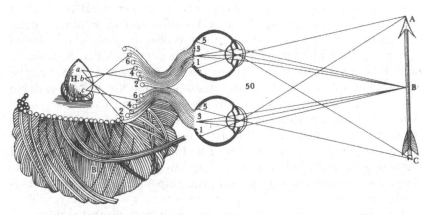

Figure 5.2, René Descartes, diagram of vision from *Treatise on Man*. *L'Homme de René Descartes* (Paris: Clerselier, 1664)

It is not those images imprinted on the external organ or on the internal surface of the brain which should be taken to be ideas – only those which are traced on the spirits of the gland H (where the seat of the common sense is located). That is to say, it is only the later figures which should be taken to be the forms or images which the rational soul united to this machine will consider directly when it imagines some object or perceives it by the senses.[60]

He makes it clear that images do not relate to what they represent. "We must at least observe that in no case does an image have to resemble the object it represents in general."[61] To prove this point he points to engravings that, according to the rules of perspective, often represent circles with ovals. Transposing this model onto sound, musical

[60] Ibid., 106.   [61] Ibid., 165.

gestures acquired meaning through conventions, which were compre-
hended through the mediation of the nerves connecting the ear to the
brain and to the "seat of imagination." Sonorous and kinesthetic forces
still existed, but those forces neither necessarily corresponded to the
sounds and meanings they created nor worked directly on the brain.

Conclusion

Ariadne and Armida articulate generalized pathos that worked by moving directly from the singer's body to the listener's ears. In their world
passions blew through the body like a strong wind on a cold day.
Clorinda and the subject of "Eccomi pronta ai baci" speak through the
mediation of musical instruments, trained voices, and elaborate narrative frames. Their passions arise from some external stimulus. These
later pieces do not depend on a connection between mind and body, a
homology between bodily sound and bodily passion. In other words,
representation is not natural but rather implies an artificial translation
of inner passions into musical sounds. This parallels Vincenzo Galilei's
assertion in the 1580s that harmony did not necessarily depend on the
inaudible sounds of the heavens vibrating within the human soul. No
longer identical to spirit, music now acts as a medium: its motions translate experiences, actions, and objects in the world into sound, as in the
Combattimento, when conventional instrumental and vocal sounds mime
the grisly details of battle described by the narrator – "thrusting" and
"clashing" swords, flailing arms and legs, and galloping horses. Because
these gestures are not natural, they need help – words or conventions –
to do their job.

Neither Armida nor Ariadne sounds very different from the *stile concitato* passages of the *Combattimento*. I want to return one final time to
Ariadne's anger and to Clorinda's as it is described by the *testo* in the
Combattimento (Example 5.3 and Example 5.6). Both passages display
anger through rapid-fire sixteenth notes. The instrumental ire of the
Combattimento only exaggerates the other two passages. But the two
moments of anger function very differently. Ariadne's anger stops and
starts; she gets worked up and then gradually she calms down – no real
person after all can sustain such a high pitch for very long. The narrator,
on the other hand, works in radical shifts that last for many measures
and can do so in large part because instrumentalists can sustain such
sounds indefinitely. The difference certainly cannot be attributed to a
supposed post-1620s discovery of the *stile concitato*. Ariadne's lament
features *concitato* moments and Monteverdi made them even more dramatic in the polyphonic version published in the 1614 sixth book of
madrigals by using the five-part texture to extend them. And the notion
of harmonic organization is not unique to Monteverdi's late pieces. After

Example 5.6, *Il combattimento di Tancredi e Clorinda*

all, Ariadne's most angry moment is organized by a pattern in the bass that turns her passage into a harmonic sequence. The difference is that in the first piece, the anger is the point and the sequence makes far less of an impression that the passion it encloses. But in "Eccomi pronta ai baci," the fifth-based motion does indeed drive the piece. Its musical structure is in fact the point.

Even though the later pieces employ gestures reminiscent of earlier practices, they were made to mean in very different ways. Since musical conventions acquire meaning from the discursive systems in which they are embedded, things can be physiologically the same and ontologically different. Gestures that in earlier compositions projected concordances between body, sound, and word now represent sensation through their musical structure. "Eccomi pronta ai baci" and the *Combattimento* bespeak a widespread occlusion of conventional practices that ultimately led to a taming of the power of song and a distancing marked by independent musical logic and fragmentation. This gradual emergence of a musical structure that privileges its own logic bespeaks a move away from an embodied sensuality that empowered Renaissance song, and toward a musical discourse that exists apart from the body, language, and the world. The body, eventually to be implicitly gendered female, would vanish from the equation, leaving the disembodied conventions to function within a codified system of representation.

The push and pull between practice and theory reminds us of the undulating manner in which experiences of embodied effects like song move, and that material transformations precede epistemological shifts. Attending to the counterpoint between mechanics and theories of sensation allows for historical consideration of the senses and suggests that though sensory phenomena may seem preeminently natural, they are in fact culturally contingent. This wedding of historical, musicological, and scientific perspectives may help explain why *L'Arianna* does not make my students weep.

Coda

I close with brief ruminations on the voices of an unlikely duo of Monteverdi's unruly women – Clorinda and Poppea. Clorinda, despite being figured in a piece that defines Monteverdi's later music, resembles most of the female figures discussed in this book; Poppea marks the beginning of an era defined by the epistemological shifts that occurred at the end of his career, showing us some of the new spaces that those shifts opened up for women. The 1643 Venetian opera, *L'incoronazione di Poppea*, presents Monteverdi's most luscious heroine – a woman who is everything Clorinda could not be: voluptuous, voracious, cunning, ambitious, and sexually charged. Neither virtuous nor chaste, Poppea sings throughout her unabashedly sensuous affair with Nero, using soaring melodies that come complete with chromaticisms and halting rhythms. The female voice is blatantly displayed, not coyly revealed. Her songs, canzonette and arias relish the technical prowess of the singing voice.

Clorinda's voice reverberates with incantations of powerful Renaissance sung speech. Wielding a transformative and animating power, her song recalls the culminating lament of *Il ballo delle ingrate*. Like the lone lamenting *ingrata*, Clorinda does not sing much until she dies. But when she finally does, her voice wields the troubling force of Petrarch's Laura and Ovid's women, rendering Tancredi "speechless and motionless" and thereby recalling Actaeon's gaze at Diana's naked body, after which her spoken invective leaves him forever speechless by turning him into a stag. Like the *ingrata* who momentarily escapes her metamorphosis, Clorinda's voice has a re-animating force. The breath of singing pushes her soul back into her body for a moment – even as her words and her wounds demand its exit. Her voice sounds most audible when she sings the brief aria-like passage after Tancredi has plunged his sword into her chest:

> Amico, hai vinto: io ti perdon, perdona
> tu ancora, al corpo no, che nulla pave,
> a l'alma sì; deh! per lei prega, e dona
> battesmo a me ch'ogni mia colpa lave.

> Friend, you have won. I do forgive you . . . forgive
> me too, oh, not this body that fears nothing,
> but this my soul. Oh pray for it, and wash
> with baptism all my faults away.

The narrator tells listeners to attend to her "voci languide" (languid voice), in which there resides "un non so che di flebile e soave" (a certain note so mournful and soft) that it snuffs out Tancredi's outrage and makes him weep. Her song is almost, but not quite, an aria. Changes in texture, style, and tonality separate this passage of dramatic reflection from the actions detailed by the narrator. Rather than speaking in recitative-style declamation as the narrator usually does, Clorinda sings in a high melodic voice. At the same time, the key abruptly moves from D major to G minor. But even though her supplication differs from the preceding agitation, and is underpinned by string chords played on one bow and with decrescendos, Clorinda's meaning is conveyed in this passage through the embodiment of interior sensations. The changes in harmonic vibrations of the major/minor motion underlying her vocal line mark her body's inner struggles. Her musical sighs, like those of Armida and Ariadne, project in sound the expiration of her spirit. The falling sigh of "al corpo no" moves to a half-step rise on the lower-pitched "a l'alma sì." In the setting of "al corpo no" and "a l'alma sì," the body that fears no harm meets the repentant soul in sounds that highlight the dissonance between – but not the categorical separation of – body and soul.

Clorinda's song brings to the fore the contested understandings of the female voice that preoccupied Renaissance thinkers. From the start her voice provokes conflicting reactions in Tancredi, who says: "E 'l tuo dir e 'l tacer di par m'alletta, barbaro discortese, a la vendetta" (Both your speech and your silence equally incite me to vengeance, savage barbarian). Speech and silence both make trouble for her, it seems. She embodies the paradox of Renaissance social mores which insisted that woman speak and sing for the entertainment and pleasure of men, while simultaneously branding those activities lascivious and dangerous. The end of the Renaissance saw the emergence of genres that depended on virtuosic women's voices but still heard in these voices the voracious incontinence of female sexuality because the female voice, like the female body, was a site of both intense pleasure and threatening excess.

Clorinda's solo song at her death makes explicit the christianized Neoplatonic links between sex, death, transformation, and song. The story ends when Tancredi baptizes her, granting her soul new and divine life.

> Non morì già che sue virtuti accolse
> tutte in quel punto e in guardia al cor le mise;
> e premendo il suo affanno a dar si volse

vita con l'acqua a chi col ferro uccise.
Mentre egli il suon de' sacri detti sciolse,
colei di gioia trasmutosse e rise,
   e in atto di morir lieta e vivace
   dir parea: "S'apre il ciel, io vado in pace."

Yet he did not die; he summoned up all his powers
for the moment and set them to guard his heart
and, repressing his grief, he turned to give
life with water to her whom with the sword he killed.
While he sounded the words of the holy rite,
she was transfigured with joy and smiled,
   and, at the point of death, happy and animated,
   she seemed to say "Heaven is opening, I depart in peace."

Her death keeps their chaste attraction separate from lascivious sex while simultaneously enacting the Neoplatonic fantasy of a divine love that wields a life-giving force. Tancredi finds in Clorinda's soul divine illumination, but he kills her body, thereby taking the Neoplatonic obfuscation of the female body to new heights. Death has always been Clorinda's only fate. As the white daughter of black, Ethiopian parents, her hidden blackness is impossible to assimilate and she must die.

Clorinda dies a humoral death, one inflected with its corollary, sex. At a moment when Galenic medicine had been cast in doubt but had not yet lost its influence on conceptions of the human body, these terms carried with them very powerful associations. The narrator tells Tancredi after he plunges his sword into Clorinda's bosom that his eyes will shed "di quel sangue ogni stilla un mar di pianto" (a sea of tears for every drop of that blood). In modern terms, the narrator seems simply to anticipate Tancredi's intense grief. But read through a Galenic lens, his words overflow with fluid, blood and immaterial spirits. The commingling of fluids, her blood and his water, certainly implies sex in any representational system. At a moment of shifting understandings of the body, the materiality of such language operates as both objective description and linguistic echo of a vanishing humoral body, a porous vessel in which internal mechanisms could be altered by the outside world. The words describe a humoral enactment of sex and her voice enacts the rebirth by reanimating her dying body with the breath of song. But the actions present a staged scene of sex, a metonymic representation of specifically heterosexual penetration which contrasts with the fluid-clashing humors of the Book 4 madrigals. One might argue that by this time the voice was less capable of doing the enactment itself, that it needed the help of actions.

While Clorinda's body is figured in decidedly Renaissance terms, Poppea's body resembles something else as she sings a different song from a different world. The epitome of the manipulative woman, she represents everything against which conduct books cautioned and embraces all of the negative attributes usually associated with female singers. When Tacitus described her in his *Annals*, the source Busenello used for the libretto, he wrote:

She was a woman possessed of all advantages but character . . . Her conversation was engaging, her wit not without point; she paraded modestly and practiced wantonness. She was never sparing of her reputation, and drew no distinction between husbands and adulterers: vulnerable neither to her own nor to alien passion, where material advantaged offered thither she transferred her desires.[1]

For Poppea, modesty functions as an independent signifier – she seduces whoever can help her. If virtue was the ideal Renaissance woman's currency, Poppea trafficked in precisely the opposite.

Poppea's flirtatious bedroom scene with Nero in Act I flies in the face of the silence and chastity mandated by Renaissance social mores. The excesses of Clorinda, Ariadne, and the *ingrate* had all remained illusionary and symbolic. They were threatening and oversexed because they inhabited female bodies, not because they enacted sexual desire. Clorinda, the warrior woman, dies a virgin; Ariadne's lusty scenes with Theseus and Bacchus occur off stage. In contrast, Poppea's sexuality dominates the opera – it is not at all figurative. Rather than trying to compensate for her essential excess by learning silence and chastity, she uses her body to get what she wants. For Clorinda love exists as Neoplatonic ascent. But for Poppea, who inhabits an opera all about pleasure, love and lust win in the end. Ensnared by Poppea's wiles, Nero abandons dignity and reason, exiles his wife, and orders the murder of his counselor Seneca.

L'incoronazione di Poppea reveals different technologies of song, of passion, and of the intersection between the two. It tells a story that the audience observes from a safe distance in a process that pushes toward cinematic voyeurism. In it, the sound of music links characters on the stage to a world enmeshed in what Carolyn Abbate calls diegetic music. Within this sound world the characters consciously use song to manipulate each other's passions – they work on each other instead of on the audience. And the characters, rather than naturally uttering generalized pathos, respond to one another. Musical conventions manipulate first the characters on stage, and then the audience. Mediated by musical structure, song no longer works directly on the bodies of the audience. Perhaps it is this mediating structure that allows for the staging of a woman whose raw sensuality would have in Renaissance times been far too unruly for the public arena.

---

[1] Tacitus, *The Annals*, trans. J. Jackson (Cambridge, MA: Harvard University Press, 1962), 3.

In her duets with Nero, Poppea's music deliberately inflames Nero's passions, making him want her and heed her every wish – namely that he banish his wife and kill his closest comrade. Poppea and Nero communicate through conventionalized musical vocabularies that are abruptly juxtaposed. Their feelings are distinct and mutable. Theirs is an economy in which passions and their musical representations are exchangeable commodities. In their Act 1 scene 3 duet, Nero tries to leave, but Poppea makes him promise he will return. She seduces him with music that features slinky chromaticisms, luscious sighs, and relentless repetitions. In this scene they never actually sing together; instead she manipulates his voice. Her "Tornerai?" (will you return) runs into his "Tornerò" (I will return). While Ariadne laments the loss of Theseus, Poppea does not allow Nero to go anywhere without permission.

Their erotic repartee continues throughout the opera. In Act 1 scene 10, Poppea reminds Nero of just how sweet were "Di questa bocca i baci" (the kisses of this mouth). She reminds him of her breasts, of the embrace of her arms. And Nero can scarcely breathe, so overcome is he by the thought of her ruby lips. Their sensual collaboration culminates in the final duet, which scholars now assume was not written by Monteverdi. The words are a simple declaration of love. The continuous melody features close imitations, luscious suspensions; the singers' voices mesh almost completely. The shared range of the two soprano voices allows for pure unisons and extremely close dissonances. Not a brief song of divine ascent, this is instead a duet of pure sensual and erotic ecstasy. But there is something cynical in this ending, for in addition to declaring love it honors victory, ambition, and desire. Nero and Poppea manipulate each other and everyone else around them to get what they want. Their musical repartee moves in perfect unison because their seductions have already worked.

Beyond Poppea's music, words, actions, and descriptions of her body attend to sensual details to which earlier works could only allude. For instance the most erotic moment in this opera of passion occurs after Seneca's death, when Lucan and Nero celebrate the beauty of Poppea and Nero's desire for her body.[2] This is not a tune of abstract love, of darting eye beams, and generalized passion such as that sung by Apollo and Orpheus in the concluding duet of *L'Orfeo*. Where Apollo promises to take Orpheus up to heaven where he can forever enjoy the harmonious image of Euridice released from the constraints of human passions, Nero and Lucan celebrate Poppea's mortal body and Nero's continued enjoyment of it. Instead of describing a fantasy of ecstasy, Lucan seduces Nero with song, using his voice and the activity of singing to push his partner

---

[2] For a reading of the homoerotics of this scene, see Wendy Heller, "Tacitus Incognito: Opera as History," *Journal of the American Musicological Society* 52/1 (1999): 39–97.

in crime toward an erotic ecstasy. The men entice each other to sing. Nero first says "cantiamo," but Lucan's ravishing melismas lead the emperor toward a celebration of Poppea's beauty. In its style – increasingly virtuosic passages that lead to the aria's conclusion – this duet recalls "O come sei gentile," "Mentre vaga Angioletta," and Orfeo and Apollo's heavenly ascent at the end of *L'Orfeo*. But the climax here differs radically. Lucan and Nero imitate each other's acrobatic vocal gestures, sing in parallel thirds, and resolve phrases in shared cadences – all musical gestures that had by this time become signs of erotic repartee. Their duet moves towards an erotic climax on the celebration of Poppea's mouth: "Cantiamo di quella bocca" (Let us sing of this mouth).

Nero sings of the pleasures and perils of Poppea's mouth – of its power to kill and to enliven the soul. The mouth is further metonymically represented by the activity of singing, which depends on just such a dangerous mouth. At this moment in the music, the virtuosic flourishes stop as Lucan fantasizes about Poppea's mouth over a descending major mode tetrachord. The sequences of close dissonances that emphasize the word "bocca," not to mention the singer's own open orifice, mark the sensuality of her mouth and song. This is a mouth that Nero has kissed and that has sung; it is not a gaping mouth of hell or a mouth that talks too much. The duet makes explicit the associations of singing with sexual activity. What makes the passage so stunning is Monteverdi's emphasis on the descending tetrachord with Nero's repeated exclamations of "Ahi Destin!" Even as the music celebrates directly the activities of the body, it functions through technologies that stand apart from the body.

Poppea anticipates the prominence of female bodies and voices that have come to characterize later opera and today's popular music scene. Audiences are now captivated by the performative power and vocal dominance of female singers. They no longer expect spiritual heights and moral improvement as they abandon themselves to the troubling but also ravishing and seductive power of the female voice. But that voice still works a kind of magic at the level of the super-sensual. It still crosses borders between the immaterial identification of subjectivity and the material body. Now song highlights an excess that marks music as radically different from speech, an excess that, by virtue of cutting across the body's interior and exterior, sounds in the end more physically embodied than plain speech. Such excess saturates especially the female voice, which emerges from a body that is other and different.

Clorinda and Poppea mark two distinct moments in early modern representations of female unruliness. That unruliness is still with us – and so too is the power of the female voice to work an ambivalent magic. To jump rather abruptly a time span of 350 years, one need only think of "Rid of Me," the 1993 recording by PJ Harvey – a favorite of academics, journalists, and teenagers alike. I bring in PJ Harvey at the very last moments of a book meant to historicize sound and to emphasize difference because I want to bring issues discussed in this book into dialogue with current discussions in musicology and critical theory that attempt to understand and perhaps capture the unruly power of song.

Whether it is the grittiness of PJ Harvey, the erotic charge of Carmen's Habañera, Lucia's mad scene, or Lulu's voice, musicologists and critical theorists alike have recently been fascinated by the super-sensuous nature of the voice, particularly of the female kind. Thus I would argue that Carolyn Abbate's uncanny moments, Barthes's "Grain of the Voice," and Poizat's cry all point to modern echoes of the force that women who envoiced Monteverdi's music possessed. For Poizat and others following Lacan, the cry comes from an unattainable materiality beyond the music. For Barthes, the grain sounds only sometimes, when voice meets language. For Derrida, music recaptures the potency of song through the dangerous supplement. For Abbate, music becomes uncanny when phenomenological sound is utterly transparent. No matter how you define its unruliness, the female voice demands attention and can, even now, captivate listeners with its intense physicality.

The grittiness of Harvey's voice in her song of rage calls to mind Roland Barthes's notion of the "grain of the voice," or the process in which voice encounters language and makes of it a sonorous collection of effects.[3] The grain sounds so clearly in Harvey's music because she emphasizes the sounds of her body – heavy breathing, screaming, and the straining of her vocal cords. By allowing her listeners to hear the making of her voice, Harvey exposes the inner realms of her body and remakes the borders between herself and her world, as well as between verbal expression and the body. "Rid of Me" characterizes rapture in terms of thirst and dismemberment. A song about rage, the pain of eroticism and love's irrational pull, it resonates with the ravenous and transformative, but mysterious, power of love articulated by the Neoplatonists. The sonorous presence of Harvey's music might be a modern equivalent of song's potential in the early modern world to challenge the limitations of despised female bodies. The furious energy of Harvey's tune calls forth the mystical power of eroticism. In the background a voice screams, "Lick my legs, I'm on fire!" The phrase comes out as pure sound, reminding us of what a material substance sound still can be and of the unruliness of the female voice.

[3] Roland Barthes, "The Grain of The Voice," in *The Responsibility of Forms: Critical Essays on Music, Art and Representation*, trans. Richard Howard (Berkeley: University of California Press, 1985), 267–278.

BIBLIOGRAPHY

Abbate, Carolyn. *Unsung Voices: Opera and Musical Narrative in the Nineteenth Century*. Princeton: Princeton University Press, 1991.

Ademollo, A. *La bell'Adriana ed altre virtuose del suo tempo alla corte di Mantova*. Città di Castello: S. Lapi Tipografo, 1888.

Alberti, Leon Battista. *Della famiglia*. Translated by G. Guarini. Lewisburg: Bucknell University Press, 1971.

    The Family in Renaissance Florence. Translated by Renée Neu Watkins. Columbia: University of South Carolina Press, 1969.

    On Painting. Translated by J. R. Spencer. New Haven: Yale University Press, 1966.

Alpers, Svetlana. "The Studio, The Laboratory and the Vexations of Art." In *Picturing Science, Producing Art*, edited by Caroline A. Jones and Peter Galison, 1998.

Altieri, Marco Antonio. *Li nuptiali*. Rome: Tipografia Romana D. C. Bartoli, 1873.

Apostle, Hippocrates G. *Aristotle's On the Soul*. Grinell, Iowa: Peripatetic Press, 1981.

Aretino, Pietro. *Sei giornate*. Edited by Giovanni Aquilecchia, 1975.

    Dialogues. Translated by Raymond Rosenthal. New York: Marsilio, 1971.

    Lettere. Edited by Paolo Procaccioli. Rome: Salerno Editrice, 1992.

    Selected Letters. Translated by George Bull. New York: Penguin Books, 1976.

Aristotle. *Generation of Animals*. Translated by A. L. Peck. Cambridge, MA: Harvard University Press, 1990.

Arkins, Brian. *Sexuality in Catullus*. New York: Hildesheim, 1982.

Armstrong, David and Ann Hanson. "The Virgin's Voice and Neck: Aeschylus, Agamemnon 245 and Other Texts." *British Institute of Classical Studies* 33 (1986): 97–100.

Armstrong, Nancy and Leonard Tennenhouse, eds. *The Ideology of Conduct: Essays on Literature and the History of Sexuality*. New York: Methuen, 1987.

Arnold, Denis. "Monteverdi's Necklace." *The Musical Quarterly* 59/3 (July 1973): 370–381.

    "Seconda Pratica: A Background to Monteverdi's Madrigals." *Music and Letters* 38 (1957): 341–352.

Austern, Linda Phyllis. "Alluring the Auditorie to Effeminacie: Music and The Idea of The Feminine in Early Modern England." *Music and Letters* 74 (1993): 343–354.

    "Nature, Culture, Myth and Musician in Early Modern England." *Journal of the American Musicological Society* 51/1 (1998): 1–49.

"'No women are indeed': The Boy Actor as Vocal Seductress in Late Sixteenth-
and Early Seventeenth-century English Drama." In *Embodied Voices: Representing Female Vocality in Western Culture*, edited by Leslie C. Dunn and
Nancy A. Jones, 83–102. Cambridge: Cambridge University Press, 1994.

Babcock, Barbara B. *The Reversible World*. Ithaca: Cornell University Press,
1978.

Bakhtin, Mikhail. *Rabelais and his World*. Translated by Helene Iswolsky.
Bloomington: Indiana University Press, 1984.

Barbaro, Francesco. "On Wifely Duties." In *The Earthly Republic: Italian Humanists
on Government and Society*, edited by R. E. Witt, E. B. Welles, and B.G. Kohl,
211–254. Philadelphia: University of Pennsylvania Press, 1978.

Bacon, Francis. *The great instauration; and, New Atlantis*. Edited by Jay Weinberger.
Arlington Heights: Harlan Davidson, 1986.

Barkan, Leonard. *The Gods Made Flesh: Metamorphosis and the Pursuit of Paganism*.
New Haven: Yale University Press, 1986.

Transforming the Passions: Ganymede and the Erotics of Humanism. Stanford:
Stanford University Press, 1989.

Barthes, Roland. "One Always Fails in Speaking of What One Loves." In *The
Rustle of Language*. New York: Hill and Wang, 1986.

S/Z. Translated by Richard Miller. New York: Hill and Wang, 1974.

Baskins, Cristelle. "Corporeal Authority in the Speaking Picture: The Representation of Lucretia in Tuscan Domestic Painting." In *Gender Rhetorics: Postures
of Dominance and Submission in History*, edited by Richard Trexler, 187–221.
Binghamton: Medieval and Renaissance Texts and Studies, 1991.

Bedini, Silvio. *The Pulse of Time*. Florence: L. S. Olschki, 1991.

Science and Instruments in 17th-century Italy. Aldershot: Variorum, 1994.

Belmonte, Pietro. *Istitutione della spesa*. Rome: Heredi Giovanni Osmarino
Gigliotto, 1587.

Belsey, Catherine. "Desire's Excess and the English Renaissance Theatre:
Edward II, Troilus and Cressida, Othello." In *Erotic Politics: Desire on
The Renaissance Stage*, edited by Susan Zimmerman, 84–103. New York:
Routledge, 1992.

The Subject of Tragedy: Identity and Difference in Renaissance Drama. New York:
Routledge, 1985.

Bembo, Pietro (1525). *Gli Asolani*. Edited by Giorgio Dilemmi. Florence: Presso
l'accademia della crusca, 1991.

Benson, Pamela Joseph. *The Invention of the Renaissance Woman: The Challenge
of Female Independence in the Literature and Thought of Italy and England*.
University Park: Penn State Press, 1992.

Biagioli, Mario and Steven J. Harris. "The Scientific Revolution as Narrative." *Configurations: A Journal of Literature, Science and Technology* 6 (1998):
243–267.

Bianconi, Lorenzo. *Music in the Seventeenth Century*. Translated by David Bryant.
Cambridge: Cambridge University Press, 1987.

Bindman, Rachel Elisa. "The Accademia dei Lincei: Pedagogy and the Natural
Sciences in Counter-Reformation Rome." Ph.D. dissertation, University of
California Los Angeles, 2000.

Block, Howard R. *Medieval Misogyny and the Invention of Western Romantic Love.* Chicago: University of Chicago Press, 1991.

Boccaccio, Giovanni. *The Corbaccio.* Translated by Anthony Cassell. Urbana: University of Illinois Press, 1975.

The Decameron. Toronto: Penguin Books, 1972.

Bonner, Mitchell. *Italian Civic Pageantry in the High Renaissance: A Descriptive Bibliography of Triumphal Entries and Selected Other Festivals for State Occasions.* Binghamton: Medieval and Renaissance Texts and Studies, 1979.

A Year of Pageantry in Late Renaissance Ferrara. Binghamton: Medieval and Renaissance Texts and Studies, 1990.

Bono, James J. *The Word of God and the Languages of Man: Interpreting Nature in Early Modern Science and Medicine.* Vol. I: *Ficino to Descartes.* Madison: University of Wisconsin Press, 1995.

Bottrigari, Ercole. *Il Desiderio.* Translated by Carol MacClintock. New York: American Institute of Musicology, 1962.

Brett, Philip, Elizabeth Wood, and Gary Thomas. *Queering the Pitch: The New Gay and Lesbian Musicology.* New York: Routledge, 1994.

Bridgeman, N. "Giovanni Camillo Maffei et sa lettre sur le chant." *Revue de Musicologie* (1956): 10–34.

Brown, Howard M. "Psyche's Lament: Some Music for the Medici Wedding in 1565." In *Words and Music: The Scholar's View; A Medley of Problems and Solutions Compiled in Honor of A. Tilman Merritt by Sundry Hands,* edited by Laurence Berman, 1–27. Cambridge, MA: Department of Music, Harvard University, 1972.

Brown, Judith. "A Woman's Place Was in the Home: Women's Work in Renaissance Tuscany." In *Rewriting the Renaissance,* edited by Margaret W. Ferguson, Maureen Quilligan, and Nancy J. Vickers, 206–224. Chicago: University of Chicago Press, 1986.

Brownlee, Kevin and Valeria Finucci, eds. *Generation and Degeneration: Tropes of Reproduction in Literature and History.* Durham, NC: Duke University Press, 2001.

Bruto, Giovanni. *The necessarie, fit and convenient education of a young gentlewoman.* Amsterdam: Theatrum Orbis Terrarum, 1969.

Burke, Peter. *The Fabrication of Louis XIV.* New Haven: Yale University Press, 1992.

The Historical Anthropology of Early Modern Italy. Cambridge: Cambridge University Press, 1987.

The Italian Renaissance: Culture and Society in Italy. Princeton: Princeton University Press, 1987.

Bynum, Caroline Walker. *Fragmentation and Redemption: Essays on Gender and the Human Body in Medieval Europe.* New York: Zone Books, 1992.

Caccini, Giulio. *Le Nuove Musiche.* Translated by H. Wiley Hitchcock. Madison: A-R Editions Inc., 1970.

Campbell, Mary Baine. *Wonder and Science: Imagining Worlds in Early Modern Europe.* Ithaca: Cornell University Press, 1999.

Carter, Tim. "'In love's harmonious consort'? Penelope and the Interpretation of *Il ritorno d'Ulisse in patria.*" *Cambridge Opera Journal* 5 (1993): 1–16.

"Intriguing Laments: Sigismondo D'India, Claudio Monteverdi and the Dido alla Parmigiana (1628)." *Journal of the American Musicological Society* 49/1 (1996): 32–70.

Monteverdi's Musical Theatre. New Haven: Yale University Press, 2002.

"Resemblance and Representation: Towards a New Aesthetic in the Music of Monteverdi." In *Con che soavità: Studies in Italian Opera, Song and Dance, 1580–1740,* edited by Ian Fenlon and Tim Carter, 118–135. Oxford: Clarendon Press, 1995.

Casseri, Giulio. *The Larynx, Organ of the Voice.* Translated by Malcolm Hast and Erling Holtsmark. Uppsala: Almqvist and Wiksells, 1969.

Castiglione, Baldesar [Baldassare]. *The Book of The Courtier (1528).* Translated by George Bull. New York: Penguin Classics, 1986.

Castiglione, Baldassare. *Il libro del cortegiano.* Translated by Giulio Carnazzi. Milano: Biblioteca Universale Rizzoli, 1987.

Chafe, Eric T. *Monteverdi's Tonal Language.* New York: Schirmer Books, 1992.

Chartier, Roger. "Social Figuration and Habitus: Reading Elias." In *Cultural History: Between Practices and Representations.* Ithaca: Cornell University Press, 1988.

Chua, Daniel. *Absolute Music and the Construction of Meaning.* Cambridge: Cambridge University Press, 1995.

Cochrane, Eric. "The End of the Renaissance in Florence." *Bibliothèque d'Humanisme et Renaissance* 27 (1965): 7–29.

Historians and Historiography in the Italian Renaissance. Chicago, 1981.

Cody, Richard. *The Landscape of the Mind: Pastoralism and Platonic Theory in Tasso's Aminta and Shakespeare's Early Comedies.* Oxford: Clarendon Press, 1969.

Cohen, H. Floris. "An Historian's Perspective on the Origins, and the Limitations, of Modern Science." In *Discipline of Medicine,* edited by L. A. van Es and E. Mandema, 21–31. Amsterdam: North-Holland, 1994.

The Scientific Revolution: A Historiographical Inquiry. Chicago: University of Chicago Press, 1994.

Collingwood, R. G. *An Essay on Philosophical Method.* 3rd edn. Oxford: Clarendon Press, 1933.

Correia, Clara Pinto. *The Ovary of Eve: Egg and Sperm and Perforation.* Chicago: University of Chicago Press, 1997.

Couliano, Ioan P. *Eros and Magic in the Renaissance.* Chicago: University of Chicago Press, 1987.

Cox, Virginia. "The Single Self: Feminist Thought and the Marriage Market in Early Modern Venice." *Renaissance Quarterly* 48/3 (Autumn 1995): 513–81.

Crabb, Ann. *A Patrician Family in Renaissance Florence: The Family Relations of Alessandra Macinghi and Her Sons, 1440–1491.* Ann Arbor: University of Michigan Press, 1980.

The Strozzi of Florence: Widowhood and Family Solidarity in the Renaissance. Ann Arbor: University of Michigan Press, 2000.

Cropper, Elizabeth. "The Beauty of Woman: Problems in the Rhetoric of Renaissance Portraiture." In *Rewriting the Renaissance: The Discourses of Sexual Difference in Early Modern Europe,* edited by Maureen Quilligan, Nancy

J. Vickers, and Margaret W. Ferguson, 175–191. Chicago: University of Chicago Press, 1986.

Cusick, Suzanne. "Gendering Modern Music : Thoughts on the Artusi–Monteverdi Controversy." *Journal of the American Musicological Society* 46 (1993): 10–26.

"Of Women, Music, and Power: A Model from Seicento Florence." In *Musicology and Difference*, edited by Ruth A. Solie, 281–305. Berkeley: University of California Press, 1993.

"On Musical Performances of Gender and Sex." Talk at University of Pennsylvania, February 24, 1996.

"'There was not one lady who failed to shed a tear,' Arianna's Lament and the construction of Modern Womanhood." *Early Music* 22 (1994): 21–45.

"Thinking from Women's Lives: Francesca Caccini after 1627." In *Rediscovering the Muses*, edited by Kimberly Marshall, 206–227. Boston: Northeastern University Press, 1993.

Dahlhaus, Carl. *Studies on the Origin of Harmonic Tonality*. Translated by Robert O. Gjerdingen. Princeton: Princeton University Press, 1991.

d'Aragona, Tullia. *Dialogue on the Infinity of Love*. Translated by Rinaldina Russell and Bruce Merry. Chicago: University of Chicago Press, 1997.

Daston, Lorraine. "The nature of nature in early modern Europe." *Configurations: A Journal of Literature, Science, and Technology* 6 (1998): 149–172.

"The Several Contexts of the Scientific Revolution." *Minerva: Review of Science, Learning and Policy* 32 (1994): 108–114.

Davidson, Arnold. "Sex and the Emergence of Sexuality." *Critical Inquiry* 14 (1987): 16–48.

Davis, Judith C. and Robert C Brown., eds. *Gender and Society in Renaissance Italy*. London: Longman, 1998.

Davis, Natalie Zemon. "History's Two Bodies." *The American Historical Review* 93, no. 1 (1988): 1–30.

"The Reasons of Misrule." In *Society and Culture in Early Modern France*, 97–124. Stanford: Stanford University Press, 1975.

"The Sacred and The Body Social in 16th Century Lyon." *Past and Present* 90 (1981): 40–70.

"Women on Top." In *Society and Culture in Early Modern France*, 124–152. Stanford: Stanford University Press, 1975.

Dear, Peter. *Discipline and Experience*. Chicago: University of Chicago Press, 1995.

Dear, Peter. *Literary Structure of Scientific Argument*. Philadelphia: University of Pennsylvania Press, 1991.

The scientific enterprise in early modern Europe: readings from "Isis." Chicago: University of Chicago Press, 1997.

Derrida, Jacques. *Of Grammatology*. Translated by Gayatri Chakavorty Spivak. Baltimore: Johns Hopkins University Press, 1976.

Descartes, René. *Discourse on Method and the Meditations*. Translated by John Veitch. Amherst: Prometheus Books, 1989.

The Passions of the Soul. Translated by Stephen Voss. Indianapolis: Hackett Publishing Company, 1989.

212

Philosophical Letters. Translated by Anthony Kenny. Oxford: Basil Blackwell, 1970.

The Philosophical Writings of Descartes. Translated by John Cottingham, Robert Stoothoff, and Dugald Murdoch. Vol. I. Cambridge: Cambridge University Press, 1985.

Dolce, Lodovico. *Dialogo: Della istitutione delle donne*. Venice: Giolito, 1560.

Dollimore, Jonathan. *Sexual Dissidence: Augustine to Wilde, Freud to Foucault*. Oxford: Clarendon Press, 1991.

Douglas, Mary. *Purity and Danger: An Analysis of the Concepts of Pollution and Taboo*. New York: Praeger, 1966.

Drake, Stillman. "Music and Philosophy in Early Modern Science." In *Music and Science in the Age of Galileo*, edited by Victor Coelho. Dordrecht: Kluwer Academic, 1992.

Durling, Robert. *The Figure of the Poet in Renaissance Epic*. Cambridge, MA: Harvard University Press, 1965.

Durling, Robert, ed. *Petrarch's Lyric Poems: The Rime Sparse and Other Lyrics*. Cambridge, MA: Harvard University Press, 1976.

Eaton, William. *Books of Secrets in Medieval and Early Modern Culture*. Princeton: Princeton University Press, 1994.

Ebreo, Leone. *Dialoghi d'amore*. Translated by S. Carmella. Bari: Laterza, 1929.

The Philosophy of Love. Translated by F. Friedeberg-Sieldy and J. H. Barnes. London: The Socino Press, 1937.

Einstein, Alfred. *The Italian Madrigal*. Princeton: Princeton University Press, 1949.

Elias, Norbert. *The History of Manners*. Translated by Edmund Jepthcott. Vol. I: *The Civilizing Process*. New York: Pantheon, 1989.

Enterline, Lynn. "Embodied Voices: Petrarch Reading (Himself Reading) Ovid." In *Desire in the Renaissance: Psychoanalysis and Literature*, edited by Valeria Finucci and Regina Schwartz, 120–146. Princeton: Princeton University Press, 1994.

"'You speak a language that I understand not': The Rhetoric of Animation in *The Winter's Tale*." *Shakespeare Quarterly* 48/1 (1997): 17–45.

Fabbri, Paolo. *Monteverdi*. Translated by Tim Carter. Cambridge: Cambridge University Press, 1994.

Fahy, Conor. "Three Early Renaissance Treatises on Women." *Italian Studies* 2 (1956): 30–55.

Falassi, Alesandro. *Time out of Time: Essays on the Festival*. Albuquerque: University of New Mexico Press, 1984.

Fallopius, Gabrielle. *Secreti diversi et miracolosi*. Venice: Ghirado Imberti, 1640.

Farge, Arlette and Natalie Zemon Davis. *Renaissance and Enlightenment Paradoxes: A History of Women in the West*. Cambridge, MA: Harvard University Press, 1993.

Feldman, Martha. "Magic Mirrors and The Seria Stage: Thoughts towards a Ritual View." *Journal of the American Musicological Society* 48/3 (1995): 423–485.

"Rore's 'selva selvaggia' The Primo Libro of 1542." *Journal of the American Musicological Society* 42 (1989): 547–642.

Fenlon, Iain. "The Monteverdi Vespers: Suggested Answers to Some Fundamental Questions." *Early Music* 5 (1977): 380–387.

Music and Patronage in 16th Century Mantua. Cambridge: Cambridge University Press, 1980.

"The Origins of the Staged Ballo." In *Con che soavità: Studies in Italian Opera, Song and Dance, 1580–1740*, edited by Tim Carter and Iain Fenlon, 13–41. Oxford: Clarendon Press, 1995.

Ferguson, Margaret. *Trials of Desire: Renaissance Defenses of Poetry*. New Haven: Yale University Press, 1983.

Ferguson, Margaret W., Maureen Quilligan, and Nancy J. Vickers. *Rewriting the Renaissance: The Discourses of Sexual Difference in Early Modern Europe*. Chicago: University of Chicago Press, 1986.

Ferrand, Jacques. *A Treatise On Lovesickness*. Translated by David A. Beecher and Massimo Ciavolella. Syracuse: Syracuse University Press, 1990.

Ficino, Marsilio. *Commentary on Plato's Symposium*. Translated by Sears Jayne. Dallas: Spring Publications Inc., 1985.

Meditations on The Soul: Selected Letters of Marsilio Ficino Translated from the Latin by Member of the Language Department of the School of Economic Science, London. Rochester: Inner Traditions International, 1997.

Sopra lo amore o ver' Convito di Platone (1469). Edited by G. Ottaviano. Milan: Celuc, 1973.

Fiertz, Markus. *Girolamo Cardano*. Translated by Helya Niman. Boston: Burkhauser, 1983.

Findlen, Paula. "From Aldrovandi to Algarotti." *British Journal for the History of Science* 24 (1991): 360.

"Between Carnival and Lent: The Scientific Revolution at the Margins of Culture." *Configurations: A Journal of Literature, Science and Technology* 6 (1998): 243–267.

"Humanism, Politics and Pornography in Renaissance Italy." In *The Invention of Pornography: Obscenity and the Origins of Modernity*, edited by Lynn Hunt, 49–108. New York: Zone Books, 1993.

Possessing Nature: Museums, Collecting, and Scientific Culture in Early Modern Italy. Berkeley: University of California Press, 1994.

Finney, Paula. "Exercises in the 16th Century." *Bulletin of the History of Medicine* 42 (1968): 422–449.

Finucci, Valeria. *The Lady Vanishes: Subjectivity and Representation in Castiglione and Ariosto*. Stanford: Stanford University Press, 1992.

The Manly Masquerade: Masculinity, Paternity and Castration in the Italian Renaissance. Durham, NC: Duke University Press, 2003.

Firenzuola, Agnolo. *On the Beauty of Women*. Translated by Konrad Eisenbichler and Jacqueline Murray. Philadelphia: University of Pennsylvania Press, 1992.

Foreman, Edward. *A Comparison of Selected Italian Vocal Tutors of the Period c. 1550–1800*. Champaign: University of Illinois Press, 1968.

Foucault, Michel. *The History of Sexuality*. Translated by Robert Harley. Vol. I. New York: Vintage Books, 1990.

The Order of Things: An Archaeology of the Human Sciences. New York: Random House Inc., 1984.

Fournier, Marian. *The Fabric of Life: Microscopy in the 17th Century*. Baltimore: Johns Hopkins University Press, 1996.

"Huygens's Design for a Simple Microscope." *Annals of Science* 46 (1989): 575.

Franco, Mark. *Dance As Text: Ideologies of the Baroque Body*. New York: Cambridge University Press, 1993.

Frantz, David O. *Festum Voluptatis: A Study of Renaissance Erotica*. Columbus: Ohio State University Press, 1989.

Freccero, John. "The Fig Tree and the Laurel." In *Literary Theory/Renaissance Texts*, edited by Patricia Parker and David Quint, 20–33. Baltimore: Johns Hopkins University Press, 1986.

Freedberg, David. *The Power of Images: Studies in the History and Theory of Response*. Chicago: University of Chicago Press, 1989.

Freitas, Roger. "Un atto d'ingegno: A Castrato in the Seventeenth Century." Ph.D. dissertation, Yale University, 1998.

French, R. K. *Dissection and Vivisection in the European Renaissance*. Aldershot: Ashgate, 1999.

Furman, Nelly. "The Language of Love in Carmen." In *Reading Opera*, edited by Arthur Gross and Roger Parker, 168–184. Princeton: Princeton University Press, 1988.

Galen. *On Semen*. Translated by Phillip De Lacy. Berlin: Akademie Verlag, 1992.

Galen. *On The Natural Faculties*. Translated by Arthur John Brock. Cambridge, MA: Harvard University Press, 1991.

García, Manuel. *Traité complet de l'art du chant*. Translated by Louis Jacques Rondeleux. Geneva: Minkoff, 1985.

Garin, Eugenia. *Renaissance Characters*. Translated by Lydia Cochrane. Chicago: University of Chicago Press, 1991.

Geertz, Clifford. *Negara: The Theatre State in Nineteenth-Century Bali*. Princeton: Princeton University Press, 1980.

Gentilcore, David. *Healers and Healing in Early Modern Italy*. Manchester: Manchester University Press, 1998.

Ginzburg, Carlo. *Clues, Myths and the Historical Method*. Translated by John and Anne Tedeschi. Baltimore: Johns Hopkins University Press, 1990.

"High and Low: The Theme of Forbidden Knowledge in the Sixteenth and Seventeenth Centuries." *Past and Present* 73 (1976): 28–41.

Giustiniani, Vincenzo. *Discorso sopra la musica*. Translated by Carol MacClintock. New York: American Institute of Musicology, 1962.

"Discorso sopra la musica de' suoi tempi." In *Le origini del melodramma*, edited by Angelo Solerti, 103–128. Turin: Bocca, 1903.

Glixon, Beth. "Scenes from the Life of Silvia Galiarti Manni, a Seventeenth Century Virtuoso." *Early Music History* 15 (1996): 97–147.

Godwin, Joscelyn. *Harmonies of Heaven and Earth: The Spiritual Dimensions of Music from Antiquity to the Avant-garde*. Rochester: Inner Traditions International, 1987.

Goffen, Rona. "Titian's Sacred and Profane Love in Marriage." In *The Expanding Discourse: Feminism and Art History*, edited by Norma Broude and Mary D. Garrard. New York: Cambridge University Press, 1992.

Titian's Women. New Haven: Yale University Press, 1997.

Goffen, Rona, ed. *Titian's Venus of Urbino*. New York: Cambridge University Press, 1997.

Goldberg, Jonathan. *Sodometries: Renaissance Texts, Modern Sexualities*. Stanford: Stanford University Press, 1992.

Goodman, David and Colin Russell. *The Rise of Scientific Europe, 1500–1800*. Sevenoaks: Hodder and Stoughton, 1991.

Gordon, Bonnie. "Singing the Female Body: Monteverdi, Subjectivity, Sensuality." Ph.D. dissertation, University of Pennsylvania, 1998.

"Talking Back: The Female Voice in Il ballo delle ingrate." *Cambridge Opera Journal* 11/1 (1999): 1–30.

Gordon, D. J. *The Renaissance Imagination*. Berkeley: University of California Press, 1980.

Gordon, Jessica. "Entertainments for the Marriages of the Princesses of Savoy in 1608." In *Italian Renaissance Festivals and their European Influence*, edited by J. R. Mulryne and Margaret Shewring, 119–141. Lewiston: The Edwin Mellen Press, 1992.

Gough, Melinda J. "Tasso's Enchantress, Tasso's Captive Women." *Renaissance Quarterly* 54/2 (2001): 523–552.

Grafton, Anthony and Lisa Jardine. *From Humanism to the Humanities*. Cambridge, MA: Harvard University Press, 1986.

Greenblatt, Stephen. *Shakespearean Negotiations: The Circulation of Social Energy in Renaissance England*. Berkeley: University of California Press, 1988.

Greene, Thomas M. " Il Cortegiano and The Choice of a Game." *Renaissance Quarterly* 32 (1979): 173–186.

"Magic and Festivity at the Renaissance Court." *Renaissance Quarterly* 40 (1987): 636–659.

"Ritual and Text in the Renaissance." In *Reading the Renaissance: Culture, Poetics, and Drama*, edited by Jonathan Hart, 17–34. New York: Garland, 1996.

Grene, Marjorie. "Aristotle-Cartesian Themes in Natural Philosophy: Some 17th-century Cases." *Perspective on Science: Historical, Philosophical, Social* 1 (1993): 66–87.

Guarini, Battista. *Opere*. Edited by Marziano Guglielmetti. Turin: U.T.E.T., 1971.

Guasco, Annibale. "Ragionamento a D. Lavinia sua figliuola della maniera del governarsi ella in corte; andando per Dama." Turin, 1586.

Guazzo, Stefano. *The Civil Conversation of M. Steeven Guazzo*. The first three books translated by George Pettie, anno 1581, and the fourth by Barth. Young, anno 1586. Edited by Edward Sullivan. New York: AMS Press, 1967.

La Civil Conversatione (1575). Edited by Amadeo Quondam. Modena: Panini, 1993.

Gunsberg, Maggie. "The Mirror Episode in Canto XVI of the *Gerusalemme Liberata*." *The Italianist* 3 (1983): 30–46.

Haar, James. *Essays on Italian Poetry and Music in the Renaissance, 1530–1600*. Berkeley: University of California Press, 1986.

Hampton, Thomas. *Writing From History: The Rhetoric of Exemplarity in Renaissance Literature*. Ithaca: Cornell University Press, 1990.

Hanning, Barbara. "Glorious Apollo: Poetic and Political Themes in the First Opera." *Renaissance Quarterly* 22/4 (1979): 485–513.

"Monteverdi's Three Genera." In *Musical Humanism: Essays in Honor of Claude Palisca*, edited by Nancy Baker and Barbara Hanning, 145–170. Stuyvesant: Pendragon, 1992.

Of Poetry and Music's Power. Ann Arbor: UMI Research Press, 1980.

Hanning, Robert and David Rosand. *Castiglione: The Ideal and the Real in Renaissance Culture*. New Haven: Yale University Press, 1983.

Hart, Jonathan, ed. *Reading the Renaissance: Culture, Poetics and Drama*. New York: Garland, 1996.

Hathaway, Baxter. *The Age of Criticism: The Late Renaissance in Italy*. Ithaca: Cornell University Press, 1982.

Hedrick, D. K. "The Ideology of Ornament: Alberti and the Erotics of Renaissance Urban Design." *Word and Image* 3 (1987): 111–137.

Heller, Wendy. "Chastity, Heroism, and Allure: Women in Opera of Seventeenth-Century Venice." Ph.D. dissertation, Brandeis University, 1995.

"The Queen as King: Refashioning Semiramide for Solo Voice." *Cambridge Opera Journal* 5/2 (1993): 93–115.

"Tacitus Incognito: Opera as History." *Journal of the American Musicological Society* 52/1 (1999): 39–97.

Henry, John. *The Scientific Revolution and the Origins of Modern Science*. New York: St. Martin's Press, 1997.

Heriot, Angus. *The Castrati in Opera*. New York: Da Capo Press, 1956.

Hilton, Wendy. "A Dance for Kings: The Seventeenth Century French Courante." *Early Music* 5 (1977): 161–172.

Hippocrates. *The Medical Works of Hippocrates*. Edited by John Chadwick and W. N. Mann. Oxford: Oxford University Press, 1950.

Hollander, Anne. *Seeing Through Clothes*. New York: Avon Books, 1973.

Howard, Jean. *The Stage and Social Struggle in Early Modern England*. New York: Routledge, 1994.

Hunt, Lynn. *Eroticism and the Body Politic*. Baltimore: Johns Hopkins University Press, 1991.

"Foucault's Subject in *The History of Sexuality*." In *Discourses of Sexuality from Aristotle to AIDS*, edited by Donna C. Stanton, 78–94. Ann Arbor: University of Michigan Press, 1993.

Isherwood, Christopher. *Music in the Service of the Kings: France in the Seventeenth Century*. Ithaca: Cornell University Press, 1973.

Jacob, James R. *The Scientific Revolution: Aspirations and Achievements, 1500–1700*. Atlantic Highlands, NJ: Humanities Press, 1998.

Jameson, Fredric. *The Political Unconscious*. Ithaca: Cornell University Press, 1981.

Jed, Stephanie. *Chaste Thinking: The Rape of Lucretia and the Birth of Humanism*. Bloomington: Indiana University Press, 1989.

Johnson, Barbara. "Muteness Envy." In *Human, All Too Human*, edited by Diana Fuss, 131–148. New York: Routledge, 1996.

Jones, Anne R. "Assimilation with a Difference: Renaissance Women Poets and Literary Influence." *Yale French Studies* 62 (1981): 135–153.

"City Women and Their Audiences: Louis Labè and Veronica Franco." In *Rewriting the Renaissance*, edited by Nancy Vickers, Margaret Ferguson, and Maureen Quilligan, 274–290. Chicago: University of Chicago Press, 1984.

The Currency of Eros: Women's Love Lyric in Europe, 1540–1620. Bloomington: Indiana University Press, 1990.

"Nets and Bridles: Early Modern Conduct Books and Sixteenth-century Women's Lyrics." In *The Ideology of Conduct: Essays on Literature and the History of Sexuality*, edited by Nancy Armstrong and Leonard Tennenhouse, 39–73. New York: Methuen, 1987.

"New Songs for the Swallow: Ovid's Philomela in Tullia d'Aragona and Gaspara Stampa." In *Refiguring Woman: Perspectives on Gender and the Italian Renaissance*, edited by Marilyn Migiel and Juliana Schiesari, 263–279. Ithaca: Cornell University Press, 1991.

Jones, Caroline A. and Peter Galison, eds. *Picturing Science, Producing Art*. New York: Routledge, 1998.

Jones, Leslie C. and Nancy A. Dunne, eds. *Embodied Voices: Representing Female Vocality in Western Culture*. Cambridge: Cambridge University Press, 1994.

Jones, Pamela. "Spectacle in Milan: Cesare Negri's Torch Dances." *Early Music* 14 (1986): 182–198.

Jordan, Constance. *Renaissance Feminism: Literary Text and Political Models*. Ithaca: Cornell University Press, 1990.

Katz, Ruth. *The Powers of Music: Aesthetic Theory and the Invention of Opera*. New Brunswick: Transaction Publishers, 1994.

Kearney, Patrick J. *A History of Erotic Literature*. London: Macmillan, 1982.

Keller, Evelyn Fox. "'The Gender/Science System' Or, Is Sex to Gender as Nature Is to Science?" *Hypathia* 2 (1987): 37–49.

Kelly, Kathleen Coyne. *Performing Virginity and Testing Chastity in the Middle Ages*. London: Routledge, 2000.

Kelso, Ruth. *Doctrine for the Lady of the Renaissance*. Urbana: University of Illinois Press, 1956.

Kendrick, Walter. *The Secret Museum: Pornography in Modern Culture*. New York: Penguin, 1987.

Kenyon, Nicholas. *Authenticity and Early Music: A Symposium*. New York: Oxford University Press, 1988.

Keyser, Dorothy. "Cross Sexual Casting in Baroque Opera: Musical and Theatrical Conventions." *Opera Quarterly* 5/4 (1988): 46–51.

Kilblansky, Raymond, Erwin Panofsky, and Fritz Saxl. *Saturn and Melancholy: Studies in the History of Natural Philosophy, Religion and Art*. London: Nelson, 1964.

King, Margaret L. *Venetian Humanism in an Age of Patrician Dominance*. Princeton: Princeton University Press, 1986.

Women of the Renaissance. Chicago: University of Chicago Press, 1990.

Kirkendale, Warren. *The Court Musicians in Florence During the Principate of the Medici*. Florence: Leo S. Olschki Editore, 1993.

Klapisch-Zuber, Christiane. *Women, Family and Ritual in Renaissance Italy*. Translated by Lydia Cochrane. Chicago: University of Chicago Press, 1987.

Klein, Joan Larsen. *Daughters, Wives, and Widows: Writings by Men about Women and Marriage in England 1500–1640*. Urbana: University of Illinois Press, 1992.

Klein, Robert and Henri Zerner, *Italian Art, 1500–1600*. (Evanston: Northwestern University Press, 1966).

Korhonen, Ann and Marjo Kaartinen, eds. *Bodies in Evidence: Perspectives on the History of the Body in Early Modern Europe*. Turku: Department of Cultural History, 1997.

Kristeller, Paul Oskar. "Learned Women of Early Modern Italy: Humanists and University Scholars." In *Beyond Their Sex: Learned Women of the European Past*, edited by Patricia H. Labalme, 91–116. New York: New York University Press, 1980.

Renaissance Thought and the Arts. Princeton: Princeton University Press, 1990.

Kristeller, Paul Oskar, ed. *The Renaissance Concepts of Man, and Other Essays*. New York: Torchbooks, 1972.

Kuehn, Thomas. *Law, Family and Women: Toward a Legal Anthropology of Renaissance Italy*. Chicago: University of Chicago Press, 1991.

Kulish, Nancy and Deanna Holtzman. *Nevermore: The Hymen and the Loss of Virginity*. Northvale, NJ: J. Aronson, 1997.

Kwint, Marius, Christopher Breward, and Jeremy Aynsley, eds. *Material Memories*. Oxford: Berg, 1999.

Lacqueur, Thomas. *Making Sex: Body and Gender from the Greeks to Freud*. Cambridge, MA: Harvard University Press, 1990.

Lao, Meri. *Sirens: Symbols of Seduction*. Rochester: Park Street Press, 1998.

Lawner, Lynne. *I modi, the Sixteen Pleasures: An Erotic Album of the Italian Renaissance*. Evanston: Northwestern University Press, 1988.

Lawrence, Amy. *Echo and Narcissus: Women's Voices in Classical Hollywood Cinema*. Berkeley: University of California Press, 1974.

Lawrence, Christopher and Steven Shapin. *Science Incarnate: Historical Embodiments of Natural Knowledge*. Chicago: University of Chicago Press, 1998.

Leonardi, Susan J. "To Have A Voice: The Politics of the Diva." *Perspectives* 13 (1987): 65–72.

Lindberg, David C. and Robert S. Westman, eds. *Reappraisals of the Scientific Revolution*. Cambridge: Cambridge University Press, 1990.

Little, Meredith Ellis. "Dance Under Louis XIV and XV: Some Implications for the Musician." *Early Music* 3 (1975): 331–341.

"Recent Research in European Dance, 1400–1800." *Early Music* 14 (1986): 331–340.

Lloyd, Genevieve. *The Man of Reason: "Male" and "Female" in Western Philosophy*. Minneapolis: University of Minnesota Press, 1994.

Lombardelli, Orazio. *Dell'uffizio della donna maritata*. Florence, 1585.

Lorenzetti, Stefano. " 'Quel celeste cantar che mi disface.' Immagini della donna e educazione alla musica nell'ideale pedagogico del rinascimento italiano." *Studi musicali* 23 (1994): 241–261.

Musica e identità nobiliare nell'Italia del Rinascimento: Educazione, mentalità, immaginario (Florence: Leo S. Olschki, 2003).

Luigini, Federico. "Il libro della bella donna." Venice, 1554.

Luthy, C. H. "Atomism, Lynceus, and the Fact of 17th Century Microscopy." *Early Science and Medicine* 49 (1996): 85–108.

MacClintock, Carol. *Readings in the History of Performance*. Bloomington: Indiana University Press, 1979.

Mace, Dean. "Pietro Bembo and the Literary Origins of the Italian Madrigal." *The Journal of Musicology* 55 (1969): 65–86.

"Tasso, *La Gerusalemme liberata* and Monteverdi." *Studies in the History of Music I: Music and Language* 1 (1983): 118–156.

Macy, Laura. "Speaking of Sex: Metaphor and Performance in the Italian Madrigal." *Journal of Musicology* 14/1 (1996): 1–45.

Maclean, Ian. *The Renaissance Notion of Woman: A Study in the Fortunes of Scholasticism and Medieval Science in European Intellectual Life*. Cambridge: Cambridge University Press, 1980.

MacNeil, Ann. *Music and Women of the Commedia dell'Arte in the Late Sixteenth Century*. NewYork: Oxford University Press, 2003.

"Weeping at the Water's Edge," *Early Music* 27 (1999), 406–418.

Marland, Hilary. *The Art of Midwifery: Early Modern Midwives in Europe*. London: Routledge, 1993.

Masson, Georgina. *Courtesans of the Italian Renaissance*. London: Secker and Warburg, 1975.

Mauss, Marcel. "Techniques of the Body." *Economy and Society* 2/1 (1979): 70–88.

May, Margaret Tallmadge. *Galen On The Usefulness of the Parts of the Body*. 2 vols. Ithaca: Cornell University Press, 1968.

Mazzotta, Giuseppe. *The Worlds of Petrarch*. Durham, NC: Duke University Press, 1993.

McClary, Susan. "Constructions of Gender in Monteverdi's Dramatic Music." In *Feminine Endings: Music, Gender, and Sexuality*, 35–53. Minneapolis: University of Minnesota Press, 1991.

Feminine Endings: Music, Gender, and Sexuality. Minneapolis: University of Minnesota Press, 1991.

"Music, the Pythagoreans, and the Body." In *Choreographing History*, edited by Susan Leigh Foster, 82–105. Bloomington: Indiana University Press, 1995.

McGee, Timothy James. "Dancing Masters and the Medici Court in the 15th Century." *Studi Musicali* 17/2 (1988): 201–224.

"Pompeo Caccini and Euridice: New Bibliographic Notes," *Renaissance and Reformation/Renaissance et Reforme* 14/2 (1990): 81–90.

McLucas, John C. "Amazon, Sorceress, and Queen: Women and War in the Aristocratic Literature of Sixteenth-Century Italy." *The Italianist* 8 (1988): 33–55.

"Clorinda and Her Echoes in the Women's World." *Stanford Italian Review* 10/1 (1991): 80–92.

Mersenne, Marin. *Harmonie Universelle* (1636–37). Translated by Roger Chapman. The Hague: M. Nijhoff, 1957.

Migiel, Marilyn. "Secrets of a Sorceress: Tasso's Armida." *Quaderni d'italianistica* 8/2 (1987): 148–166.

Minor, Andrew Collier. *A Renaissance Entertainment: Festivities for the Marriage of Cosimo I, Duke of Florence, in 1539*. Columbia: University of Missouri Press, 1968.

Molho, Anthony. *Marriage Alliance in Late Medieval Florence*. Cambridge, MA: Harvard University Press, 1994.

Monteverdi, Claudio. *Madrigali guerrieri e amorosi*. edited by Gian Francesco Malipiero. New York: Dover, 1990.

Mounsey, Chris, ed. *Presenting Gender: Changing Sex in Early-modern Culture*. Lewisburg: Bucknell University Press, 2001.

Morlini, Girolamo. *Novelle e favole*. Rome: Salerno, 1983.

Muir, Edward. "Images of Power: Art and Pageantry in Renaissance Venice." *American Historical Review* 84/1 (1979): 16–52.

Murata, Margaret. "The Recitative Soliloquy." *Journal of the American Musicological Society* 32 (1979): 45–73.

Musacchio, Jacqueline Marie. *The Art and Ritual of Childbirth in Renaissance Italy*. New Haven: Yale University Press, 1999.

Nagler, A. M. *Theatre Festivals of the Medici*. New Haven: Yale University Press, 1964.

Neville, Jennifer. "The Italian Ballo as Described in Fifteenth Century Dance Treatises." *Studies in music, Australia* 18 (1984): 38–51.

Newcomb, Anthony. "Courtesans, Muses or Musicians? Professional Women Musicians in Sixteenth-Century Italy." In *Women Making Music: The Western Art Tradition 1150–1950*, edited by Jane Bowers and Judith Tick, 90–115. Urbana and Chicago: University of Illinois Press, 1985.

The Madrigal at Ferrara. Princeton: Princeton University Press, 1980.

Newman, Karen. *Fashioning Femininity and English Renaissance Drama*. Chicago: University of Chicago Press, 1991.

"The Politics of Spectacle: La Pellegrina and the Intermezzi of 1589." *MLN* 10/1 (1986): 95–114.

Norman, Buford and Michèle Vialet. "Sexual and Artistic Politics under Louis XIV: The Persephone Myth in Literature." In *Images of Persephone*, edited by Elizabeth T. Hayes, 45–75. Tallahassee: University of Florida Press, 1994.

Nye, Katharine Park and Robert A. "Review of Making Sex: Body and Gender from the Greeks to Freud." *New Republic* 204/7 (1991): 53–55.

Ong, Walter J. *Ramus: Method and the Decay of Dialogue*. Cambridge, MA: Harvard University Press, 1983.

Ordern, Kate van. "Sexual Discourse in the Parisian Chanson: A Libidinous Aviary." *Journal of the American Musicological Society* 48/1 (1995): 1–42.

Orgel, Stephen. *The Illusion of Power: Political Theater in the English Renaissance*. Berkeley: University of California Press, 1975.

Le trasformationi di Lodovico Dolce (1533). New York: Garland, 1979.

Ossi, Massimo. "A Sample Problem in Seventeenth-Century Imitatio: Claudio Monteverdi, Francesco Turini, and Battista Guarini's 'Mentre vaga angioletta.'" In *Music in Renaissance Cities and Courts: Studies in Honor of Lewis Lockwood*, edited by Jessie Ann Owens and Anthony Cummings, 253–269. Warren, MI: Harmonie Park Press, 1997.

Ovid. *Heroides and Amores*. Translated by Grant Showerman. Edited by E. H. Warmington. Cambridge, MA: Harvard University Press, 1914.

    Metamorphoses. Translated by Frank Justus Miller,. Revised by G. P. Goold. Cambridge, MA: Harvard University Press, 1977.

Pagel, Walter. "Religion and Neoplatonism in Renaissance Medicine (Review)." *Journal of the History of Philosophy* 26 (1985): 318–320.

Palisca, Claude. *Studies in the History of Italian Music and Music Theory*. Oxford: Clarendon Press, 1994.

    The Florentine Camerata: Documentary Studies and Translations. New Haven: Yale University Press, 1989.

Paré, Ambroise. *Of Monsters and Marvels (1573)*. Translated by Janis L. Pallister. Chicago: University of Chicago Press, 1982.

    The Works of that Famous Chirurgion Ambrose Parey. Translated by Thomas Johnson. London: T. Cotes and R. Young, 1634.

Parisi, Susan. "Ducal Patronage of Music in Mantua 1587–1627: An Archival Study." Ph.D. dissertation, University of Illinois at Urbana, 1989.

Park, Katharine. "The Criminal and the Saintly Body: Autopsy and Dissection in Renaissance Italy." *Renaissance Studies* 47 (1994): 1–33.

    "The Organic Soul." In *The Cambridge History of Renaissance Philosophy*, edited by Quentin Skinner, Charles B. Schmitt, Eckhard Kessler, and Jill Kraye, 455–464. Cambridge: Cambridge University Press, 1988.

    "The Rediscovery of the Clitoris." In *The Body in Parts*, edited by David Hillman and Carla Mazzio, 171–195. New York: Routledge, 1997.

Park, Katharine and Lorraine Doston. *Wonders and the Order of Nature 1150–1750*. New York: Zone Books, 1998.

Parker, Patricia A. *Inescapable Romance: Studies in the Poetics of a Mode*. Princeton: Princeton University Press, 1979.

Parkinson, G. H. R., ed. *The Renaissance and 17th-century Rationalism*. London: Routledge, 1993.

Paster, Gail Kern. *The Body Embarrassed: Drama and The Disciplines of Shame in Early Modern England*. Ithaca: Cornell University Press, 1993.

    "Nervous Tension: Networks of Blood and Spirit in the Early Modern Body." In *The Body in Parts: Fantasies of Corporeality in Early Modern Europe*, edited by David Hillman and Carla Mazzio, 107–129. New York: Routledge, 1997.

Pirrotta, Nino. "Music and Cultural Tendencies in Fifteenth-Century Italy." In *Music and Culture in Italy from the Middle Ages to the Baroque*, 80–113. Cambridge, MA: Harvard University Press, 1984.

    "Monteverdi's Poetic Choices." In *Music and Culture in Italy from the Middle Ages to the Baroque*, 271–317. Cambridge, MA: Harvard University Press, 1984.

    "Theater, Sets, and Music in Monteverdi's Operas." In *Music and Culture in Italy from the Middle Ages to the Baroque*, 254–271. Cambridge, MA: Harvard University Press, 1984.

Plato. *Timaeus*. Translated by Donald J. Zeyl. Indianapolis: Hackett Publishing Company, 2000.

Poizat, Michel. *The Angel's Cry: Beyond the Pleasure Principle in Opera*. Translated by Arthur Denner. Ithaca: Cornell University Press, 1992.

Pompilio, Angelo and Paolo Fabbri. *Il Corago o vero alcune osservazioni per metter bene in scena le composizioni drammatiche*. Florence: Leo S. Olschki Editore, 1983.

Porter, William. "Peri's Dafne." *Journal of the American Musicological Society* 18/2 (1965): 170–197.

Press, Simon Reynolds and Joy. *The Sex Revolts*. Cambridge, MA: Harvard University Press, 1996.

Quint, David. *Epic and Empire: Politics and Generic Form from Virgil to Milton*. Princeton: Princeton University Press, 1990.

Rabelais, François. *The Histories of Gargantua and Pantagruel*. Translated by J. M. Cohen. Harmondsworth: Penguin, 1982.

Reiner, Stuart. "La vag'Angioletta (and Others)." *Studien zur Italienisch-Deutschen Musikgeschichte* 9 (1974): 26–89.

"Preparations at Parma – 1618, 1627–1628." *Music Review* 25 (1964): 273–354.

Ribe, Neil. "Cartesian Optics." *Isis* 97 (1988): 42.

Robb, Nesca. *Neoplatonism of the Italian Renaissance*. London: George Allen and Unwin Ltd., 1935.

Rogers, Mary. "An Ideal Wife at the Villa Maser: Veronese, the Barbaros and Renaissance Theories of Marriage." *Renaissance Studies* 7/4 (1993): 379–398.

Rosand, Ellen. "Barbara Strozzi, virtuossima cantatrice: The Composer's Voice." *Journal of the American Musicological Society* 31/2 (1978): 241–282.

"The First Opera Diva: Anna Renzi." *Historical Performance* 3/1 (1990): 3–7.

"Monteverdi's Il ritorno d'Ulisse in patria and the Power of 'Music.'" *Cambridge Opera Journal* 7/3 (1995): 179–183.

"Monteverdi's Mimetic Art: L'incoronazione di Poppea." *Cambridge Opera Journal* 1/2 (1989): 113–137.

Opera in Seventeenth-Century Venice: The Creation of a Genre. Berkeley: University of California Press, 1991.

"Operatic Ambiguity and the Power of Music." *Cambridge Opera Journal* 4/1 (1992): 75–80.

Rosenthal, Margaret F. *The Honest Courtesan: Veronica Franco, Citizen and Writer in Seventeenth-Century Venice*. Chicago: University of Chicago Press, 1992.

Rosenthal, Margaret and Anne Rosalind Jones, eds. *Veronica Franco: Poems and Selected Letters*. Chicago: University of Chicago Press, 1998.

Rosselli, John. "The Castrati as a Professional Group and a Social Phenomenon, 1550–1850." *Acta Musicologica* 60/2 (1988): 143–179.

Rubin, Gayle. "The Traffic in Women: Notes on the Political Economy of Sex." In *Toward an Anthropology of Women*, edited by Rayna R. Reita. New York: Monthly Review Press, 1975.

Ruggiero, Guido. *Binding Passions: Tales of Marriage, Magic, and Power at the End of the Renaissance*. Oxford: Oxford University Press, 1993.

The Boundaries of Eros: Sex Crimes and Sexuality in Renaissance Venice. New York: Oxford University Press, 1985.

Russell, Colin. *Science and Social Change in Britain and Europe*. New York: St. Martin's Press, 1983.

Russo, Mary. "Female Grotesques, Carnival and Theory." In *Feminist Studies/ Critical Studies*, edited by Teresa de Lauretis. Bloomington: Indiana University Press, 1986.

Sansone, Matteo and Roger Savage. "*Il corago* and the Staging of Early Opera: Four Chapters from an Anonymous Treatise circa 1530." *Early Music* 17 (1984): 495–515.

Saslaw, James M. *Ganymede and the Renaissance: Homosexuality in Art and Society*. New Haven: Yale University Press, 1986.

   The Medici Wedding of 1589: Florentine Festival as Theatrum Mundi. New Haven: Yale University Press, 1996.

   The Poetry of Michelangelo: An Annotated Translation. New Haven: Yale University Press, 1991.

Savage, Roger. "Daphne Transformed." *Early Music* 17 (1989): 485–495.

Sawday, Jonathan. *The Body Emblazoned: Dissection and the Human Body in Renaissance Culture*. New York: Routledge, 1996.

Scary, Elaine. *The Body in Pain: The Making and Unmaking of the World*. New York: Oxford University Press, 1985.

Schechner, Richard. *Between Theater and Anthropology*. Philadelphia: University of Pennsylvania Press, 1985.

Schibonoff, Susan. "Botticelli's Madonna del Magnificat: Constructing the Woman Writer in Early Humanist Italy." *PMLA* 109 (1994): 190–206.

Schmitt, Brian P. Copenhave and Charles B. *A History of Renaissance Philosophy*. New York: Oxford University Press, 1992.

Schrade, Leo. *Monteverdi: Creator of Modern Music*. London: W. W. Norton, 1950.

Schwartz, Regina and Valeria Finucci. *Desire in the Renaissance: Psychoanalysis and Literature*. Princeton: Princeton University Press, 1994.

Seville, Isidore of. *Isidore of Seville: The Medical Writings, an English Translation*. Translated by William D. Sharp. Philadelphia: American Philosophical Society, 1964.

Seznec, Jean. *The Survival of the Pagan Gods: The Mythological Tradition and Its Place in Renaissance Humanism and Arts*. Translated by Barbara F. Sessions. Princeton: Princeton University Press, 1961.

Shah, Mazhar H. *The General Principles of Avicenna's Canon of Medicine*. Karachi: Naveed Clinic, 1966.

Shapin, Steven. *The Scientific Revolution*. Chicago: University of Chicago Press, 1996.

Shewring, Margaret and J. R. Mulryne. *Italian Renaissance Festivals and Their European Influence*. Lewiston: Edwin Mellen Press, 1992.

Siegel, Rudolph E., ed. *Galen On the Affected Parts*. New York: S. Karger, 1976.

Silverman, Kaja. *The Acoustic Mirror: The Female Voice in Psychoanalysis and Cinema*. Bloomington: Indiana University Press, 1988.

Silverman, Lisa. *Tortured Subjects: Pain, Truth, and the Body in Early Modern France*. Chicago: University of Chicago Press, 2001.

Simons, F. Kent and P. *Patronage, Art and Society in Renaissance Italy*. Oxford: Clarendon Press, 1987.

Siraisi, Nancy G. *Avicenna in Renaissance Italy: The Canon and Medical Teaching in Italian Universities after 1500*. Princeton: Princeton University Press, 1987.

Medieval and Early Renaissance Medicine: An Introduction to Knowledge and Practice. Chicago: University of Chicago Press, 1990.

"The Music of the Pulse in the Writings of Italian Academic Physicians." *Journal of Mediaeval Studies* 50 (1975): 689–710.

Skinner, Quentin, Charles B. Schmitt, Eckhard Kessler, and Jill Kraye, eds. *The Cambridge History of Renaissance Philosophy.* New York: Cambridge University Press, 1988.

Smith, Bruce R. *Homosexual Desire in Shakespeare's England: A Cultural Poetics.* Chicago: University of Chicago Press, 1994.

Smith, Pamela. *The Business of Alchemy: Science and Culture in the Holy Roman Empire.* Princeton: Princeton University Press, 1994.

Solerti, Angelo. *Gli albori del melodramma.* 3 volumes. Turin: Bocca, 1903.

Le origini del melodramma. Turin: Bocca, 1903.

Le vite di Dante, Petrarca e Boccaccio scritte fino al secolo decimosesto. Milan: Vallardi, 1904.

"Un balletto musicato da Claudio Monteverdi sconosciuto a suoi biografi." *Rivista Musicale Italiana* 7 (1904).

Sommerville, Margaret R. *Sex and Subjectivity: Attitudes to Women in Early Modern Society.* London: Arnold, 1995.

Soranus. *Gynecology.* Translated by Owsei Temkin. Baltimore: Johns Hopkins University Press, 1956.

Spackman, Barbara. "Inter musam et ursum moritur: Folengo and the Gaping 'Other' Mouth." In *Refiguring Woman: Perspectives on Gender in the Italian Renaissance,* edited by Marilyn Migiel and Juliana Schiesari, 19–35. Ithaca: Cornell University Press, 1991.

Speroni, Sperone. "Dialogo d'amore." In *Trattatisti del Cinquecento,* edited by Mario Pozzi, 511–563. Milan–Naples: Ricciardi, 1978.

Stallybrass, Peter. "The Body Enclosed: Patriarchal Territories: The Discourses of Sexual Difference in Early Modern Europe." In *Rewriting the Renaissance: The Discourses of Sexual Difference in Early Modern Europe,* edited by Margaret M. Ferguson, Nancy J. Vickers, and Maureen Quilligan, 123–142. Chicago: University of Chicago Press, 1986.

"Transvestitism and the Body Beneath: Speculating on the Boy Actor." In *Erotic Politics: Desire on the Renaissance Stage,* edited by Susan Zimmerman, 64–84. New York: Routledge, 1992.

"We Feast in our Defense: Patrician Carnival in Early Modern England and Robert Herrick's Hesperides." *English Literary Renaissance* 16 (1986): 234–252.

"Worn World: Clothes and Identity on the Renaissance Stage." In *Subject and Object in Renaissance Culture,* edited by Maureen Quilligan, Peter Stallybrass, and Margreta de Grazia, 289–337. Cambridge: Cambridge University Press, 1996.

Stallybrass, Peter and Ann R. Jones. "Fetishizing Gender: Constructing the Hermaphrodite in Renaissance Europe." In *Body Guard: The Cultural Politics of Gender Ambiguity,* edited by Julia Epstein and Kristina Straub, 88–111. New York: Routledge, 1991.

Stallybrass, Peter and D. S. Kastan. *Staging the Renaissance: Reinterpretations of Elizabethan and Jacobean Drama.* New York: Routledge, 1991.

Stanivukovic, Goran V., ed. *Ovid and the Renaissance Body*. Toronto: University of Toronto Press, 2001.

Stevens, Denis. *The Letters of Claudio Monteverdi*. Cambridge: Cambridge University Press, 1980.

"Madrigali Guerrieri et Amorosi." In *The Monteverdi Companion*, edited by Denis Arnold and Nigel Fortune, 227–257. New York: W. W. Norton and Company, 1968.

Stone, Lawrence. *The Family, Sex and Marriage in England 1500–1800*. New York: Harper and Row, 1977.

Uncertain Unions: Marriage in England 1660–1753. New York: Oxford University Press, 1992.

Strainchamps, Edmond. "The Life and Death of Caterina Martinelli: New Light on Monteverdi's L'Arianna." *Early Music History* 5 (1985): 155–186.

Strong, Roy. *Splendor at Court: Renaissance Spectacle and the Theater of Power, National Portrait Gallery, London, Great Britain*. Boston: Houghton Mifflin, 1973.

Strunk, Oliver. *Source Readings in Music History: The Renaissance*. New York: W. W. Norton and Company, 1965.

Sutton, Julia. *Courtly Dance of the Renaissance: A New Translation and Edition of the "Nobiltà di dame" (1600)*. New York: Dover, 1995.

Tacitus. *The Annals*. Translated by John Jackson. Cambridge, MA: Harvard University Press, 1962.

Taruskin, Piero Weiss and Richard. *Music in the Western World*. New York: Schirmer Books, 1984.

Tasso, Torquato. *Gerusalemme liberata*. Edited by Marziano Guglielminetti. Milan: Garzanti, 1987.

Jerusalem Delivered: An English Prose Version. Translated by Ralph Nash. Detroit: Wayne State Press, 1987.

Talvacchia, Bette. *Taking Positions: On the Erotic in Renaissance Culture*. Princeton: Princeton University Press, 1999.

Tinagli, Paolo. *Women in Italian Renaissance Art*. Manchester: Manchester University Press, 1997.

Tomlinson, Gary. "Madrigal, Monody and Monteverdi's Via naturale all'immitatione." *Journal of the American Musicological Society* 34 (1981): 60–108.

Metaphysical Song: An Essay on Opera. Princeton: Princeton University Press, 1999.

Monteverdi and the End of the Renaissance. Berkeley: University of California Press, 1987.

"Music and the Claims of Text: Monteverdi, Rinuccini and Marino." *Critical Inquiry* 8 (1981–82): 565–589.

Music in Renaissance Magic: Toward a Historiography of Others. Chicago: University of Chicago Press, 1993.

"Rinuccini, Peri, Monteverdi and the Humanist Heritage of Opera." Ph.D. dissertation, University of California, 1981.

Tomlinson, Gary, ed. *Strunk's Source Readings in Music History*. Edited by Leo Treitler. Revised edition. Vol. III. New York: W.W. Norton and Company, 1998.

Bibliography

Traub, Valerie. *Desire and Anxiety: Circulations of Sexuality in Shakespearean Drama.* New York: Routledge, 1992.

Treadwell, Nina. "Restaging the Sirens: Musical Women in the Performance of Sixteenth Century Italian Theater." Ph.D. dissertation, University of Southern California, 2003.

Trexler, Richard C. "Ritual Behavior in Renaissance Florence." *Medievalia et Humanistica: Studies in Medieval and Renaissance Culture* 4 (1973): 125–144.

Trotti, Bernardo. *Dialoghi del matrimonio e vita vedovile.* Turin, 1578.

Turner, Victor. *From Ritual to Theater: The Human Seriousness of Play.* New York: Performing Arts Journal Publications, 1982.

Udine, Federico Luigini da. "Libro della bella donna." [1540s].

Ulrich, Bernhard. *Concerning the Principles of Voice Training during the Cappella Period and Until the Beginning of Opera 1474–1640.* Translated by John Seale. Edited by Edward Foresman. Minneapolis: Pro Musica Press, 1973.

Verheyen, Egon. *The Palazzo del Tè in Mantua.* Baltimore: Johns Hopkins University Press, 1977.

Vickers, Nancy. "Diana Described: Scattered Women and Scattered Rhyme." *Critical Inquiry* 8/2 (Winter 1981): 265–279.

"Members Only." In *The Body in Parts*, edited by David Hillman and Carla Mazzio, 3–23. New York: Routledge, 1997.

Vives, Juan Luis. *The Education of a Christian Woman.* Chicago: The University of Chicago Press, 2000.

Walker, D. P. "The Astral Body in Renaissance Medicine." *Journal of the Warburg and Courtauld Institute* 21 (1958): 119–133.

Music, Spirit, and Language. Edited by Penelope Gouk. London: Variorum Reprints, 1985.

"Musical Humanism in the 16th and early 17th Centuries." *Music Review* 2 (1941): 1–13, 111–121, 220–227, 288–308.

Studies in Musical Science. London: The Warburg Institute, 1978.

Wear, Andrew. "Medicine in Early Modern Europe 1500–1700." In *The Western Medical Tradition 800 BC to AD 1800*, ed. Lawrence Conrad et al. Cambridge: Cambridge University Press, 1995.

Weinberg, Bernard. *A History of Literary Criticism in the Italian Renaissance.* Chicago: University of Chicago Press, 1974.

Weinberg, Julius R. *A Short History of Medieval Philosophy.* Princeton: Princeton University Press, 1969.

Whenham, John. *Duet and Dialogue in the Age of Monteverdi.* Ann Arbor: UMI Press, 1982.

Claudio Monteverdi, Orfeo. Cambridge: Cambridge University Press. 1986.

Whigham, Frank. "Interpretations at Court: Courtesy and the Performer–Audience Dialectic." *New Literary History* 143 (1983): 623–641.

White, Allon. *Carnival, Hysteria, and Writing: Collected Essays and Autobiography.* New York: Oxford University Press, 1993.

White, Allon and Peter Stallybrass. *The Politics and Poetics of Transgression.* Ithaca: Cornell University Press, 1983.

Wilkie, David J. and J. S. Furley *Galen On Respiration And The Arteries.* Princeton: Princeton University Press, 1984.

Wilson, Catherine. "Visual Surface and Visual Symbol." *Journal of the History of Ideas* 49 (1988): 85.

Wistreich, Richard. "'La voce è grata assai, ma . . .': Monteverdi on Singing." *Early Music* 12 (1994): 6–21.

Wittkower, Rudolf and Margot. *Born Under Saturn: The Character and Conduct of Artists; A Documented History from Antiquity to the French Revolution.* London: Weidenfeld and Nicolson, 1963.

Wofford, Susan L. "The Social Aesthetics of Rape: Closural Violence in Boccaccio and Botticelli." In *Creative Imitation: New Essays on Renaissance Literature in Honor of Thomas M. Greene,* edited by Margaret W. Ferguson, G W. Pigman III, Wayne A. Rebborn, and David Quint, 191–229. Binghamton: Medieval and Renaissance Text Studies, 1992.

Wynne-Davies, Marion. "'The Swallowing Womb': Consumed and Consuming Women in Titus Andronicus." In *The Matter of Difference: Materialist Feminist Criticism of Shakespeare,* edited by Valerie Wayne, 129–153. Ithaca: Cornell University Press, 1991.

Yates, Frances Amelia. *The French Academies of the Sixteenth Century.* London: Warburg Institute, 1947.

Yavneh, Naomi. "The Ambiguity of Beauty in Tasso and Petrarch." In *Sexuality and Gender in Early Modern Europe,* edited by James Turner, 133–157. Cambridge: Cambridge University Press, 1992.

Yolton, John W., ed. *Philosophy, Religion and Science in the 17th and 18th Centuries.* Rochester: University of Rochester Press, 1994.

Zacconi, Lodovico. *Prattica di musica.* Bologna: Forni, 1592.

Zanier, Giancarlo. "Platonic Trends in Renaissance Medicine." *Journal of the History of Ideas* 48 (1987): 509–519.

Zonta, Giuseppe. "Trattati del Cinquecento sulla donna." Bari: Laterza, 1913.

INDEX

Abbate, Carolyn 204, 207
academies 181, 182
actresses 41
affections, primary 188
Agnelli, Scipione 67
Alberti, Leon Battista 142, 179
anatomy 138–139, 180–181, 182
    see also body, understanding of and
    beliefs about
Andreini, Isabella 145
Andreini, Virginia 145
dell'Anguillara, Giovanni Andrea 58,
    159
d'Aragona, Tulia 41, 87, 89, 94–95,
    116–117
Arcadelt, Jacques, "Il bianco e dolce
    cigno" 113–114
Aretino, Pietro 76, 97–98, 99–103
    Monteverdi and 87, 88, 117, 118, 126
Aristotle 20–25
    on sensory experience 182,
        193–194
    on voice production 19
    on women 73, 80, 115
Aristoxenus 185
Artusi, Giovanni 43, 81–82, 108, 185
    debate/dispute with
        Monteverdi 81–82, 108, 122, 183,
        185–188, 190
Augustine of Hippo 66, 99, 107
Austern, Linda 4
Avicenna 32

Bacon, Francis 181, 189–190
Baird, Julianne 18
Bakhtin, Mikhail 78–79
Ballarmine, Robert 107 *
Barbaro, Francesco 50, 74, 75
Bardi, Giovanni de 107
Barkan, Leonard 63
Barthes, Roland 139–140, 141, 207

Basile, Adriana 132, 133, 144–145, 148,
    149, 153–154, 155
    Monteverdi and 12, 114, 133, 144–145,
        146–148, 149, 153–154
basso continuo 166, 183
Beatty, Warren 32
Bembo, Helena 76
Bembo, Pietro 76, 87, 89, 91, 98, 128
    Castiglione and 92, 93
    Ferrand and 90
    Ninfo and 94
Bentivoglio, Caterina 37
birds, singers and 154–156
blazon 45, 131, 139–143, 165
blood, circulation of 13, 46
Boccaccio, Giovanni 54–56, 90
body
    as parts 139–143 (*see also* blazon)
    and singing *see* singing as physical
        activity
    understanding of and beliefs about 13,
        31–35, 46, 77–80, 111–114, 115,
        165–166, 179 (*see also* anatomy; voice)
    see also sensation
body fluids 79–80
body temperature 21–22, 32–35, 46
botanical gardens 180–181
Botticelli, Sandro 56
Bottrigari, Ercole 43, 154
Brancaccio, Giulio Cesare 146, 159
breathing 21, 33, 78
Brunelleschi, Filippo 179
Bruto, Giovanni 40
Busenello, Gian Francesco 204

Caccini, Francesca 36, 37
Caccini, Giulio 12, 25, 26, 30–31, 36, 81,
    146, 149
    and ornamentation 41–42, 43–44
Caccini, Lucia 36
Caccini, Margherita 36

Index

Index

"Cor mio, mentre vi miro" 89–91, 122 (*see also* "Cor mio, mentre vi miro" *under* Monteverdi)
"Gorga di cantatrice" 131–139, 140–141, 143–144, 150–156 (*see also* "Mentre vaga Angioletta" *under* Monteverdi)
L'Idropica 47, 59, 84
"Io mi son giovinetta" 109
Guasco, Annibal 35–36, 147, 148
Guasco, Lavinia 35–36, 147, 148
Guazzo, Stefano 74

Hargis, Ellen 18
harmony 168
Harvey, PJ 206–207
Harvey, William 13, 46
hearing 192–198
Herophilus 20, 77
Hippocrates 31, 90
historical performance movement 17–18
humoral theory 20–25, 32, 79–80, 91, 106

Index of Forbidden Books 99
instrument 45, 76, 176, 183, 189
intonation *see* tuning
Isidore of Seville 79

Johnson, Barbara 83
Jones, Pamela 51

laboratories 180–181
Lacan, Jacques 207
Lacquer, Thomas 111
Leonardo da Vinci 19, 138
Lipking, Lawrence 49
love
  music and 91
  writings on and beliefs about 88–103
  see also sex/sexuality
Lucian 97
Luppi, Leonora 39
Luppi, Silvia 39
Luzzaschi, Luzzasco 12, 14, 132, 136, 137

Macey, Laura 112–114, 129
MacNeil, Ann 58–59, 85
Macy, Laura 76
Madonna 32
madrigals 76, 86–88, 110–111, 112–114, 117, 165
  texts 108–109
Maffei, Camillo 23–25, 26–27, 31, 35–37, 78

male singers 4–6, 146, 154, 159–160
  see also castrati
Marenzio, Luca 136
Margherita of Savoy 3
  wedding celebrations 4, 47–51, 81
Marino, Giambattista, and Marinist style 46, 128–129, 132
Marot, Clement 141
marriage manuals 50
Martinelli, Caterina 3–4, 36, 37, 38–39, 81, 144
Mattheson, Johann 164
Mazziere, Ginevra 39
Mazzotta, Giuseppe 66
McClary, Susan 87, 113–114, 129, 158
Medici-Gonzaga, Elenora 81
Mei, Girolamo 106, 108
men
  identity 4–6
  see also male singers
menstruation 79–80
Mersenne, Marin 25–26
Michelangelo 138
microscopes 191–192
Monteverdi, Claudia Cattaneo 12
Monteverdi, Claudio 2, 38, 147–148
  audience and circulation of works 88
  contemporary views of music by 104
  debate with Artusi *see under* Artusi
  influence 188
  letters 35, 67, 176, 178
  and ornamentation 41–42
  and science 164, 182
  and singers 12, 15, 23, 24–25, 114, 146–147; his children 35, 36
  texts 86–87, 88, 89, 108–109
  theory of music 187–189, 190–191
  and transition 7, 164–166
  "A un giro sol de' begli occhi lucenti" 86
  "Anima mia, perdona" 186
  L'Arianna 50, 81; Arianna's lament 67–69, 81, 83–85, 161–162, 166–170, 171, 172, 174, 175, 176, 177–179, 183, 194, 198–200; crying at 3, 83–85, 161, 167, 200; Monteverdi on 167; performers 59, 81, 83; text 47–51, 56–59
  Il ballo delle ingrate 3, 47–73, 77, 78–79, 81, 83–84, 85, 201; dance aspects 63–64
  "Chiome d'oro" 45–46, 164

231

Index